W9-ABI-644

Gramley Library
Salem Academy and College
Winston-Sa em, N.C. 27108

Relationships of Sympathy

Relationships of Sympathy

The Writer and the Reader in British Romanticism

THOMAS J. McCARTHY

SCOLAR PRESS

Gramley Library
Salem Academy and College
Winston-Salem, N.C. 27108

© Thomas J. McCarthy, 1997

All rights reserved. No part of this publication may be reproduced, stored in a retrieval system, or transmitted in any form or by any means, electronic, mechanical, photocopying, recording, or otherwise without the prior permission of the publisher.

Published by
SCOLAR PRESS
Gower House
Croft Road
Aldershot
Hants GU11 3HR
England

Ashgate Publishing Company
Old Post Road
Brookfield
Vermont 05036–9704
USA

British Library Cataloguing in Publication Data

McCarthy, Thomas J.
    Relationships of Sympathy: The Writer and the Reader in
British Romanticism.
    (Nineteenth Century series)
    1. Romanticism—Great Britain.   2. Authors and readers—Great
Britain—History—19th century.   3. English literature—
19th century—History and criticism.
    I. Title.
    920.9'145'09034

    ISBN 1–85928–315–2

Library of Congress Cataloging-in-Publication Data

McCarthy, Thomas J., 1962–
    Relationships of sympathy: the writer and the reader in British
Romanticism/Thomas J. McCarthy.
        p.   cm.
    Includes index.
    ISBN 1–85928–315–2 (cloth)
    1. English literature—19th century—History and criticism.
    2. Authors and readers—Great Britain—History—19th century.
    3. Romanticism—Great Britain.   4. Sympathy in literature.
    I. Title.
    PR457.M4   1997
    820.9'145—dc20   96–41036
                                                                CIP

ISBN 1 85928 315 2

Typeset in Sabon by Manton Typesetters, 5–7 Eastfield Road, Louth, Lincolnshire, LN11 7AJ and printed in Great Britain by Hartnolls Ltd. Bodmin Cornwall.

Gramley Library
Salem Academy and College
Winston-Salem, N.C. 27108

Contents

The Nineteenth Century
General Editor's Preface

The aim of this series is to reflect, develop and extend the great burgeoning of interest in the nineteenth century that has been an inevitable feature of recent decades, as that former epoch has come more sharply into focus as a locus for our understanding not only of the past but of the contours of our modernity. Though it is dedicated principally to the publication of original monographs and symposia in literature, history, cultural analysis, and associated fields, there will be a salient role for reprints of significant texts from, or about, the period. Our overarching policy is to address the spectrum of nineteenth-century studies without exception, achieving the widest scope in chronology, approach and range of concern. This, we believe, distinguishes our project from comparable ones, and means, for example, that in the relevant areas of scholarship we both recognize and cut innovatively across such parameters as those suggested by the designations 'Romantic' and 'Victorian'. We welcome new ideas, while valuing tradition. It is hoped that the world which predates yet so forcibly predicts and engages our own will emerge in parts, as a whole, and in the lively currents of debate and change that are so manifest an aspect of its intellectual, artistic and social landscape.

Vincent Newey
Joanne Shattock

University of Leicester

Acknowledgements

I would like to thank a number of people who were in one way or another instrumental in the conception and/or writing of this book: Paul Betz, for introducing me to Romantic literature with his inimitably passionate intelligence, and for his sincere encouragement over the years; Wayne Knoll, for teaching me to care about literature and to take my writing and my ideas seriously, for his giddy outbursts of excitement in class, and mostly for his friendship; Roy Park, for his enthusiastic guidance which helped to inspire my desire to undertake Romantic scholarship; Curtis Perry, for his intellectual camaraderie in Cambridge, and particularly for his invaluable assistance with the organization and focus of Chapter 3; Mark Nevins, for countless discussions on life, literature and everything in between, and for always generously sharing his overflowing font of ideas; David Perkins, for helping me formulate and hone the ideas for this book, and for his keen intellectual guidance throughout its early drafts; Philip Fisher, for his incisive feedback on the early drafts of this book and for urging me to pursue its publication; James Engell, for his kind and generous comments on earlier versions of this book; and John Mannering, for many useful suggestions during the final manuscript preparation.

I would like to acknowledge in a special way the late Timothy Healy, S.J., who made it possible for me to attend Oxford University, where so much of what I love about literature was wonderfully deepened and nurtured.

For Clare,
my sympathetic beloved

Introduction

> How can I approach the unknowable of the other? How can another help me understand that which has never before been felt in this particular way by anyone else, the unnameable that leaves one locked in one's aloneness?[1]

The roots of sympathy

'He projected his mind out of his own particular being, and felt and made others feel, on subjects in no way connected with himself, except by force of contemplation, and that sublime faculty, by which a great mind becomes that which it meditates on.'[2] Coleridge's writings on Shakespeare played a significant role in defining the most important critical and aesthetic concept of the Romantic period in England, the imagination. The resurgent admiration for Shakespeare was due to the widespread belief, expounded in eighteenth-century philosophy and aesthetics, and culminating in the Romantic ethos, that being a great poet meant being a great human being, which, in turn, was determined by one's capacity for self-transcendence. Indeed, breaking down barriers and challenging conventional notions of the self were typical of Romantic thought. Yet as Professor Bate illustrated, and as Coleridge's references to 'contemplation' and 'meditates' implies, the self became the centre of inspiration and knowledge for the Romantics. Thus the Romantic revolution corresponded to a simultaneous intensification of the importance of the self and the loss of self.

The particular idea of the imagination that Coleridge no doubt had in mind was the idea of sympathy, whose roots lie in the Greek, *sumpatheia* ('feeling with'). 'One of the major themes of mid- and late eighteenth-century thought, both moral and aesthetic',[3] sympathy became crucial to Romantic writers' basic understanding of the self:

> Among the more common romantic dicta which had their roots in the preceding century was the insistence that the imagination, by an effort of sympathetic intuition, is able to penetrate the barrier which puts space between it and its object, and, by actually entering into the object, so to speak, secure a momentary but complete identification with it.[4]

Much of the preoccupation with sympathy was an attempt to respond to Hobbes's claim that human beings are fundamentally selfish. In his *Inquiry Concerning Virtue, or Merit* (1699), Shaftesbury argued for the inherent link between self-interest and public interest by means of what he called the 'natural affections'. Hume's *Treatise of Human Nature* (1739), whose similar connection between sympathy and morality 'was one starting point for the fascination with sympathy that later swept the century',[5] asserted that sympathy is the chief source of moral distinctions. 'The sentiments of others can never affect us, but by becoming, in some measure, our own.'[6] Only by first making the Other present to us through sympathy – knowing and being moved by him – can one act as a truly moral being. In *The Theory of Moral Sentiments* (1759), which 'opened the floodgate to the rising tide of interest in the sympathetic imagination',[7] Adam Smith 'represents the experience of sympathy as an epistemological and an aesthetic problem'.[8] That is, Smith demonstrated that sympathy represents more than simply feeling; it is a critical and aesthetic doctrine.

By offering sympathy as the nexus of intellect and feeling, imagination and the passions, Smith set sympathy on an irreversible course. Alexander Gerard's *Essay on Genius* (1774) exemplifies the influence that sympathy exercised on a broad range of related concepts. Gerard's vivid description of genius could equally well describe sympathy as it was coming to be understood in the latter part of the late eighteenth century. 'The mind is enraptured with the subject', writes Gerard, 'and exalted into an extasy. In this manner the fire of genius, like a divine impulse, raises the mind above itself, and by the natural influence of the imagination actuates it as if it were supernaturally inspired.'[9] Remarkably like Coleridge's account of Shakespeare's 'sublime faculty', Gerard's use of 'divine impulse' and 'supernaturally inspired' suggests an almost inexplicable process. Both passages refer to an intellectual process so charged with emotion that it 'raises the mind above itself' and into the object of its contemplation. This action – a simultaneous self-involvement and self-transcendence – is the trademark of accounts of sympathy during this period. Given that this was an age in which the critical valuation of Shakespeare and the importance of sympathy were both on the ascendant, it is no coincidence that the very quality for which Shakespeare was most admired was this ability to apparently lose himself in the Other. Elizabeth Montague praised his ability to evoke as well as to enact sympathy. His plays, she wrote, unfold

> the internal state of the persons interested, and never fail to command our sympathy. Shakespeare seems to have had the art of the Dervise, in the Arabian tales, to throw his soul into the body of another man, and be at once possessed of his sentiments, adopt his passions, and rise to all the functions and feelings of his situation.[10]

Note the metaphor of rising with which the process culminates, again suggesting the temporary movement out of and beyond the boundaries of one's own self.

By the beginning of the nineteenth century, then, Hazlitt could remark in his lectures that Shakespeare 'had only to think of any thing in
order to become that thing, with all the circumstances belonging to
it'.[11] This power which became the object of Romantic writers' admiration can be understood as a simultaneous exercising of the intellect and
the emotions, an event most often depicted as the physical metaphor of
reaching, rising or lifting oneself out of oneself and into the other's
body and being. Absorption in the Other, however, demands a great
degree of self-consciousness, an ostensibly paradoxical dialectic which
illustrates sympathy's roots in moral as well as aesthetic theory. As Bate
points out, two of the premises of British eighteenth-century philosophy
and criticism were that 'there is a natural and instinctive sympathy for
one's fellow man . . . and that, because of its primary importance in the
constitution of man, identification by sympathy, which is achieved
through the imagination, characterizes the highest moral and aesthetic
exertion'.[12] Indicative of certain assumptions current among early nineteenth-century writers and readers alike, and a principal reason for the
exalted position of the poet in the estimation of ordinary people, was
Shelley's statement in *A Defence of Poetry* that 'a man, to be greatly
good, must imagine intensely and comprehensively; he must put himself
in the place of another and of many others; the pains and pleasures of
his species must become his own'.[13] Shelley equates moral as well as
existential worth with the capacity for sympathy, or 'a going out of our
own nature', to know and to feel what the Other feels.

Sympathy and empathy: pointed concept and elusive terminology

In *The Creative Imagination*, James Engell observes that in the early
nineteenth century, sympathy 'becomes that special power of the imagination which permits the self to escape its own confines, to identify
with other people, to perceive things in a new way, and to develop an
aesthetic appreciation of the world that coalesces both the subjective
self and the objective Other'.[14] In addition to summarizing effectively
the key components of sympathy as understood by Romantic writers,
Engell's statement aptly (if unwittingly) captures the most salient aspect
of sympathy, in both early nineteenth century and twentieth century
writing: its complex and elusive nature. Engell includes within his definition of sympathy the ability to 'escape' the self, to 'identify with other
people', to 'perceive things' and, finally, to 'coalesce' subject and object
– four distinct activities, each of which represents a complex and problematic phenomenon, yet all of which somehow find common ground
under the umbrella term, 'sympathy'. These four components continue

to figure prominently in discussions of sympathy today. Indeed, the problem today is, in a sense, no different from the difficulty faced in the early nineteenth century, when sympathy was closely associated, even interchangeable, with a range of related concepts. One cluster of concepts emphasized the importance of feeling and included 'enthusiasm', 'ardor' and 'passion'. Another group, attempting to describe heightened intellectual capacity, included 'genius', 'invention', 'instinct' and 'knowledge'. Terms emphasizing 'the moral sense', especially as part of the century-long effort to rebut Hobbes, include 'fellow-feeling' and 'disinterested'. There is an enormous overlapping element among these terms and there are terms which defy categorization, such as 'projection' and one of the period's most important terms, 'sensibility'. The subtle, multiplex, even diffuse, nature of sympathy is its most characteristic feature.

In this century, the study of sympathy has been taken up by psychologists, psychoanalysts, sociologists and philosophers. As the Romantics' understanding of sympathy influenced their assumptions about the ability of one person to know another, it also strongly influenced the way they wrote and read literature. A purely historical study of sympathy in the Romantic period would become mired in the limitations of their knowledge of the human mind. In order to lend fresh insight and perspective to their ideas of sympathy, therefore, and ultimately to provide a criterion for evaluating the merit and practicability of their approach to literature, my analysis will be grounded in twentieth-century writings on the psychology of sympathy.

Before investigating the central issues elaborated by modern discussions of sympathy, we must first confront a problem of terminology. It is best articulated by Lauren Wispé in a seminal article in sympathy studies, 'The Distinction Between Sympathy and Empathy: To Call Forth a Concept, a Word Is Needed', in which he writes:

> Whatever will be written about empathy applies in principle also to the concept of sympathy. As a matter of fact, however, there has been so little recent research on so-called sympathy that the discussion must be in terms of empathy and empathy research . . . Empathy – however defined – has become the word of choice in psychology.[15]

Despite its 'substantial history' in the early twentieth century, in the past several decades 'the concept of sympathy fell into theoretical and terminological disfavour in social psychology'[16] as well as in psychotherapy and clinical psychology. To complicate matters even further, 'the crux of the problem is that although empathy is a word in common usage – which probably makes matters worse – there is little agreement among psychologists about the construct, or the process, of empathy'.[17]

The only consensus regarding empathy and sympathy among psychologists today, then, is that the terms seem to defy precise definition or understanding. Thus, the problem is twofold. Not only is the word 'sympathy' used interchangeably with 'empathy', but whichever term is used invites confusion in so far as it engenders an array of ideas and concepts.

This is not to imply that there is no basis for distinction between sympathy and empathy; most psychologists agree that there are two relatively distinct concepts which the various uses of 'sympathy' and 'empathy' are an attempt to differentiate. Wispé believes a blurring of distinctions has occurred. 'Sympathy and empathy are two different psychological processes, and . . . they should not be called by the same word.'[18] The problem is that the very same process designated by one psychologist as sympathy is likely to be called empathy by another. The literature is full of such instances. To take just one example, this is how Wispé distinguishes between sympathy and empathy: 'In empathy the self is the vehicle for understanding, and it never loses its own identity. The feelings . . . are "in the other". By contrast, sympathy is concerned with communion rather than accuracy, and self-awareness is reduced rather than augmented.'[19] Robert Katz makes the same distinction, but applies exactly the opposite labels:

> When we have sympathetic feelings in our encounters with others, we become even more sharply aware of ourselves. Our self-consciousness is intensified . . . The empathizer tends to abandon his self-consciousness . . . his own identity fuses with the identity of the other. When we empathize, we lose ourselves in the new identity we have temporarily assumed. When we sympathize, we remain more conscious of our separate identity.[20]

As further testament to the inexact state of affairs, it is not uncommon for even an author to contradict himself, often within the same work. Later in the same book, for instance, Katz contradicts his account of empathy above as a loss of self by stating that in empathy 'we feel how [the other] must be feeling and at the same time do not lose touch with our own responses to the event'. He also describes empathy as an 'alternating between subjective involvement and objective detachment'.[21] He cannot decide, it would seem, whether empathy is essentially subjective or objective or some combination of the two.

One basis for distinguishing sympathy from empathy cited by a number of psychologists is that sympathy is 'feeling sorry for another', distinguishing it from empathy which is 'understanding another, knowing what he or she is going through, knowing what her experience is like'.[22] For Eisenberg and Strayer, who embrace this view, 'empathy involves sharing the perceived emotion of another – "feeling with" another', whereas 'sympathy is "feeling for" someone, and refers to feelings of sorrow, or feeling sorry, for another. That is to say, sympathy often involves feelings of concern ... Often sympathy is the consequence of empathizing'.[23] According to this school of thought, sympathy is akin to pity and applies exclusively to situations involving another's suffering. Wispé agrees, stating it even more unequivocally. Sympathy, he contends, 'is exactly the psychological process that involves the painful awareness of someone else's affliction as something to be relieved ... This precludes sympathizing with someone's happiness'.[24]

While this is a compelling argument, other psychologists – such as Katz – disagree entirely, using sympathy as a broad category of intense emotional and intellectual phenomena, virtually indistinguishable from the above definitions of empathy. Most of the phenomena described in Scheler's *The Nature of Sympathy* (1913), for example, correspond closely to recent writings on empathy. Alexander Sutherland, writing at the turn of the century, believed that sympathy is 'that general tendency which makes men grieve at the pains and rejoice in the pleasures of their fellows'.[25] James Sully wrote that 'in sympathizing with a person, we are occupied with his feelings as such, and are ourselves in a state of resonant feeling'.[26] Yet another turn-of-the-century psychologist determined that sympathy 'is in a very great degree intellectual, that it rests upon intellectual operations'.[27]

Therefore, while many modern psychologists – not to mention common speakers – regard 'feeling sorry for' someone else as belonging to the realm of sympathy, there is no consensus for this being the basis for a distinction between sympathy and empathy. Wispé's definitive examination of the two terms makes it clear that they are just that – two terms for one body of psycho-emotional concepts and phenomena. Reaching a distinction should be less important than appreciating the fundamental issues at stake, regardless of the terms which are rather arbitrarily applied to those issues. Indeed, proponents of the 'distinction' school of thought seem to find certainty where there is none in terms of the difference between sympathy and empathy. For instance, it is at best specious to distinguish between the way in which 'sympathy intensifies both the representation and the internal reaction to the other person's predicament'[28] and the designation of empathy as 'an emotional response that stems from another's emotional state or condition and that is congruent with the other's state or situation'.[29]

The failure to reach a clear definition of empathy or sympathy or both, is less a sign of intellectual weakness than an indication of the richness of the psychological phenomena toward which the two terms are reaching. Eisenberg and Strayer, in their introductory chapter to an extensive series of essays investigating empathy, imply this: 'In part because of its wide-ranging application, the notion of empathy is, and always has been, a broad, somewhat slippery concept – one that has provoked considerable speculation, excitement, and confusion.'[30] The distinctions which, as we have seen, they proceed to make between this 'slippery' concept and its twin, sympathy, can hardly be taken as more than a suggestion, given the lengths to which they go to illustrate empathy's indefinite boundaries. In an essay in a volume entitled *Empathy II*, psychologist John J. Hartman finds similar evidence for uncertainty: 'as a term, "empathy" has evolved in such a way that it means many different things to many different people'.[31] Kenneth Clark makes a similar implication in his comment that 'the available literature does neglect a clear definition and a comprehensive theoretical approach to this important phenomenon',[32] though to be more precise it is not that empathy itself is neglected, but that its definition is elusive.

In other words, it is as if the chaos stems from the very breadth and suggestiveness of the term – which Wispé's study indicates to be 'empathy' – whether the phenomenon to which it corresponds be called sympathy or empathy. Hence Deutsch and Madle's conclusion in a recent article: 'Despite the variety of conceptualizations of empathy, few empirical advances have been made. One reason for this paucity of significant research appears to be a lack of consensus for operational definitions of empathy.'[33] As early as 1937, in his influential work, *Pattern and Growth in Personality*, Gordon Allport attests to the term's imprecision: 'It is regrettable that with passing years the original meaning of empathy as "objective motor mimicry" became hopelessly confused and lost to view. The term has broadened out to mean any process of successful understanding or inference.'[34] At the time Allport's book was published, empathy was less than 30 years old, having been coined by Edward Titchener in 1909 as a translation of the German *Einfuhlung* ('feeling into') made famous by Theodor Lipps 'to explain how a person grasped the meaning of aesthetic objects and the consciousness of other persons . . . *Einfuhlung*, understood in this very general sense, became the way of understanding all forms of psychic participation'.[35]

This notion of a 'freemasonry among all men',[36] as Titchener called it, is the broad way from which we must approach the general concept embodied by the words sympathy and empathy. This does not mean that we will be unable to reach a more precise and useful understanding of, and distinction between, the terms. Rather, it is the only starting-point supported by recent literature and the most effective view from which to commence identifying and delineating specific components of the intellectual and emotional phenomenon of 'psychic participation'. For the time being, the basic distinction is that empathy is the comprehensive understanding of another's experience, and sympathy is the

feelingful response to that achieved understanding. Yet this will be seen
to be clearly inadequate, because empathy is also an emotional phenomenon, just as sympathy is also an intellectual one. Thus, while
countless writers have attempted to articulate definite distinctions between sympathy and empathy, reading these many accounts makes clear
that what matters is not the terminology but certain key issues which
consistently form the basis of these discussions and writings, most
notably the way in which the self participates intellectually and emotionally in the experience of the Other. Thus, for most of this chapter,
the two terms will be used interchangeably, depending upon the particular choice of the writer under discussion. The final part of my argument, however, will establish guidelines for a new understanding of the
terms, particularly with respect to the sympathetic nature of the relationship between reader and text.

While the goal of this investigation is not to develop criteria for
distinguishing sympathy from empathy, certain guidelines will emerge
as we undertake the more important task of exploring the key issues in
twentieth-century writings on empathy and sympathy. The one element
of the phenomenon of 'psychic participation', whether it is called by the
name of sympathy or empathy, about which virtually all psychologists
agree is that it is a psycho-emotional activity – that is, both intellectual
and emotional. The other principal issues to be addressed all centre
around the question of what exactly happens in empathy or sympathy:
what *is* sympathy? The various avenues of inquiry and debate pursued
within the disciplines of psychology, psychotherapy, sociology and philosophy can be divided into three major issues. First is the degree to
which the self is involved in the Other, versus the extent to which the
self is differentiated from the Other, and whether sympathy entails a
blurring of self and Other; to what extent does (must) a loss of self
accompany sympathy? Second, and closely related, is the degree to
which heightened Other-awareness is accompanied by greater insight
into the sympathizer's own identity; a key question here is the relative
extent to which the focus in sympathy is on the self versus the Other.
Finally, is sympathy essentially an act of communication or an act of
understanding? Does the sympathizer actively shape the event or does
he/she play a more reactive, interpretive role?

Intellect and feeling, cognition and affect

Titchener's introduction of 'empathy' into the language defined it as
'the tendency to feel oneself into a situation ... on the analogy of
sympathy, which is feeling together with another'.[37] Whether 'feeling

into' or 'feeling with' another, feeling is allied with knowing to create, if not a bond, a shared experiential space between the sympathetic self and the Other. In this respect, studies of empathy since Titchener, and particularly in recent decades, have in common the belief in empathy as a form of knowing. Much as the Romantic writers overturned the neo-classical belief in science and reason in favour of the imagination, with its fusion of intellect and passion, as the human faculty best suited for the revelation of truth, twentieth-century clinical psychologists have advocated empathy as a means of seeking the truth in the therapy setting.[38] In his book, *A Preface to Empathy*, David Stewart acknowl-edges empathy's roots in and kinship with science: both represent a search for knowledge and truth. But like his Romantic counterparts, Stewart asserts that scientific knowing is inadequate to the truth of human nature: 'When science is thought to be the only way to truth and to insight, especially in personal behavior, it then constitutes one of the obstructions which it is the purpose of empathy to overcome.'[39] He distinguishes between the 'empathic knower' and the 'scientific knower',[40] in the object as well as the means of their inquiry:

> If you do not go beyond the scientific phase, you cannot say that you know a person. At best, you may say that you have scientific knowledge about a human being, a living creature, a biological entity. But the basis of scientific knowledge of a human being, an incomplete knowledge of that being as person, is spontaneous identification, the first stage of the same process which naturally completes itself in the personal act of empathy. This initial crude identification requires psychological completion in an act of delib-erate re-identification, one person with another, in order to qualify as an act of empathy.[41]

What is here being called empathy, then, is a form of knowing which demands the involvement of something beyond purely intellectual facul-ties. Feeling is an essential element of empathic and sympathetic know-ing. For Katz this bipolar – both feelingful and intellectual – approach is vital to grasping and understanding the truth of the Other, 'what is individual and distinctive in a person . . . When the knower employs his own feeling and does not rely exclusively on concepts that are necessar-ily abstract and stereotyped, he understands more profoundly'.[42] For Joseph Lichtenberg, the 'empathic process' is not merely 'an under-standing of emotions'.[43] That is, empathy consists of feeling as well as understanding.

Martin Buber, who has written profoundly and subtly about the interrelationship between persons, calls this kind of total self-engage-ment in the Other 'imagining the real', which he describes as 'not a looking at the other, but a bold swinging – demanding the most inten-

sive stirring of one's being – into the life of the other'.[44] 'Stirring' and
'swinging' 'into the life of the other' recall the physical images of self-
transcendence characteristic of late eighteenth-century Shakespeare criticism; they suggest, among other things, involvement so elemental between self and Other so as not merely to bring about emotional identification with and understanding of the Other, but to move and transform
the sympathizing self incalculably, if temporarily. In *The Empathic Imagination*, psychiatrist Alfred Margulies likewise envisions the empathic
act as a combining of all human faculties. He uses the example of a
patient's dreams to illustrate the way in which the therapist enters into
and experiences the other's world, not merely his or her feelings, thoughts
or troubles: 'For a moment, I live the near ecstatic experience in all of
its vividness; I feel the seductive pull and fear of larger-than-life intensity and euphoria, the connection to the cosmic, the dissolution of
boundaries. I can now better understand.'[45]

Understanding alone, however, is not the goal of sympathy. What all
these accounts share is the suggestion that in so far as empathy and
sympathy engage a deeper part of the self – indeed the total self – and
diverge away from the purely scientific toward the emotional, they must
be recognized as essentially imprecise phenomena. More specifically,
these accounts illustrate that some sort of 'dissolution of boundaries', a
blurring of self and Other, is necessary in order not simply to achieve
knowledge and understanding of another, but actually, somehow, to
experience the Other. David Stewart illustrates this wholly unscientific
blurring of distinction that occurs in empathy, due largely to the fundamental role played by emotion:

> In science, scientific knowing and the scientific object are required
> by logical discipline to be distinct and clearly independent of one
> another to facilitate provisionally the efforts of science. But when
> the psychologist sets out to know another person as agent like
> himself, he finds that the neat dichotomy necessary in scientific
> work is no longer present . . . He cannot draw a clear line between
> his intentions and those of his fellow agent. He knows the other by
> identification with himself, he projects or introjects, not sure at
> first whether he has mistakenly identified, either in one direction or
> another. Still, his feelings are essential in understanding the feelings
> of the other, though he can never be completely sure either of his
> feelings as belonging independently to himself, or, of the other's as
> belonging independently to the other.[46]

As a scientist, the therapist must seek to understand; as one seeking
understanding, the therapist must feel, for 'feelings are essential in
understanding'.

Absorption and blurring of identities

The crux of scholarly debate on this issue is whether self and Other merge in sympathy or whether the sympathizer maintains consciousness of his/her distinct identity at all times throughout the process. Many psychologists agree with Stewart's conception of successful empathy as being necessarily uncertain in the boundaries it draws between self and Other. Katz describes this blurring of identities: 'We reverberate to the emotions of the other person and are no longer aware of our separate identity.'[47] The word 'reverberate' points to a problematic image used frequently in literature on empathy and sympathy. As early as 1889 the image is used by James Sully to describe sympathy: 'the mind of the person affected does not consciously represent or dwell on the feeling which affects him, but simply vibrates in common with it'.[48] 'Reverberate' and 'vibrate' imply a back-and-forth movement and suggests that empathy is a process, rather than a singular activity or moment. Psychoanalyst Theodor Reik employs the same image in explaining the analyst's own inner dynamic in any successful relationship with a client. After the essential initial 'stage of observation', the therapist must 'vibrate unconsciously in the rhythm of the other person's impulse and yet be capable of grasping it as something outside himself and comprehending it psychologically, sharing the other person's experience and yet remaining above the struggle'.[49] For Reik the analyst's own concomitant psychological and emotional state is crucial not only to achieving significant involvement in the client's own inner experience, but also to preventing the analyst from losing his/her own identity in the process. He describes the process further: 'The first step in sharing the unconscious emotion is the condition of psychological comprehension: his own hidden affective impulse comes to be a means of cognition, but until it is mastered there can be no objectively valid knowledge of the inner processes of the other person.'[50] Detached assessment, at once the goal and the prerequisite of empathizing, becomes inevitably intertwined with shared emotion.

Several modern accounts of empathy and sympathy delineate some sort of multi-step process, like the one portrayed by the 'reverberating' of Katz and Reik, and all of them progress from observation through active immersion in the other's experience to objective evaluation of the experience. Katz himself identifies four phases of empathy: 1) an involuntary identification, in which 'we are projected into the other person by our own fantasy, response, or feeling'; 2) 'incorporation', or 'the act of taking the other person into ourselves'; 3) 'reverberation', or 'the dialectic between the actual me and the me which is identified with the other person'; and 4) 'detachment', in which 'we break our identifica-

Gramley Library
Salem Academy and College
Winston-Salem, N.C. 27108

tion and deliberately move away to gain the social and psychic distance necessary for objective analysis'.[51] Edith Stein describes a similar process in different terminology: emergence of the experience, the fulfilling explication, and comprehensive objectification of the explained experience.[52] Sully's process of sympathy involves observation, interpretation – recalling past emotional experiences, implying that one must understand before one can sympathize – and finally 'a higher form of sympathy' requiring an effort of 'the constructive imagination'[53] (like the Romantics' 'shaping spirit'). Such a process, as opposed to a momentary phenomenon, is important because it provides a mechanism whereby the sympathizer can lose him/herself temporarily in the Other while still ultimately differentiating between self and Other. This twofold dynamic is most often characterized, as Reik has done above, by the terms cognitive and affective – intellect and emotion – the two key elements in sympathy.

Psychologist Carl Rogers has provided the definitive account of this essentially twofold process of loss of self through immersion in the Other while maintaining, or finally re-establishing, distinct self-awareness. In a seminal 1958 article, he said 'empathy is the ability to sense the client's private world as if it were your own without ever losing the "as if" quality'.[54] Since that time, the 'as if' caveat has become central to our understanding of the empathic process. Katz, for instance, makes explicit reference to it in describing empathy: 'We are involved in as-if behavior. We become self-forgetful. Abandoning our own self, we seem to become fused with and absorbed in the inner experience of the other person.'[55] Note the placement of 'seem' in conjunction with 'fused' and 'absorbed'; rather than mitigating their impact, 'seem' serves to clarify the physical images of oneness. David Woodruff Smith's recent phenomenological study of perception, consciousness and empathy makes the 'as if' quality the fulcrum between loss of self, and total, direct experiencing of the Other:

> Empathy is understanding another's experience from the other's point of view, projecting oneself into the other's place as subject of her experience. Thus, in empathic perception, I see 'her' as another 'I', a fellow subject whose selfhood I understand through empathy and my own self-awareness. As self-awareness in consciousness is a direct awareness of oneself as 'I', so other-awareness in empathic perception is a direct awareness of another person as 'her' or 'him' or 'you', understood as if 'I'.[56]

While some psychologists argue that 'you' or 'she' becomes part of and one with 'I', 'at least for a moment',[57] the Rogerian school insist that separateness is maintained throughout. Significantly, this does not mean that absorption in the Other is in any measure hampered or attenuated.

Gramley Library
Salem Academy and College
Winston-Salem, N.C. 27108

As an illustration of this, Rogers cites a description of what is called 'the nondirective attitude', in which

> counselor participation becomes an active experiencing with the client of the feelings to which he gives expression, the counselor makes a maximum effort to get under the skin of the person with whom he is communicating, he tries to get within and to live the attitudes expressed instead of observing them ... in a word, to absorb himself completely in the attitudes of the other.[58]

Nevertheless, the *illusion* of blurring, or loss of self, which often accompanies this absorption remains just that, for the 'as if' element means that the empathizer's self-absorption in the Other stops short of self-abnegation, without – paradoxically – sacrificing utter immersion in the Other.

Even before Rogers and the mid-twentieth-century surge in writing on empathy, two works on sympathy early in the century base their analysis on a very similar concept. Joseph Jones, in *Sociality and Sympathy* (1903), describes a situation in which person 'A' sympathizes with person 'B', who is in pain. Although through cognition sympathy is often aided by memories of like experiences, the 'as if' quality enables the self to venture beyond the bounds of its own experiences and into the life of the Other:

> A now feels pain not in terms of a mere remembered self, but in terms of the self, at the moment presented to him in B. Through the recognized ... attributes in B, the experience has indeed become actually A's again, but A's pain by what might be called the illusion of the sympathetic state is the pain of this alter ego-B ... It is *sui generis* among experiences, for the pain is felt centered in another being; and this is what we mean by sympathy.[59]

The 'illusion' of oneness between A and B, the equivalent of Rogers's 'as if', represents the key to this process, for while Jones asserts that 'this oneness of self is the essential mark of sympathy', he adds that 'the subject is conscious from first to last of a difference between himself and the object ... There is seldom if ever an absolute blending of the subject's self with the object'.[60]

A decade later, Max Scheler attacks the problem of sympathy in much greater depth and detail, and one of his conclusions likewise foreshadows later work in empathy, such as that by Rogers and Smith. He describes fellow-feeling, his highest form of sympathy, as a twofold process in which what is traditionally called empathy, or objective understanding, is followed by sympathy, or affective response: 'that is, my commiseration and his suffering are phenomenologically two different facts, not one fact'.[61] The self is not lost in the Other. The beauty of sympathy, according to Scheler, lies precisely in its difference from such related concepts as imitation, emotional contagion or infection (attributing the other's emotion to myself), and what he calls empathy (attributing my emotion to the Other). In true fellow-feeling, he avers,

> there is no reference to the state of one's own feelings. In commiserating with B, the latter's state of feeling is given as located entirely in B himself: it does not filter across into A, the commiserator, nor does it produce a corresponding or similar condition in A. It is merely 'commiserated with', not undergone by A as a real experience ... We are able to savour their joy without thereby needing to get into a joyful mood ourselves.[62]

Maintaining the distinction between self and Other is paramount in Scheler's influential conception of sympathy, despite the fact that the goal remains absorption in the Other. The point is to understand, appreciate and 'savour' the other's feelings and experiences without, however, losing oneself in the process, for without the separate sympathizing self there would be no sympathy. The paradox is that the goal of complete immersion in the life of the Other entails the need to remain two distinct beings. So, too, with current empathy theory. 'There appears to be recent agreement that an empathic response requires self-other differentiation.'[63]

Sympathy, self-knowledge and personal identity

The blurring of self–Other distinction – symbolized by a loss of self – and objective detachment are one pair of extremes which must be balanced in sympathy and empathy. But there is another opposite of a loss of self, and that is intense subjective involvement, or a focus on self. All the accounts we have examined illustrate that the role of the self is far more important than that of the Other, the object of sympathy. Now we shall explore exactly why this is so as we address the relationship between sympathy and identity, that is, how the psycho-emotional phenomenon of heightened Other-awareness can lead to greater insight into oneself and is intimately connected to personal identity. In a characteristic moment, Katz describes empathy as 'a pendulum-like action, alternating between subjective involvement and objective detachment',[64] suggesting that the focus is either on one's own feelings or on none at all, and that the self, far from being lost or melted into the other person's identity, is the cornerstone of the empathic process. Near the turn of the century, before empathy had emerged on the scene, Jones claimed that in addition to being 'a direct function of my consciousness of kind', sympathy is also 'the recognition of my most fundamental self'.[65] By defining 'consciousness of kind', or the condition of Other-awareness, as the recognition of oneself in another, Jones links inextricably the idea of sympathy with the notion of personal identity, a pairing not only suggested by the Romantic admirers of Shakespeare, but also embraced by empathy studies in recent decades.

It is paradoxical that an act of sympathy or empathy is fundamentally about the self at least as much as it is about the Other. Yet, as Stewart argues, 'empathy, far from blurring personal identity, makes it possible'.[66] This begins, he explains, when

> the other person will display behavior which appears foreign to your original feelings of identification with him. You then try to imagine something similar in your own experience in order to understand and accept the increasingly foreign elements in the other's behavior. This enables you, not only to understand the other better, but also better to understand yourself.[67]

Thus it is the effort demanded by difference which helps not only to create empathic understanding, but also to gain insight into oneself. Even when one is able to draw on one's own similar experience as a means to empathic insight into the Other, thereby minimizing difference, effort is required and bears fruit in the form of personal insight. Stewart illustrates this by using a typical clinical and therapy scenario:

> The recovered alcoholic has an appreciation of the active drinker's behavior for having been through the same experience, but in empathy, instead of criticizing or judging, the recovered man uses this means to knowledge of the other to know himself better, to strengthen his sobriety, and reciprocally to introduce the 'know-how' of sobriety to the active addict.[68]

Earlier we saw that some psychologists locate sympathy's distinguishing feature in the painful nature of the feelings involved and in the attendant desire to take action in order to alleviate the other's suffering. In the quote above, Stewart makes the same claim for empathy, offering further evidence of the arbitrariness with which the two terms are defined. More important, however, the scenario of the recovered alcoholic demonstrates that sympathy is a process, rather than a moment of emotional attachment, whose motive and end are not merely the understanding or benefit of another, but also insight into oneself.

Margulies equates empathy with wonder, both of which phenomena correspond to 'a searching attitude of simultaneously knowing and not-knowing', and he posits that the search for the Other is really a search for one's own self: 'The quest for empathy leads to the irreducible paradox of the self – which defines and finds itself through the other in its own reflective and interpersonal spiral.' This spiral, like the 'vibration' and 'reverberation' we saw earlier, is a dialectical process wherein 'we will unavoidably find ourselves reflected within our gaze toward the other. I look for you and see myself; I have no choice but to draw on what I know and feel'.[69] Katz uses a similar image for the process, portraying empathy as a medium through which the other person 'is a source for our own self-understanding, a mirror in which we are reflected'.[70] In other words, the sympathizing (or empathizing) person may be said to be one who loses him/herself for a time *in* the Other, but who avoids losing him/herself *to* the Other. In this way, one's own identity, far from being lost in the quest for the Other, becomes equally a subject and an object of the search itself. As a consequence, 'when empathy is lacking, our self-awareness and self-respect are diminished. We then experience ourselves more as objects and less as persons'.[71]

The quest for personal identity, however, can lead to the very opposite, a reification of the other person by a desire to control, instead of understand and feel, his/her experience. Twentieth-century theory has emphasized empathy's function of counteracting the basic egotistic drive within the human psyche, therefore also denoting empathy as a manifestly effortful process. Psychologist Martin Hoffman explains that '[e]mpathy may be uniquely suited for bridging the gap between egoism and altruism, since it has the property of transforming another person's misfortune into one's own feeling of distress. Empathy thus has elements of both egoism and altruism'.[72] This is why, near the turn of the century, before empathy had emerged on the scene, James Sully wrote that sympathy 'is the great force which binds the individual to his social environment', and that 'the giving of sympathy is largely a matter of exchange'.[73] Scheler reiterates this notion in his account of sympathy: 'It is precisely in the act of fellow-feeling that self-love, self-centered choice, solipsism and egoism are first wholly overcome.'[74] More recently, Wispé likewise called sympathy 'the basis for the social bond'.[75] In other words, the very struggle for survival stimulates the ego in the strongest terms, while likewise giving rise to sympathy and co-operation. Jones explains this phenomenon on a macro, or social, level:

> Society, if it means anything, means a structure built out of the great life-needs of the creature. It is this thing of activity and struggle that must be varied and transformed through sympathetic and altruistic dispositions, if there is ever to arise a society which is conscious and psychic in its bone and marrow.[76]

Written in the wake of Darwinian evolution theory, Jones's book conveys a sense of anxiety and urgency about the need for sympathy to play an active role in human relations.

The human struggle is no less complicated nearly a century later, and psychologists and sociologists confront the issue of power on the individual, psychological level. Kenneth Clark regards power and empathy as the two crucial elements in our achieving an understanding of what it means to interact with and understand one another. He observes, 'I must now view empathy and power as inextricable components of human dynamics. Power and empathy may be seen as conflicting or counterbalancing dynamics in the individual's struggle for some sort of equilibrium in his or her interaction with others.'[77] In this light, the key to the empathic process lies in recognition of the fact that psychological participation in another's experience, no less than social survival, represents a 'struggle' of sorts: to reiterate, empathy is an effortful process.

Significantly, Margulies uses the very same image in explicating empathy as 'the listening dialectic that emerges in the ongoing struggle to enter another's reality'.[78] The strong suggestion underlying this and much of recent empathy literature is that what is needed is a communicative and creative process, not merely a mirroring or echoing, on the one hand, or a one-dimensional quest for personal identity, on the other. Thus Margulies: 'The therapist must strive for a position of tension between knowing and not-knowing. Empathy is not merely a resonating with the other, but an act of will and creativity.'[79] Effort, struggle and conflict – not simply either loss of the self to the Other or loss of the Other within the personal identity of the self – must characterize the empathic process, making its goal communication, not simply listening or echoing.

Communication and context

One manifestation of this egotistic impulse lies in the attempt to determine the meaning created within the context of the empathic process. The interpersonal psychological implications of this drive may be seen, therefore, by shifting attention away from the dichotomy of self and Other, and examining the linguistic context in which sympathy occurs. Stewart writes that 'as a knower of people, I do not primarily seek to control them, but to become acquainted with them'.[80] Yet control takes subtle forms, and in the effort to achieve insightful understanding of another and oneself, even empathy can hamper genuine understanding and communication.

In a pivotal article in empathy studies, Arnett and Nakagawa explain what they see as the problem with our understanding of empathy:

> Empathic listening literature in speech communication largely presupposes a fundamental dualism between two independently existing subjects, correlative to the communicative functions of speaking and listening. Based upon the necessity to reconcile the presumed separation between self and other, the empathic listener's task is to infer the psychological intentions or internal states of the

speaker. Accordingly, subjective experience becomes the final arbiter of meaning ('Meaning is in people, not in words.').[81]

The central place of the assumed distinction between self and Other constantly threatens to make the empathic process a purely subjective or purely objective determination of meaning. Arnett and Nakagawa refer to this as the 'internal bias' because it regards the self as the sole source of meaning rather than seeking meaning in the actual encounter *between* two persons. As a result, the dialectic nature of the empathic process – what Margulies and Clark described as the interpersonal 'struggle' – is lost, and meaning becomes purely a function of the empathizer's capacity to determine the content and nature of the other's experience. Central to what is called the 'inference theory' of empathy, then, the internal bias 'results in focusing attention on "getting in touch with one's own self" and "attempting to understand the other's self". This concentration on self reifies the notion into a possessable entity'.[82]

Perhaps the quintessential example of the 'internal bias', Reik's account of 'the third ear' conceives of the empathizer as a combination of detective, translator and narcissist:

> The psychoanalyst who hopes to recognize the secret meaning of this almost imperceptible, imponderable language has to sharpen his sensitiveness to it, to increase his readiness to receive it. When he wants to decode it, he can do so only by listening sharply inside himself, by becoming aware of the subtle impressions it makes upon him and the fleeting thoughts and emotions it arouses in him ... [Thus] he can arrive at its unconscious motives and meanings ... The only way of penetrating into the secret of this language is by looking into oneself, understanding one's own reactions to it.[83]

For Reik, the role of listener – and analogously, I shall argue, reader – hinges less on identifying with the other person than on 'decoding' a 'secret' 'language' and unearthing 'unconscious motives and meanings', a process at once highly subjective and objectifying. Instead of assuming a concept of self, and empathizing 'by using the self-concept to make inferences about the internal states of other people', Arnett and Nakagawa argue that the concept of self must be regarded as a product of the dialogical context in which human beings confront and know one another.

> We need to explore and develop alternatives ... to the internal, inference-based approach that grounds many empathic studies. The internal assumption of empathic listening must cease to view the person's internal feelings as most important; rather, the meaning given birth between partners in relationship may be the pivotal point for inquiry.[84]

Arnett and Nakagawa suggest that 'the pursuit of the self' in empathic listening 'results in a shift from self as "being-in-the-world" to self as "being-attempting-to-possess-the-world"'.[85] Yet, in apparent contradiction to this, the thesis of Stewart's book is that empathy makes both personal identity and communication possible. As a 'deliberate identification with another, accompanied by growing insight into both oneself and the other', empathy is 'a technique necessary to . . . interpersonal communication'.[86] The key to successful empathic process is not simply ignoring the self, but recognizing its limitations and its contextual – that is, interpersonal – grounding: 'in self-discipline I shall resist wanting to control you, an easy substitute for knowing you, a harder task'. The goal of the empathizing person, according to Stewart, is 'to integrate myself as a living pattern in order the better to know and be known'.[87] The fundamental desire to integrate the self 'as a living pattern' and thereby 'to know and be known' is where Stewart meets Arnett and Nakagawa, who 'suggest a shift from psyche to the linguisticality of human relationships, analogous to the Copernican revolution. The self, like the earth, can no longer be viewed as the center, but the person must be studied as situated in relationship with the ecological system or relational system between persons'.[88]

As the title of their article implies, Arnett and Nakagawa advocate a change in the assumptions people read into the idea of empathy. Taking their argument as a starting-point – particularly in view of the remarkably arbitrary distinction between 'sympathy' and 'empathy' and the need for an adequate way of focusing on and describing the central idea in both – perhaps what is needed is an idea rather than a word. The idea, I submit, is that human beings are capable of understanding and responding feelingfully to another person's experience, and what is important is not so much *how* this takes place cognitively and emotionally or the name we assign it, as that it *can and does* take place and that this interpersonal medium is the context for the ongoing creation of the self. The 'linguisticality' means that this self is not a given; rather, understanding occurs in the same context – the same moment, the same text – as communication. This 'dialogical or hermeneutical transaction "between" persons'[89] will form the basis for the next chapter, in which we will examine Romantic assumptions about reading and the text.

Notes

1. A. Margulies (1989), *The Empathic Imagination*, New York: W. W. Norton, 36.

2. S. T. Coleridge (1930), *Shakespearean Criticism*, 2 vols, T. Raysor (ed.), Cambridge, MA: Harvard University Press, vol. I, 212.
3. J. Engell (1981), *The Creative Imagination: Enlightenment to Romanticism*, Cambridge, MA: Harvard University Press, 143.
4. W. J. Bate (1945), 'The Sympathetic Imagination in Eighteenth-Century Criticism', *Journal of English Literary History*, 12, 144.
5. Engell, *The Creative Imagination*, 55.
6. D. Hume (1888), *A Treatise of Human Nature*, L. A. Selby-Bigge (ed.), Oxford: Clarendon Press, 441.
7. Engell, *The Creative Imagination*, 149.
8. D. Marshall (1988), *The Surprising Effects of Sympathy: Marivaux, Diderot, Rousseau and Mary Shelley*, Chicago: University of Chicago Press, 5.
9. A. Gerard (1774), *An Essay on Genius*, B. Fabian (ed.) (1966), Munich: W. Fink, 68. Earlier, in his *Essay on Taste* (1759), Gerard had addressed sympathy directly: 'The force of sympathy . . . enlivens our ideas of the passions infused by it to such a pitch, as in a manner converts them to the passions themselves' (in Bate, 'The Sympathetic Imagination', 169–70).
10. E. Montague, *Essays on the Writings and Genius of Shakespeare* (1769), 37, in Engell, *The Creative Imagination*, 154. W. Richardson likewise wrote, 'He is the proteus of the drama' and 'changes himself into every character', *Philosophical analysis and illustration of some of Shakespeare's remarkable characters* (1774), 38, 10, in Engell, *The Creative Imagination*, 8.
11. W. Hazlitt (1930–34), *The Complete Works of William Hazlitt*, 21 vols, P. P. Howe (ed.) after edn of A. R. Waller and A. Glover, London: J. M. Dent, vol. 5, 50.
12. Bate, 'The Sympathetic Imagination', 159.
13. P. B. Shelley (1967), 'A Defence of Poetry', in David Perkins (ed.), *English Romantic Writers*, New York: Harcourt, Brace and World, 1076.
14. Engell, *The Creative Imagination*, 143–4.
15. L. Wispé (1986), 'The Distinction Between Sympathy and Empathy: To Call Forth a Concept, a Word Is Needed', *Journal of Personality and Social Psychology*, 50, 316.
16. Wispé, 'The Distinction', 315.
17. Ibid., 317.
18. Ibid., 314.
19. Ibid., 318.
20. R. L. Katz (1963), *Empathy: Its Nature and Uses*, New York: Free Press, 9.
21. Katz, *Empathy*, 39, 27.
22. D. W. Smith (1989), *The Circle of Acquaintance: Perception, Consciousness and Empathy*, Dordrecht: Kluwer, 115.
23. N. Eisenberg and J. Strayer (1987), 'Critical Issues in the Study of Empathy', in N. Eisenberg and J. Strayer (eds), *Empathy and Its Development*, Cambridge: Cambridge University Press, 5, 6.
24. Wispé, 'The Distinction', 318.
25. A. Sutherland (1898), *The Origin and Growth of the Moral Instinct*, 2 vols, London: Longmans, Green, vol. 2, 302.
26. J. Sully (1889), *Outlines of Psychology*, 2 vols, London: Longmans, Green, vol. 2, 111.

27. A. Bain (1903), as quoted in J. Jones, *Sociality and Sympathy*, in J. M. Baldwin and J. M. Cattell (eds), vol. 5, no. 1, *The Psychological Review*, New York: Macmillan, 3–4.
28. Wispé, 'The Distinction', 318.
29. Eisenberg and Strayer, 'Critical Issues', 5.
30. Ibid., 3.
31. J. J. Hartman (1984), 'Discussion' of N. Gregory Hamilton, 'Empathic understanding' (pp. 217–22), in J. Lichtenberg, M. Borstein and D. Silver (eds), *Empathy II*, Hillsdale, NJ: Analytic Press, 224.
32. K. B. Clark (1980), 'Empathy: A Neglected Topic in Psychological Research', *American Psychologist*, 35, (2) February, 187.
33. F. Deutsch and R. Madle (1975), 'Empathy: Historic and Current Conceptualizations, Measurement, and a Cognitive Theoretical Perspective', *Human Development*, 18, 282.
34. G. W. Allport (1937), *Pattern and Growth in Personality*, New York: Holt, Rinehart and Winston, 536.
35. L. Wispé, 'History of the Concept of Empathy', in Eisenberg and Strayer, *Empathy and Its Development*, 20.
36. E. B. Titchener (1915), *A Beginner's Psychology*, New York: The Macmillan Company, 293.
37. Ibid., 198.
38. See, for instance, J. Strayer, 'Affective and Cognitive Perspectives on Empathy', in Eisenberg and Strayer, *Empathy and Its Development*.
39. D. Stewart (1956), *A Preface to Empathy*, New York: Philosophical Library, 3.
40. Stewart, *A Preface*, 135.
41. Ibid., 15.
42. Katz, *Empathy*, 15, 17.
43. J. Lichtenberg (1984), 'The Empathic Mode of Perception and Alternative Vantage Points for Psychoanalytic Work', Lichtenberg, Borstein and Silver, 115.
44. M. Buber (1965), *The Knowledge of Man*, M. Friedman and R. G. Smith (tr.), London: George Allen and Unwin, 81.
45. Margulies, *The Empathic*, 34.
46. Stewart, *A Preface*, 136–7.
47. Katz, *Empathy*, 5.
48. Sully, *Outlines*, 508.
49. T. Reik (1949), *Listening with the Third Ear: The Inner Experience of a Psychoanalyst*, New York: Farrar, Straus, 468.
50. Reik, *Listening*, 468–9.
51. Katz, *Empathy*, 41, 42, 44, 46.
52. E. Stein (1970), *On the Problem of Empathy*, W. Stein (tr.), The Hague: Martinus Nijhoff, 10 ff.
53. Sully, *Outlines*, 511.
54. C. R. Rogers (1958), 'Characteristics of a Helping Relationship', *Personality Guidance Journal*, 37, 13.
55. Katz, *Empathy*, 5.
56. Smith, *The Circle*, 112 (my emphasis).
57. Reik, *Listening*, 464.
58. N. J. Raskin (1947), 'The Nondirective Attitude', unpublished manu-

script, in C. R. Rogers (1951), *Client-Centered Therapy*, Boston: Houghton Mifflin, 29.

59. Jones, *Sociality*, 8.
60. Ibid., 8, 9.
61. M. Scheler (1970), *The Nature of Sympathy*, P. Heath (tr.), Hamden, CT: Archon Books, originally published in German (1913), 13.
62. Scheler, *The Nature*, 41.
63. Deutsch and Madle, 'Empathy: Historic and Current', 271.
64. Katz, *Empathy*, 27.
65. Jones, *Sociality*, 11.
66. Stewart, *A Preface*, 20.
67. Ibid., 10.
68. Ibid., 17.
69. Margulies, *The Empathic*, xii, 58.
70. Katz, *Empathy*, 79.
71. Ibid., 8.
72. M. L. Hoffman (1981), 'Is Altruism Part of Human Nature?', *Journal of Personality and Social Psychology*, 40, 133. Stewart, *A Preface*, 13, touches on a similar idea when he remarks that 'empathy is the therapeutic corrective of self-pity and of pain'.
73. Sully, *Outlines*, 508. A decade later James Baldwin uses similar terminology, referring to sympathy as 'some form of social instinct'. J. M. Baldwin (1902), *Social and Ethical Interpretations in Mental Development*, New York: Macmillan, 45.
74. Scheler, *The Nature*, 98.
75. L. Wispé (1978), 'Toward an Integration', in L. Wispé (ed.), *Altruism, Sympathy, and Helping: Psychological and Sociological Principles*, London: Academic Press, 319.
76. Jones, *Sociality*, 86.
77. Clark, 'Empathy: A Neglected Topic', 188.
78. Margulies, *The Empathic*, 21.
79. Ibid., 18.
80. Stewart, *A Preface*, 16.
81. R. C. Arnett and G. Nakagawa (1983), 'The Assumptive Roots of Empathic Listening: A Critique', *Communication Education*, 32, October, 370.
82. Arnett and Nakagawa, 'The Assumptive Roots', 371.
83. Reik, *Listening*, 147.
84. Arnett and Nakagawa, 'The Assumptive Roots', 374–5.
85. Ibid., 372.
86. Stewart, *A Preface*, 41.
87. Ibid., 8, 16.
88. Arnett and Nakagawa, 'The Assumptive Roots', 375.
89. Ibid., 375.

CHAPTER ONE

The hermeneutics of sympathy

In a hermeneutic enterprise, reading necessarily intervenes but, like computation in an algebraic proof, it is a means toward an end, a means that should finally become transparent and superfluous; the ultimate aim of a hermeneutically successful reading is to do away with reading altogether.[1]

My head has grown giddy in following the windings of the drawing in Raphael, and I have gazed on the breadth of Titian, where infinite imperceptible gradations were blended in a common mass, as into a dazzling mirror.[2]

any system built on the passiveness of the mind must be false, as a system.[3]

Schleiermacher's hermeneutics

Though it is doubtful that Friedrich Schleiermacher ever met any of the English Romantic writers, he articulated in a more systematic, philosophical way what writers across the English Channel believed about how one reads a text. In formulating a universal hermeneutics, Schleiermacher not only established a new understanding of written texts as human utterances, but also refashioned the role of the reader from being merely an exegete or objective interpreter of a distant piece of writing to being a listener in an ongoing dialogue. Just as he is considered 'the founder of modern hermeneutics'[4] for his revolutionary conception of the relationship between reader and author, so too were the Romantic writers in England reshaping the way a text was received and understood. Although not expressed as a set of hermeneutic principles, nevertheless Romantic ideals centred around establishing an intimacy between author or poet and reader based on the same psychological and emotional phenomena which characterize and animate a personal relationship.

As an illustration of the connection between Schleiermacher and the English Romantics, E. S. Shaffer has examined some parallels between Schleiermacher and Coleridge in an essay entitled, 'The Hermeneutic Community: Coleridge and Schleiermacher'. According to Shaffer, Schleiermacher and Coleridge both recognized 'the need for a freshly formulated hermeneutic method which could overcome distance in time and space and recapture the moment of intimate communion in speech, the moment of "immediate understanding" (*Hermeneutics*, p. 192)'.[5] In traditional hermeneutics, this distance was a given: the exegete approached an ancient or obscure text as an alien attempting to decode the language and thereby glean meaning. For Schleiermacher, and for Coleridge and his Romantic contemporaries, hermeneutics could be applied equally effectively to a contemporary text or a conversation. 'For both men the human intimacy of spontaneous, spoken intercourse with a friend was linked with especial closeness to the exercise of the hermeneutic gift and the formulation of hermeneutic rules more refined than those of ordinary understanding.'[6] In another illustration of the parallel between Schleiermacher and the English Romantics, Karl Morrison has written that for Schleiermacher 'the great war was against blind instinct, thoughtless habit, dead obedience, everything inert and passive – all symptoms of stifled humanity and freedom'.[7] Compare this with the language of Shelley's *Defence of Poetry*, which endeavours to show that 'poetry . . . reproduces the common universe of which we are portions and percipients, and it purges from our inward sight the film of familiarity which obscures from us the wonder of our being'.[8]

Similarly, when Shelley writes that 'Reason is the enumeration of quantities already known; imagination is the perception of the value of those quantities, both separately and as a whole,'[9] he is echoing a distinction made implicitly by Schleiermacher between genuine understanding and traditional hermeneutics, particularly with respect to the so-called hermeneutical circle. In his day Schleiermacher saw three 'specialized' hermeneutics: biblical exegesis, classical studies and the law. He wanted to formulate a universal or general hermeneutics, for these three 'failed to do justice to the actual goal of interpretation: to understand in the fullest sense of the word'.[10] For Schleiermacher, interpretation rooted in rational analysis can yield at best a one-dimensional view of a particular aspect of a text. In his 'full-scale reconception of hermeneutical theory',[11] he shifted the emphasis from objective determination of meaning in a text to a highly subjective and interactive process of understanding wherein meaning is produced through an act of sympathetic imagination on the part of the reader. For Schleiermacher, as for Shelley, sympathy is the key to the process by which a man would come to understand another and thus to arrive at genuine meaning. In *Defence*, Shelley proclaims that 'a man, to be greatly good, must imagine intensely and comprehensively; he must put himself in the place of another and of many others'.[12] Schleiermacher, propounding a similar conception of how successfully to approach the written word, stated that 'before the art of hermeneutics can be practiced, the interpreter must put himself both objectively and subjectively in the position of the author'.[13]

Schleiermacher transforms hermeneutics from the art of explaining or interpreting texts into 'the act of a living, feeling, intuiting human being'.[14] It is a 'general' hermeneutics because he turns hermeneutics away from being seen as a specifically disciplinary matter belonging to theology, literature and the law, and toward an art of understanding any utterance in language. Because he believed that 'every problem of interpretation is, in fact, a problem of understanding',[15] his hermeneutics was a mixture of objective and subjective elements, thought as well as feeling. According to Richard Niebuhr, Schleiermacher's art demanded two talents: 'the first is the ability . . . to feel language as a living reality and to penetrate "into the core of the language in its relation to thought". The second is the ability to know men as individuals . . . by the direct understanding of the "genuine meaning of a man and his distinctive characteristics"'.[16] Far from merely ransacking a text for a hidden meaning, Schleiermacher's idea is that a reader involves him/herself on an unprecedented personal level – not unlike Shelley's sympathetically active poet – in an effort to know the text as an utterance of a particular individual.

The basis of Schleiermacher's radical conception of hermeneutics as the art of understanding can be found in his comparison of reading to listening. In an address before the Prussian Academy of Sciences he urged interpreters of written words to exercise the fullest sympathetic principles of personal conversation, as he himself did:

> very often in private conversation I resort to hermeneutical opera-tions, if I am not content with the ordinary level of understanding but wish to explore how, in my friend, the transition is made from one thought to another, or if I would seek out the views, judg-ments, and endeavors that are connected with the fact that he expresses himself in one way rather than in another with respect to the subject of our conversation.[17]

'Artistic interpretation', he wrote, 'has the same aim as we do in ordi-nary listening.'[18] That is, hermeneutics shifted from a purely textual and scientific matter to a psychological, even emotionally charged, interactive event. Because any text was a product of a human mind, Schleiermacher reasoned, the endeavour to understand it could only bear fruit if that person behind the written words was taken into account. Just as in personal conversation he recommends listening broadly and imaginatively – seeking deeper levels of dialogue and in-sight by actively making connections – so, too, does interpretation of a text demand awareness of the deeper level of engagement with the words, a 'listening' beyond the words on the page.

According to Gadamer, because 'Schleiermacher saw . . . individuality as a mystery that could never be quite grasped', the barrier dividing one person from another, like that between an interpreter and a text, 'is to be overcome by feeling, an immediate, sympathetic and conatural understanding'.[19] Thus this new hermeneutics was not merely a way of more effectively grasping the meaning of the written words, but more importantly it was a part of a larger epistemology. 'Entirely consistent with his theory of knowledge',[20] according to Thomas Torrance, this hermeneutics regarded thinking as a form of inward speech and speech as an external form of thinking. Therefore in order to truly understand written words, one must make the necessary connections with their corresponding thoughts, including those not explicitly written. The interpreter must not forget, Torrance continues, 'that he is concerned with speech or language, with what is spoken and heard in acts of communication between subject and object. That must not be forgotten even when it is a written text that is to be understood'.[21] Schleiermacher's hermeneutics is quintessentially a theory of understanding because he views reading as a human encounter rather than as an exegetical or purely intellectual task. Because, according to Schleiermacher, 'every act of understanding is the reverse side of an act of speaking', 'the success of an act of interpretation depends on one's linguistic competence and on one's ability for knowing people'.[22]

In the Introduction we saw that a key component of current definitions of sympathy is the 'as if' quality, whereby one person is able to enter into the life of another and participate in a profound sympathetic relationship with that Other, without losing his/her own separate identity, precisely because he/she acts *as if* he/she were that other person. Here, too, Schleiermacher's conception of a two-way dialogue between the interpreter, or reader, and the author hinges on the reader's acting – thinking, feeling, imagining – *as if* the author were present with the reader in an ongoing conversation. According to Niebuhr, 'the act of interpreting appeared to him to be something personal and creative as well as scientific, an imaginative reconstitution of the selfhood of the speaker or writer . . . an effort of empathy'.[23] Indeed, that Schleiermacher lived this psychological hermeneutics is attested by a description written by Henrich Steffens, his friend and colleague at the University of Halle:

> He was lively in all of his movements and his facial features were most telling . . . He appeared in fact to look right through a person . . . a hearty sympathy moved him inwardly and an almost childlike goodness pervaded this visible calm . . . While he was engrossed in the most lively conversation, nothing escaped him. He saw everything that was going on about him on all sides; he heard everything, even the softest conversation of others.[24]

In addition to intense listening, two qualities appear in this account which correspond to basic elements of sympathy: it is an active, creative effort on the part of the interpreter, as well as an interactive exchange involving both reader and author. The latter recalls Torrance's statement that 'communication between subject and object' is crucial to achieving an understanding of a text, just as it is in any genuine dialogue.

Taking hermeneutics to unprecedented levels, Schleiermacher 'insisted that along with the traditional philological discipline, and pressing beyond it, there must be another in which we probe into the author's mind and reach an understanding with him through reproducing in ourselves the basic determinations of his spirit'.[25] The key word here is (the second) 'with': Schleiermacher does not envision the interpreter merely reaching an understanding *of* the author, which would suggest not only that there is an objective truth about the text, but also that the reader is in a position to grasp it by an act of investigation or exegesis. For understanding to occur the interpreter and author must interact through the language, just as the sympathetic listener re-creates and participates in the life of the speaker by a process involving simultaneous awareness of both self and Other. Put differently, 'both the speaker and the hearer must share the language and the subject of their discourse'.[26] This relationship between subject and object, reader and author, is essentially a subjective process – one dependent on the reader/interpreter for its movement and life; it is, as Torrance describes it, an act of *re*production on the part of the interpreter which sets the dialogue in motion. Nevertheless, just as in a conversation, the hermeneutical activity is equally dependent on both subject and object. As James Torrance puts it, 'in this act of reconstruction ... it follows that between an author and his interpreter there is an act of communication; a dialogue ... in which the interpreter in terms of his own self-consciousness or self-understanding can understand something of the mind, the purposes, the intention of the author'.[27] Understanding is not a sudden flash of recognition or the inevitable product of arduous analysis, but a dynamic realization involving self and Other as human beings engaged in relationship.

The truth of this for Schleiermacher rests on his fundamental belief that language, whether written or spoken:

> is the medium of communication between one subject and another, and that it is only in terms of our own self-understanding (of our own cognitions and conations and feelings ...) that we can understand the mind of another. Only in terms of our own self-understanding can we project ourselves into the mind of another and 'relive', 'reconstruct', his experiences and so rediscover ourselves.[28]

The 'art of understanding',[29] as Schleiermacher calls his hermeneutics, is as much active as it is interactive, that is, it demands that the interpreter actively engage in the inner life of the author, as imagined through his written words. Thus 'one vibrated in unison with the speaker as one understood'.[30] 'Vibrate' is an image commonly used in twentieth-century accounts of sympathy and empathy, and as used here by Palmer contributes to an appreciation for Schleiermacher's hermeneutics as involving motion and emotion on the part of the interpreter. Translator James Duke notes Schleiermacher's fondness for the image of 'interplay', which 'connotes movement, and it is striking how often Schleiermacher refers to the motion of and within hermeneutics. To him understanding is a dynamic process, an ongoing operation that proceeds more by craft than by mechanics'.[31] Thomas Torrance calls it a 'dialogical encounter . . . in which the interpreter, as well as the author, takes part'.[32] This sympathetic activity 'can be carried out . . . only through a movement in which the interpreter traces the creative process lying behind a work . . . and then reconstructs it by a movement of participation'.[33] Morrison likewise finds that 'Schleiermacher's doctrines of participatory bonding focused on movement.'[34] The emphasis on movement is significant for it points up the way in which the creative and recreative, the subjective and objective elements, are intertwined in Schleiermacher's theory of understanding.

In order to understand this theory, it is necessary to understand what he meant by the hermeneutical circle. This is especially important since the basis of the theory is that understanding is a referential operation. What we understand forms itself into systematic unities, or circles made up of parts. The circle as a whole defines the individual part, and the parts together form the circle – for example, a sentence and its words. Understanding is 'circular' in that 'by dialectical interaction between the whole and the part, each gives the other meaning'.[35] Fundamental to the formulation of this circle is a hermeneutical gap, which can be defined as the breach or distance arising from the separateness of human existence. Just as we saw in many definitions of sympathy in the Introduction, the distinctness of the two individuals – also seen here as 'parts' of the 'whole' which is the relationship to be created between them – is a necessary prerequisite to their eventually becoming part of the seamless whole of the circle. As Morrison notes, 'the distance between speaker and hearer . . . was the fundamental precondition for hermeneutics'.[36] It is only in the process which joins the parts that genuine understanding of those parts emerges. 'Because within this "circle" meaning comes to stand, we call this the hermeneutical circle.'[37]

The concept of the circle – of whole and parts – can be applied in two particular ways. First, all or part of a text may be considered as a part within the context of the author's whole life and thought. In this conception, the reader attempts to understand how that particular part, or 'statement, as a fact in the person's mind, has emerged', as well as 'to sense how the thoughts contained in the statement will exercise further influence on and in the author'. These two elements in the hermeneutic process Schleiermacher calls the 'subjective-historical' and the 'subjective-prophetic', respectively.[38] The other way in which the hermeneutic circle is applied conceives of the reader and author as *parts*, and their relationship – initiated by the author in the text itself and brought to dynamic fruition through the reader's sympathetic participation in the author's inner life – as the *whole*. This movement on the part of the reader is 'an effort to bridge the distance between the self and the other'.[39] As mentioned above, this conception is contingent on an apparent paradox: the gap, or separateness of the individual parts, is a *sine qua non* of the process; but equally important is the fact that the individual identities remain intact despite their co-operation in the whole, brought about by the reader's sympathetic act. In *'I Am You': The Hermeneutics of Empathy in Western Literature, Theology, and Art* (1988), Karl Morrison locates this paradox at the heart of Schleiermacher's hermeneutics: 'Schleiermacher's maxim that the interpreter should transform himself into the author of the text preserved the individuality of the "I" and the "you", even while it posited their identity in human nature. Correspondingly, Schleiermacher's conception of the hermeneutic gap included a principle of uncertainty.'[40]

This uncertainty, arising from the sympathetic identification of distinct subject and object, is the prerequisite for knowledge of the Other in any relationship, according to Morrison's analysis. Hence, 'the concepts set forth by the sentence, "I am you", were at work in the central hermeneutic proposition that interpreters could, and should, transform themselves into the author'.[41] For Morrison, there is a fundamental connection not only between sympathy and hermeneutics, but also between the known and the unknown, which accounts for the unscientific, conversational nature of Schleiermacher's theory of understanding. In fact, Morrison points out, Schleiermacher held that 'the play leading to participatory union involved conflict ... The contrary powers interpenetrated and became one, even as in a dialectic ... conflict was the necessary authentication of participatory bonding'.[42] Similarly, in writing on Schleiermacher, Gadamer asserts that 'there is a polarity of familiarity and strangeness on which hermeneutic work is based'.[43]

Part of the 'strangeness' lies in the uniquely psychological turn which Schleiermacher gives hermeneutics. He consistently argues that 'since we have no direct knowledge of what was in the author's mind, we must try to become aware of many things of which he himself may have been unconscious, except insofar as he reflects on his own work and becomes his own reader'.[44] From this element in Schleiermacher, we learn not only that the reader's role is to know the Other/author as a person, but also that there is something in the very role as reader which puts one in a position to understand in a uniquely thorough and profound way. The ultimate goal of the hermeneutical circle, then, takes the reader beyond the text. 'To put oneself in the position of the author', Schleiermacher writes, 'means to follow through with this relationship between the whole and the parts. Thus it follows, first, that the more we learn about an author, the better equipped we are for interpretation.'[45] Gadamer explains that 'what is to be understood is now not only the exact words and their objective meaning, but also the individuality of the speaker, that is, the author'.[46] Schleiermacher believed in taking the art of understanding so far that not only would the interpreters transform themselves into the author of the text under review, but that they would come to understand 'the author better than the author understood himself'.[47]

Schleiermacher believed that one needed a grammatical and a psychological understanding. The grammatical proceeds from the general to the particularities of the text, that is, understanding 'the exact words and their objective meaning', while the psychological reveals 'the individuality of the speaker' or author. Thus he asserted that 'understanding a speech always involves two moments: to understand what is said in the context of the language with its possibilities, and to understand it as a fact in the thinking of the speaker'.[48] Each of these elements, in turn, call for both comparative and divinatory interpretation by the reader. In the comparative method the reader (listener, interpreter) seeks to understand the similarities between him/herself and the author by regarding the words within the context of the author's entire life and work. The divinatory method is, in Gadamer's words, a 'placing of oneself within the mind of the author, an apprehension of the "inner origin" of the composition of a work, a recreation of the creative act'.[49] In so far as it corresponds to the event in which 'the interpreter by an act of sympathetic imaginative intuition can divine what is in the author's mind',[50] the divinatory method is rooted in the same psychological phenomenon which makes interpersonal relationships rewarding. Torrance echoes this language, declaring that it is an 'approach through which the interpreter in an act of imaginative and sympathetic understanding appreciates the individuality of the author that comes to expression in his style'.[51]

Style was for Schleiermacher an essential feature of a text, because it represents the essential link between who a person is and how he/she conveys his/her thoughts and feelings in language. More than markings on a page, a text was for Schleiermacher an utterance; he regarded language as an expression not merely conveying meaning, but creating it out of the depths of the individual. The sympathy employed in the divinatory method reveals what Morrison calls the 'negative content' of the language – the ineffable, impalpable 'hiddenness' of the text. 'In his search for meaning', Morrison goes on, 'the interpreter sought the unsaid in the text.'[52] 'The unsaid' suggests what is crucial for Schleiermacher – namely, that whether written or spoken, language must be regarded not as a text, but as an utterance. Thus it is that a reader or listener is in the privileged position of seeing into the inner life of an author or speaker, through the window of his/her words. Because texts are 'pure expressive phenomena', in Gadamer's words, the goal of hermeneutics is 'to grasp every text as an expression of life'.[53] Torrance posits:

> Schleiermacher saw that to understand a text we must see it as the outward literary creation of a living mind. Therefore the interpreter must penetrate through the outward text, by an act of empathy and imagination, and enter into the mind of the author to understand both the author and his work in their wholeness.[54]

A text, then, was only complete when it engaged and 'interacted' with a sympathetically imaginative reader. As Wilhelm Dilthey explains it, the result of Schleiermacher's innovations in hermeneutics means that the literary 'work carries an insatiable need to complete its own individuality through contemplation by other individualities'.[55] Schleiermacher 'was convinced that words were only shadows of perceptions and feelings, and, without enabling others to participate in those ineffable realities, they imparted no understanding of what they said'.[56] Thus 'interpretation presupposes not only the treatment of language as a movement of human life and its expression, but an understanding of the interpersonal structure of human life and existence as the "whole" within which communication takes place'.[57] As an illustration of his insistence that texts be understood as utterances – speech acts to be listened to and interacted with – in his *Introductions to the Dialogues of Plato* Schleiermacher goes so far as to assert that the dialogue is superior to the written word in matters of instruction and communication. The purpose of language for Schleiermacher is *to express* – thoughts, feelings, ideas – and, when done with a listener or reader in mind, to communicate with the other individual(s). It was the study of the *Dialogues* which helped Schleiermacher to realize the difference between traditional hermeneutics and his divinatory method, and also the inherent connection between interpretation of a text and fruitful communication between two human beings:

> Plato himself ... complains [in the Phaedrus] of the uncertainty which always attaches to written communication of thoughts, as to

whether the mind also of the reader has spontaneously conformed
to such communications, and in reality appropriated it to itself, or
whether, with the mere ocular apprehension of the words and
letters a vain conceit is excited in the mind that it understands
what it does not understand.[58]

'Communication', and not merely interpretation or discovery of textual
meaning, is the natural product of Schleiermacher's hermeneutic of
understanding.

Niebuhr explains that this possibility for communication between
reader and author 'is based upon the sensitivity that every man has for
all others, a sensitivity which, Schleiermacher declares, "appears to rest
on the fact, that each individual carries in himself a minimum of all
others"'.[59] Morrison similarly notes that Schleiermacher believed each
person to be 'a compendium of humanity' – that is, 'each personality
embraced in some sense the whole of human nature'.[60] The basis, in
other words, for his new hermeneutic of divination lies in the assumption of a common bond, or natural sympathy, among human beings.
For Schleiermacher this clearly meant a spiritual, even holy, source of
interconnectedness which made possible a profound understanding of
the text as a human utterance – in other words, not simply because
there was a shared language in which the utterance was spoken or
written. 'Interpretation', therefore, 'was possible because of an "ind-
welling form of knowing" through which the individual participated in
the Absolute, "infinite humanity", or "the higher World Spirit".'[61]
Thus 'Schleiermacher places the individual in the community of uttered
thought not as a monad that stands in either an external or predeter-
mined relationship to all other individuals but rather as a particular
rational life in which consciousness of self and of community or kind
nourish each other organically.'[62]

A fundamental element in sympathy studies is that the sympathizing
subject never actually loses himself in the Other, but on the contrary
must have a heightened self-awareness in order fully to participate in
the inner life of the Other. Not surprisingly, then, Schleiermacher's
theory of interpretation, which is rooted in sympathy and aims to create
communication and relationship between subject and object, emphasizes the interactive growth of both individuals. According to Niebuhr,
this is 'the basic conviction' that informs Schleiermacher's hermeneutics:
'speaking and interpreting presuppose participation in a common humanity but at the same time they give a new concreteness to that which
is distinctly human in our experience of others and of ourselves'.[63] The
reader's interaction with the text, and subsequently with the author, is
dependent upon the existence of the 'higher Spirit' or sympathy, but it
also represents an effort to reach a greater understanding of one's own

humanity. According to Morrison, 'the concept that individuals belonged to a developing organic whole, in which they had a common identity, enabled Schleiermacher to assume an identity between subject and object, whether between an interpreter and an author, or between a particular human being and the Absolute'.[64] A reader can know the author through the sympathy of the divinatory method precisely because he/she shares a common humanity with every person and therefore already possesses a part of that author.

English Romantic readers

What we have just learned about Schleiermacher's hermeneutics may be divided into three categories of ideas, all implicitly bound together by the belief that successful reading and understanding spring from sympathy. First is the notion that the reader must enter into and participate in the inner life of the Other, which demands a high degree of emotional and intellectual activity on the part of the reader. Second is the presupposition that a common bond of humanity exists which makes the process of sympathy more natural, if not inevitable. The third prong hinges on the understanding of a written text as an utterance; entailed here are the conception of reading as listening, the reader's identification of and interest in the author as a person, and the idea that sympathetic reading is ultimately a dialogical and communicative act akin to a relationship between two people. Nothing as systematic or philosophical as Schleiermacher's hermeneutics was produced in England during that same period. Nevertheless, despite Marilyn Butler's statement that 'we do not know much about how the reader in the age of sensibility understood his participatory role, nor whether his intellect or opinions were commonly engaged along with his sympathies',[65] by examining critical writings of the Romantic era, along with some help from modern psychology of sympathy, we can infer what some of those opinions and assumptions were. This section looks closely at many of the literary reviews which appeared in the early nineteenth century, as well as at prose writings of Hazlitt, Wordsworth and others, against the backdrop of Schleiermacher's hermeneutics. As summarized in the three points above, Schleiermacher's theories of reading can be found operating in these Romantic critical writings, shedding fresh light on the importance of sympathy in the way Romantic readers oriented themselves to literature.

We must first illustrate the extent to which sympathy was a value in this period, both as a way of interacting and as a way of reading. Hazlitt's *Essay on the Principles of Human Action* (1805) is famous for its defence of the disinterested and sympathetic elements of human nature and its assertion that self-love is not the sole basis for human action. 'The imagination', writes Hazlitt,

> by means of which alone I can anticipate future objects, or be interested in them, must carry me out of myself into the feelings of others by one and the same process by which I am thrown forward as it were into my future being, and interested in it. I could not love myself, if I were not capable of loving others.[66]

Sympathy is a component of the imagination; what allows me to care about another's fate is precisely what allows me to care about my own.

In an essay published much later and centering on similar themes, 'Self-Love and Benevolence' (1828), Hazlitt makes a graphic case for the prevalence of sympathy in everyday life:

> Suppose that by sudden transformation your body were so contrived that it could feel the actual sensations of another body, as if your nerves had an immediate and physical communication; that you were assailed by a number of objects you saw and knew nothing of before, and felt desires and appetites springing up in your bosom for which you could not at all account ... This miracle takes place every day in the human mind and heart ... Do I not by imaginary sympathy acquire a new interest (out of my self) in others as much as I should on the former supposition by physical contact or material magnetism? and am I not compelled by this new law of nature (neither included in physical sensation nor a deliberate regard to my own individual welfare) to consult the feelings and wishes of the new social body of which I am become a member ... ?[67]

We saw in the Introduction that accounts of sympathy (and empathy) liken it to physical phenomena such as melting, interpenetration, echoing and vibration. Here, too, the state which Hazlitt calls 'a new sympathetic body' can be understood as a 'physical communication' involving 'material magnetism'. The sense of sympathy as profoundly moving and interactive is so vivid that physical metaphors are seemingly unavoidable.

In an essay on 'People of Sense', he derides the incapacity of 'this class of reasoners' to avail themselves of the impalpable in human experience – in other words, Morrison's 'negative content' and Schleiermacher's wholly unscientific divinatory approach to the Other. This is because 'they proceed by rule and compass, by logical diagrams, and with none but demonstrable conclusions'. As a consequence, fumes Hazlitt, 'they are only half-alive. They can distinguish the hard edges and determinate outline of things; but they are alike insensible to the stronger impulses of passion, to the finer essences of thought'.[68] What they are lacking is 'taste', which Hazlitt equates with sympathy in the essay 'Thoughts on Taste'. While the concept of taste is applied specifically to a person's response to art – 'Taste (as it relates to the productions of art) is strictly the power of being properly affected by works of genius . . . it is entire sympathy with the finest impulses of the imagination, not antipathy'[69] – Hazlitt clearly has in mind the more general sense of a supple intellect and sensibility in human encounters. 'Who is it', he asks:

> that, in looking at the productions of Raphael or Titian, is the person of true taste? He who finds what there is, or he who finds what there is not in each? . . . he who broods over the expression of the one till it takes possession of his soul, and who dwells on the tones and hues of the other till his eye is saturated with truth and beauty, for by this means he moulds his mind to the study and reception of what is most perfect in form and colour, instead of letting it remain empty.[70]

Sympathy means contemplating, or 'brooding' and 'dwelling', and then becoming so 'possessed of' and 'saturated with' it that one is 'moulded' to its very essence.

These are strong terms and speak of the passion with which Hazlitt and others believed in sympathy as a means to understanding and truth.[71] Like Schleiermacher, in other words, Romantic readers and writers felt that the success of a work of literature depended not only on its content and style (the 'parts'), but equally on its readers' capacity to 'divine' its deepest source and meaning in the writer (the 'whole'). Schleiermacher wrote that 'complete knowledge always involves an apparent circle, that each part can be understood only out of the whole to which it belongs, and vice-versa'.[72] A passage from his essay, 'On Depth and Superficiality', shows Hazlitt's implicit agreement with Schleiermacher's psychological version of the hermeneutical circle, as he argues for a combination of analytical and synthetic understanding as the best avenue to truth:

> The depth of the understanding . . . may be explained to mean, that there is a pile of implicit distinctions analysed from a great variety of facts and observations, each supporting the other, and that the mind, instead of being led away by the last or first object or detached view of the subject that occurs, connects all these into a whole from the top to the bottom, and by its intimate sympathy with the most obscure and random impressions that tend to the same result, evolves a principle of abstract truth.[73]

Like interlocutors in a discussion, the parts interact through the mediation of the active mind, simultaneously remaining distinct and contributing to the identity of the whole. In what hermeneutics depicts as a circular process, the mind seizes upon all the particular pieces of the picture and, connecting them by means of its sympathetic imagination, derives a comprehensive vision of the truth. In the essay, 'On Reason and Imagination', Hazlitt gives further evidence of his kinship with Schleiermacher's idea of the relationship between feeling and understanding, positing that 'the boundary of our sympathy is a circle which enlarges itself according to its propulsion from the centre – the heart'.[74]

Similarly, in a review of *The Excursion* in the *British Critic* in 1814, the (anonymous) critic speaks of the 'metaphysical' character of Wordsworth's poetry in terms remarkably reminiscent of Schleiermacher's hermeneutics. The process of 'combining and abstracting' once again echoes his divinatory approach to closing the hermeneutical gap:

> Since his poetry is the shadow of his philosophy, the result of intense reflection and a peculiar way of combining and abstracting, its interest depends in a great measure on a right understanding of the process which formed it. But there are few who have music enough in their souls to unravel for themselves his abstruser harmonies ... they can delight and improve those only, who have fancy enough to transport themselves into the poet's circumstances and mood of mind, and leisure enough to work out with him the speculations and feelings consequent thereupon.[75]

Most striking is that not only must the efficacious reader enter into the inner life of the poet – subtle and esoteric enough by itself – but he/she must also 'work out *with*' the poet the hidden and more complex origins of his thoughts and feelings. The reviewer's use of 'with' suggests that nothing short of a collaborative relationship must take place between reader and author, initiated by what amounts to the reader's active listening skills.

Clifford Siskin has recently written that 'in the late eighteenth and early nineteenth centuries, the self was made to feel by being remade into an active agent – one whose primary activity is feeling'.[76] The connection between feeling and being an active agent is especially true for the reader at this time. If the reader fails to 'bring a portion of the same meditative disposition, innocent tastes, calm affections, reverential feelings, philosophic habits, which characterize the poet himself', says one reviewer of 'The Recluse', writing in the *British Review* in 1815, then the poem remains unappreciated and unfinished. This same critic laments some readers' lack of sympathetic imagination in reading Wordsworth:

> Mr. Wordsworth has not unfrequently ... given his readers credit for too great quickness of apprehension and too liberal a good-nature: he has supposed that they would humor his disposition; fall in with his frame of mind, and understand his intention, when, in fact, they have wanted the first stimulus of curiosity ... [and] were

too opinionated or too indifferent even to prepare themselves to listen.[77]

Echoing Hazlitt's view of taste as the opposite of antipathy and indifference, this critic adds a further link between a reader's 'disposition' – not merely his/her skills or innate capacity – and his/her ability to understand. Interpreting a work successfully depends upon whether or not the reader engages his/her mind and heart in the process and 'prepares himself to listen', to the text as well as to the 'unsaid' in the author him/herself.

Another element of Schleiermacher's hermeneutics echoed by the English Romantics is the conviction that all sympathy and understanding of a written work takes place within the context of a common humanity. In striking similarity to Schleiermacher's notion that each person was 'a compendium of humanity', Hazlitt remarked that Shakespeare's mind 'contained a universe of thought and feeling within itself',[78] adding that 'If we know what one man feels, we so far know what a thousand feel in the sanctuary of their being. Our feeling of general humanity is at once an aggregate of a thousand different truths, and it is also the same truth a thousand times told.'[79]

A review by Thomas Noon Talfourd of *The Works of Charles Lamb* (1818) published in *The Champion* in 1819 eloquently testifies to many critics' belief that sympathy is the most important means of judging literary merit in a work of art and aesthetic taste in a reader, precisely because it is the noblest attribute of our common human nature. Comparing Lamb to Shakespeare, Talfourd writes:

> He throws himself into a myriad varieties of sentiment and passion, and seems to live and breathe only in his characters ... The quality of which we speak ... pervades the whole range of his faculties – leading them, as by a divine affinity, to find the deep and pure springs of cordiality and love which are scattered every where through this our human nature – and giving them an intuitive perception of those things to which they are naturally attracted. It is a kind of intellectual magic, like the power of those magicians who are represented in oriental story, as finding out hidden treasures where all appeared barren to the common eye, and as able to open by a word the rich veins of precious ore ... He seems to 'live along' the golden fibres of affection by which the great brotherhood of man is mysteriously bound together. [80]

This profound and extensive sympathy, inspired by a 'divine affinity' – reminiscent of Schleiermacher's method of 'divining' the author – is responsible for Lamb's keen creative powers as well as his uncommon awareness of 'the great brotherhood of man'. To identify the process if we can: first, Lamb's pervasive and profound understanding of human nature instinctively leads his imagination to those objects and individuals which are most apt to further elicit his insight and evoke his sympathy; he then engages in dynamic relationship with those objects and individuals – whether fictional characters, readers or personal memories – thereby deepening his store of sympathy with, and knowledge of, human nature. The oxymoronic 'intellectual magic' is in keeping not only with the discussion of the elusive nature of sympathy in the Introduction, but also with Talfourd's notion of the 'mysterious' bond among humankind.

A characteristic of greatness in a writer, then, was his/her ability to evoke the reader's sympathy, to stimulate the divinatory hermeneutic process through language which draws the reader into and beyond the words on the page and heightens his/her consciousness of the 'higher World Spirit'. As put by a reviewer of *The Excursion* in the *British Critic* in 1815, 'in painting with words, no less than with colours, those artists are always considered as the best, who make us feel as well as see their work, and excite sympathy as well as admiration'.[81] For Talfourd, Hazlitt was such a writer. In a review of the first volume of *Table Talk* (1821) in the *London Magazine*, Talfourd marvels at the extraordinary degree to which Hazlitt makes the reader part of the events, thoughts and feelings described from his life:

> If he gives a character of a favorite book, he not merely analyzes its beauties, but makes us partakers of the first impression it left on his own heart, recalling some of the most precious moments of his existence, and engrafting them into our own. We, too, seem to have been stunned with him on the first perusal of the Robbers, to have luxuriated with John Buncle, to have shed over the Confessions of Rousseau delicious tears, to have 'taken our ease at our inn', on the borders of Salisbury Plain, and 'shaken hands with Signor Orlando Frescobaldo, as the oldest acquaintance we have'. There is no other critic who thus makes his comments part of ourselves for ever after, as is the poet's sweetest verse, or the novelist's most vivid fiction ... He puts a heart into his abstrusest theories. No other writer mingles so much sturdiness with so much pathos; or makes us feel so well the strength of the most delicate affections.[82]

Talfourd is a critic whose writing both praises and enacts sympathy, illustrating the important connection between the reader's need to be a kind of active listener and the fact that this hermeneutic method can give rise to a fruitful dialogue with not only the text but also the author. Part of the reason why Hazlitt's reflections are 'engrafted' (note once again the physical image) into the reader is that Talfourd has clearly, if unwittingly, adopted a divinatory approach to reading. As a result, he is capable of *feeling* the 'unsaid' as well as *knowing* what Gadamer calls the 'dark Thou',[83] the human spirit behind the words.

For Schleiermacher as for the Romantics, feeling was an essential element not only of efficacious writing and reading, but also of the sense of community and relationship which writing and reading could generate and give expression to. Morrison observes that 'Schleiermacher invoked the principle of a common humanity, rendered articulate through feeling:'[84] 'articulate' is the key adjective here, signalling the identity between language and feeling in the conception shared by Schleiermacher and the Romantics that literature is an utterance. For many Romantic readers, poetry was the language which most perfectly expressed and evoked the feeling of what Morrison called 'infinite humanity'. In *Sketches of the Poetical Literature of the Past Half-Century* (1851), D. M. Moir consistently praises poetry which expresses 'genuine feeling', a determination based largely on reader response. He comments, for instance, that 'the most beautiful specimens of [the poet Thomas] Moore's "words wed to verse" are those in which he has unbosomed sentiments and reflections, loves and longings and regrets, common to the whole of mankind, and which find, accordingly, a sympathetic echo in every bosom'.[85]

In the essay 'On Reason and Imagination', Hazlitt asserts that 'the object and end' of literature is 'to enable us to feel for others as for ourselves, or to embody a distinct interest out of ourselves by the force of imagination and passion'.[86] For him poetry 'communicates to the imagination' and 'penetrates our whole being',[87] a process which embodies the interplay of mind and object which Schleiermacher describes between reader and text. According to Hazlitt,

> wherever any object takes such a hold of the mind as to make us dwell upon it, and brood over it, melting the heart in tenderness, or kindling it to a sentiment of enthusiasm; – wherever a movement of imagination or passion is impressed on the mind, by which it seeks to prolong and repeat the emotion, to bring all other objects into accord with it, and to give the same movement of harmony . . . to the sounds that express it – this is poetry.[88]

Again the description of the interaction between text and reader is marked by active, physical images: the poem 'takes hold of the mind' and 'melt[s] the heart', while the corresponding 'movement' of the imagination or passion is 'impressed on the mind'. Moreover, just as Schleiermacher's hermeneutics is based on dynamics of speaking and listening, so Hazlitt's account of the process is informed by an analogy with oral expression, or music, in the 'harmony' which the imagination or passion strives to achieve with 'the sounds that express it'. *Othello*, writes Hazlitt in 'On Poetry in General', is so powerful not merely because the passions depicted are intense and the tragedy great, but more precisely because seeing or reading about those passions and events 'makes us drink deeper of the cup of human life . . . and calls the springs of thought and feeling into play with tenfold force'.[89]

Conversely, when language fails to produce feeling in its readers, it likewise fails to strike the chord of sympathy and understanding. Hazlitt deems Bentham 'the leader' of 'people of sense' because he 'does not write to be understood . . . The language he adopts is his own . . . a technical and conventional jargon, unintelligible to others, and conveying no idea to himself in common with the rest of mankind, purposely cut off from human sympathy'.[90] Richardson's romances are weak and unappealing, claims Hazlitt, because 'the sympathy excited is not a voluntary contribution, but a tax . . . The heart does not answer of itself like a chord in music'.[91] Similarly, he derides even Crabbe's best verses because they 'are of a sort that chill, rather than melt the mind; they repel instead of haunting it'.[92] So the mind must be responsive and active, but it cannot be so if the writing fails to pique it and engage its sympathy. It is as if only when the mind is 'melted' does it become supple enough to wrap itself around and work its way into the cavernous regions of the work.

Belief in art as the vehicle for the artist's self-expression was taken for granted after 1800. Indeed, it seems that only when a work is such an utterance from within is the reader able to 'listen' hermeneutically, in Schleiermacher's sense of this dynamic. By looking closely at a sampling of contemporary criticism and reviews of Byron's works it becomes clear that for Romantic readers the emphasis on feeling in language led to their tendency to approach the written word as speech rather than as a text. As a result they presumed that the feelings, experiences and events in a work of literature were those of the author himself. This may be due largely to the nature of Byron's poetry and dramatic works along with the fact that his noble birth and flamboyant personal style surrounded him with an air of the exotic and passionate. Whatever the reason, his poetry generated intense interest in himself as a man, a technique once again recalling Schleiermacher's psychological and divinatory hermeneutics.

A lengthy review of *Childe Harold*, Canto IV, written by John Wilson and appearing in *Blackwood's Edinburgh Magazine* in May 1818, epitomizes this phenomenon. Wilson begins with the bald statement, 'it is impossible to speak of his poetry without also speaking of himself, morally, as a man . . . In his poetry, more than any other man's, there is felt a continual presence of himself – there is everlasting self-representation or self-reference'. Unlike critics in 1590 or 1990, Wilson refuses to acknowledge the possible creation by Byron of a fictional narrator, instead interpreting the 'I' as Byron's own voice. However, this technique does not in the least detract from the poetry's success, which is measured according to the (appearance, at least, of) genuine feeling expressed by Byron and called up in the reader. '[P]erhaps that', he continues, 'which to cold and unimpassioned judgment might seem the essential fault of his poetry, constitutes its real excellence, and gives it power.'[93] Its excellence lies in the author's presence before the reader, for this personal element invests the language with power to express and evoke real sympathy. It is a power 'that hurries us along with it like a whirlwind' as it 'awoke and stirred up all the profoundest feelings and energies of our souls'.[94]

In a particularly impassioned passage, Wilson's identification of Childe Harold and Byron is so complete that the two become one, and the critic's evaluation of the poetry becomes similarly inseparable from his intense sympathy with the collective Byronic persona:

> 'The wondrous Childe' passes before our eyes, and before our hearts, and before our souls. And all love, and pity, and condemn, and turn away in aversion, and return with sympathy; and 'thoughts that do lie too deep for tears' alike agitate the young and the old ... when they think on the features of his troubled countenance, – when they hear the voice of his lofty mournings, – when they meditate on all the 'disastrous chances that his youth has suffered'. There is round him a more awful interest than the mere halo round the brow of a poet. And in his feelings, his passions, his musings, his aspirings, his troubled scepticism, and his high longings after immortality, his eagle-winged raptures, his cold, dull, leaden fears, his agonies, his exultation, and his despair, – we tremble to think unto what a mysterious nature we belong, and hear in his strains, as it were, the awful music of a revelation.[95]

This palpably personal response to the poem is possible only due to the reader's presumption that the speaker in the poem is not merely a fictional creation, but a living human being whom this reader can understand in an extra-textual – that is, psychological and emotional – way. Wilson explains that 'it can only be the simple, natural, human force of the vivid utterances of intense passion, that produces in minds of every description so strong a sympathy with Byron in all his different moods'.[96] 'Utterances' imply a listener and, when that person engages in the equivalent of Schleiermacher's hermeneutics, they very often call forth a sympathetic 'utterance' from the listener/reader.

Butler's observation that 'the first three decades of the nineteenth century saw the emergence of a heightened interest in the personality of the artist'[97] both accounts for, and is explained by, this identification of the speaker with the author.[98] The passions on the page elicit reflection and even speculation about Byron himself:

> We have no hesitation in saying, that Byron's creations are not so much poems, as they are glorious manifestations of a poet's mind.

> Having in himself deep sense of beauty – deeper passions than probably any other great poet ever had – and aspiring conceptions of power, the poetry in which he expresses himself must be full of vivid portraiture of beauty, deep spirit of passion, and daring suggestions of power.[99]

That Byron had 'aspiring conceptions of power', for instance, is a notion derived solely from his poetry, which Wilson understands as a 'manifestation of the poet's mind'. It is as if the critic knew Byron from personal interaction and was subsequently able to observe in the poetry expressions of the poet's thoughts and emotions. But in fact Wilson's implicit hermeneutic moves him to 'divine' the inner life from the poetry.

Another critic, reviewing cantos IX–XI of *Don Juan* in the *British Magazine* in 1823, admits to using this divinatory method. Despite 'possessing not the slightest personal knowledge of him', the critic states that 'Lord Byron once stood with us in the light of a dear friend.'[100] Still another critic sees in the actions and expressions of Byron's heroes that the poet himself is struggling with his faith, constantly 'relapsing into his gloom of unbelief'.[101] In a passage remarkably sympathetic and psychological, Wilson enters into the realm of speculation and unknown about the poet, as he 'looks deeply into his Poetry' and finds the mind and heart of Byron. Reviewing 'The Lament of Tasso' in *Blackwood's Edinburgh Magazine* in 1817, he says it is a composition

> in which Lord Byron has allowed his soul to sink down into gentler and more ordinary feelings. Many beautiful and pathetic strains have flowed from his heart, of which the tenderness is as touching as the grandeur of his nobler works is agitating and sublime. To those, indeed, who have looked deeply into his Poetry, there never was at any time a want of pathos; but it was a pathos so subduing and so profound, that even the poet himself seemed afraid of being delivered up unto it; nay, he seemed ashamed of being overcome by emotions which the gloomy pride of his intellect often vainly strove to scorn; and he dashed the weakness from his heart, and the tear from his eyes, like a man suddenly assailed by feelings which he wished to hide, and which, though true to his nature, were inconsistent with the character which that mysterious nature had been forced, as in self-defence, to assume.[102]

This highly metaphorical account, punctuated by 'seemed', 'like' and 'as', is indicative of the boldly subjective nature of the review. What he does not know for fact, Wilson none the less 'knows' by an intuition and understanding akin to Schleiermacher's 'subjective-historical' and 'subjective-prophetic' methods of divination. He recreates in his imagination the inner workings of Byron's psyche; and this reconstruction is, as Schleiermacher avers, itself a creative process. 'Hermeneutics and criticism', he wrote, 'are related such that the practice of either one presupposes the other. In both, the relationship to the author is general and varied.'[103]

In a letter to Lady Beaumont in 1807, Wordsworth demonstrates how to read a poem and engage in this sort of 'general and varied' relationship with the poet. His description recalls the hermeneutical circle, in the way the interaction of whole and parts contribute to full understanding. Speaking of the sonnet, 'With Ships the Sea was Sprinkled Far and Nigh', he first equates himself with the First Person speaker, saying 'I am represented in the Sonnet as casting my eyes over the sea' and repeatedly identifying himself with the 'I' of the poem. He then illustrates how a reader should enter the mind of the poet and imaginatively follow its movements and contours:

> My mind may be supposed to float up and down among [the multitude of ships] in a kind of dreamy indifference with respect either to this or that one, only with a pleasurable state of feeling with respect to the whole prospect. 'Joyously it showed', this continued till that feeling may be supposed to have passed away, and a kind of comparative listlessness or apathy to have succeeded, as at this line, 'Some veering up and down, one knew not why'. All at once, while I am in this state, comes forth an object, an individual, and my mind, sleepy and unfixed, is awakened and fastened in a moment.[104]

The phrases 'may be supposed' and 'a kind of', both used twice, characterize the subjective, unscientific nature of Wordsworth's reading. Like Schleiermacher, he emphasizes the role of feeling in understanding. Moreover, his comments suggest that the process of the poet's mind being aroused and fixing on an object must be repeated in the reader himself if he is fully to appreciate the poem. According to this process, the mind is aroused by an object, but being once 'rouzed, all the rest comes from itself'. Finally, he says the poem invites the reader 'to rest his mind as mine is resting',[105] thus giving a clear notion that a text's meaning lies beyond merely interpreting the words on the page, and that in order to realize this the reader must endeavour to understand the poet's imagination.

When James Montgomery claims in a review of *Poems, in Two Volumes* (1807) in the *Eclectic Review* in 1808 that 'Mr. Wordsworth is himself a living example of the power which a man of genius possesses, of awakening unknown and ineffable sensations in the hearts of his fellow-creatures',[106] the implied corollary is that once 'awakened' the reader must respond with concomitant emotion and imagination if he is to 'answer' the poet's call. Because of the prevalence of sympathy as a value in this period, I submit, both parties contribute equally to the communicative act, which is comprised of both writing and reading, speaking and listening.[107]

'Interpretive listening'

At virtually the same time, Schleiermacher and English Romantic readers and writers were developing a theory of reading, dependent on the reader responding actively to a text which is itself alive with feeling. This process entails not merely standing before the text as spectator, and not even mirroring the words or sentiments in his/her own mind, but participating in the creative act through a process which emphasizes difference and individuality in order to then attain a genuinely sympathetic understanding. The ostensible goal is to understand the author, but ultimately what is achieved in Schleiermacher's and Romantic hermeneutics/sympathy is a form of communication: an interpretive art which is psychological as well as emotional.

What all this points to may be what is posited in a recent article entitled, 'Interpretive Listening: An Alternative to Empathy', in which communication psychologist John Stewart deals with issues we have seen in Schleiermacher and throughout Romantic writing. Stewart shares Schleiermacher's desire to understand understanding within an interpersonal context but, whereas Schleiermacher approached textual interpretation through an analogy with listening, Stewart is mainly concerned with speech communication and listening and uses hermeneutics as a way of illustrating and supporting his theory.

There are two kinds of hermeneutics, he contends: reproductive and interpretive. Schleiermacher's belongs in the former category (along with Dilthey and E. D. Hirsch) because of its focus on finding the meaning of a text and reaching an understanding of the author's intent. This view of 'the development of understanding as a process whereby an interpreter/listener recreates the objectifiable meaning originally created by the author/speaker'[108] assumes that there is an objective inner reality to which the author's language merely gives expression. According to Stewart, this psychological approach is like empathic listening in that both are processes which occur solely within the interpreter and thus deny the fundamentally interactive nature of any (successful) interpretive or listening event. Moreover, the goal of 'laying one's self aside' is not only impossible but also counter-productive, because it fails to acknowledge that genuine understanding is an *inter*personal phenomenon. Stewart takes issue with Schleiermacher, then, for treating 'a fundamentally communicative phenomenon as if it were an individual process'.[109] By contrast, hermeneutics of the interpretive variety (developed by Heidegger, then Gadamer and Ricoeur) insists that hermeneutical understanding is 'a participation in shared meaning'[110] and 'can be defined no longer as an inquiry into the psychological intentions which are hidden beneath the text, but rather as the explication of the being-in-the-world displayed by the text'.[111]

Although Stewart attempts to distance himself from Schleiermacher, it becomes evident in his explication of what he calls 'interpretive listening' that this active, communicative function of reading is suggested in the writings of both Schleiermacher and the Romantics. Clearly, Schleiermacher's belief that a reader could 'come to understand the author better than the author understood himself' indicates a psychologizing element to his theory; however, his hermeneutics suggests this same communicative phenomenon, as do other writings of the period, in emphasizing that the reader must be as alive to the text as he/she would be in a conversation. Examination of Stewart's argument in light of Romantic notions of reading – which we have shown to be informed by the same principles as Schleiermacher's hermeneutics – actually illustrates that Stewart's and Schleiermacher's hermeneutics are more complementary than contradictory. For while Stewart emphasizes the communicative element in hermeneutics, he fails to recognize the active component of sympathy, which is crucial to Schleiermacher's listener/interpreter. By opposing empathy or empathic listening to interpretive listening, Stewart betrays a lack of understanding of empathy, which, as we have seen in the Introduction, is both an active and interactive phenomenon.

Stewart first emphasizes that instead of just being 'open to what the other means, so that he or she can reproduce it', the listener must be 'open to the meanings that are being developed *between* oneself and one's partner'.[112] Niebuhr makes it clear that he finds such a dynamic at work in Schleiermacher's hermeneutics:

> The dialectic between the divinatory and comparative methods, through which the interpreter is required to come to an increasing knowledge of himself as he reaches after the inner meaning of the author, indicates that the discipline of interpretation arises out of and belongs to the dialogue of life with life.[113]

Schleiermacher knew that this 'dialogue of life with life' cannot occur within the interpreter's head, but entails a personal engagement in the life of the Other. This is why he calls for sympathy by the reader, as a way of entering into the other's thoughts and feelings. The openness which sympathy produces, then, is not merely reproductive, but creates an altogether new psychological and emotional space in which to interact and understand. This 'between' is a key element in hermeneutics and in sympathy, as Martin Buber explains: 'the meaning is to be found neither in one of the two partners nor in both together, but only in their dialogue itself, in this "between" which they live together'.[114]

A second point advanced by Stewart is that 'language – or more accurately "languaging" – is a mode or medium of human be-ing; it is not a tool or system we use but a way we be who we are'.[115] In other words, as Ricouer implies in his concept of 'the being-in-the-world displayed by the text', the words in a text or speech do not simply serve to express an inner meaning already existent prior to and apart from those words. As a result, understanding or interpreting must attend to the utterance itself as a self-revelatory event at which the reader/listener is crucially present. Schleiermacher appreciates this fact, as evidenced in his statement that 'every act of understanding is the reverse side of an act of speaking'.[116] Niebuhr explains that this self-revelation is completed – and to that extent occurs – only through the reader's active participation. 'The immediate self-consciousness of the author can never pass wholly over into communication but remains at the level of self-disclosure, which itself can be appropriated only by an act of intuition or divination on the part of the interpreter.'[117] In other words, the speech act or written word is an utterance and not a text, in so far as it is in itself incapable of communicating anything, but requires the active presence of a listener or reader. The communicatory act, then, lies as much in the sympathetic or interpretive listening as in the original utterance and hence is a two-way event.

It is precisely because 'Schleiermacher understood thinking and feeling to be co-present functions of the self' that he recognizes the dialogic, interactive aspect of interpretation. He believed, in Niebuhr's words, that 'a thinking . . . that merely takes up the thoughts of others as they lie in the language and that fails to register its own thoughts in the language also, betrays a stultified humanity, for it indicates the individual's failure to recognize his organic responsibility in the community of uttered thought'.[118] What Stewart calls the 'fusion of horizons' (after Gadamer and Ricoeur) corresponds to participation in this 'community of uttered thought', or Morrison's 'higher World Spirit', invoked by Schleiermacher and the Romantics alike to signify the context in which sympathy and genuine understanding occur. For Hazlitt, understanding and communication, both dependent on sympathy, were mirror images of the same phenomenon:

> Language is the medium of our communication with the thoughts of others. But whoever becomes wise, becomes wise by sympathy; whoever is powerful, becomes so by making others sympathise with him. To think justly, we must understand what others mean: to know the value of our thoughts we must try their effect on other minds.[119]

Stewart would disagree that the power of language rests in sympathy because he fails to appreciate the active and creative aspect of sympathy. His insistence that language is a communication event blinds him to the corollary of that thesis, which is that the success of language depends upon a sympathetic act.

It seems that Stewart is implicitly aware that the 'fusion of horizons' entails sympathy, but in his zealous efforts to avoid psychology and to reject any concept of 'losing oneself in the Other', he likewise avoids embracing any other aspect of sympathetic participation. His description of this 'fusion' actually recalls Schleiermacher's hermeneutical circle as well as the 'universal spirit' which for him and the Romantics represents the basis for all acts of understanding:

> When one understands another, one does not disregard oneself in order to place oneself in the place of the other. In Gadamer's words, the process of understanding 'is not the empathy of one individual for another, nor is it the application to another person of our own criteria, but it always involves the attainment of a higher universality that overcomes, not only our own particularity, but also that of the other'.[120]

The distinction between self and Other is equally important for Schleiermacher and Romantic writers, but for them separateness of actual identity does not have to preclude oneness of experience through sympathy. Coleridge, like his contemporaries, admires Shakespeare in part because 'he becomes all things, yet forever remaining himself'.[121] This is why 'in every one of his various characters we still feel ourselves communing with the same human nature. Every where we find individuality ... union of the universal with the particular'.[122] Likewise Hazlitt writes in his *Essay On The Principles of Human Action*, 'I always remain perfectly distinct from others, the interest I take in their past or present feelings being ... never any thing more than the effect of imagination and sympathy.'[123] This combination of fusion and distinctness is possible, I would argue, because of the demand placed on the reader to take an active part in the text. Shakespeare was a great poet in part because 'he felt and made others feel, on subjects [in] no way connected with himself, except by force of contemplation, and that sublime faculty, by which a great mind becomes that which it meditates on'. As Coleridge makes clear, that faculty is sympathy, which completes the communication of the text, the utterance, by making the reader into 'an active creative being'. The 'conversation' between interpreter and text, then, can happen only after the reader is transformed into a participant, a process which must 'come from within, – from the moved and sympathetic imagination'.[124]

In emphasizing the separateness of the 'partners' – reader and author, listener and speaker – Stewart wants to shift attention away from the psychology of the hermeneutic event and toward the event itself. According to his understanding of empathy, empathic listening focuses on what happens *inside* the listener and communicator and is based on the belief that one person can participate in the inner life of another. Interpretive listening, by contrast, focuses on what transpires *between* the communicator and listener/interpreter (or writer and reader) and as such is an encounter, a conversation. This is preferable, Stewart avers, because 'as Arnett and Nakagawa clarify, the empathic paradigm encourages a "reification of self"'. It is more important to focus on what is being 'co-produced by the communicators than on the psychological states "behind" the talk'.[125] Stewart erroneously assumes that empathy and communication do not share any goals or functions: objectification or reification are by no means necessary products of empathic listening. As this chapter has endeavoured to illustrate, sympathy and hermeneutics do share an active and interpretive element. Coleridge revels in this 'between' state while simultaneously embracing sympathy's psychological aspects. In poetry, he says, 'the reader should be carried forward, not merely or chiefly by the mechanical impulse of curiosity, or by a restless desire to arrive at the final solution; but by the pleasurable activity of mind excited by the attractions of the journey itself'.[126] It is the 'activity' or 'play' (as Stewart calls it) of the 'journey' – that is, the reading event – as much as anything else which Coleridge believes should fire the reader.

None the less, the aesthetic nature of the relationship between self and Other, specifically the problem of reification raised by Stewart, is an important one for the hermeneutics of sympathy. David Marshall argues that the aesthetics on which Romantic literature is based '(with its emphasis on subjectivity and affect) centered on the question of the effects that a work of art had on its reader or beholder'. This rise in subjectivity meant that 'discussions of sympathy [at the time] turn on the theatrical relations that make the possibility of fellow feeling a problem of representation'. Therefore, he argues, a 'surprising effect' of sympathy is its danger of reifying the notion of self, in so far as it represents others 'as spectacles before us'. The result of this purely aesthetic sympathy which makes the Other into an object is an interpretive experience devoid of participatory elements and a hermeneutic 'in which people face each other as spectators and spectacles'.[127] Moreover, when sympathy is a desired effect rather than a condition in which human beings – reader, listener, beholder – achieve understanding, then true sympathy is impossible.

Michael Fried finds a similar tension between theatricality (or the desire for effect) and genuine participation at work in the relationship between painting and beholder in eighteenth-century French painting. As we have demonstrated with popular literature, Fried similarly shows that popular paintings were those which fully engaged, or 'absorbed', the beholder. This demanded active qualities from the beholder and from the painting itself, though both remain physically still. 'A painting, it was claimed, had first to attract . . . and then to arrest . . . and finally to enthrall . . . the beholder, that is, a painting had to call to someone, bring him to a halt in front of itself, and hold him there as if spellbound and unable to move.'[128] Diderot illustrated through his painting and criticism that genuine absorption is generated not by paintings blatantly directed at the beholder and depicting exaggerated passion, but by paintings depicting characters who themselves were absorbed in a situation or emotion. Natural, unself-conscious expression, like language as utterance, is what absorbs the beholder. Thus Diderot makes the 'distinction between . . . natural, spontaneous, largely automatic realizations of an intention or expression of a passion on the one hand and conventional, mannered, and (in the pejorative sense . . .) theatrical simulacra of those on the other'.[129]

With the absorption of the beholder as a goal and as a primary criterion of successful art, Diderot, like Schleiermacher and English Romantic writers, promoted 'the de-theatricalization of the relationship between painting and beholder'.[130] This meant that he valued paintings in which the beholder could place, or locate, him/herself in the painting and participate in its characters and its beauty. As a result, says Fried:

> in Diderot's writings on painting and drama the object–beholder relationship as such, the very condition of spectatordom, stands indicted as theatrical, a medium of dislocation and estrangement rather than of absorption, sympathy, self-transcendence; and the success of both arts, in fact their continued functioning as major expressions of the human spirit, are held to depend upon whether or not the painter and dramatist are able to undo that state of affairs, to de-theatricalize beholding and so make it once again a mode of access to truth and conviction.[131]

Diderot equates theatricality with alienation of the beholder (and, analogously, reader, listener and audience). In order once again to 'locate' the beholder in the painting and make him/her no longer merely a spectator, Diderot calls for 'the constitution of a new sort of beholder – a new "subject"'. Fried cites several passages from Diderot's criticism (his 'salons') illustrating this new subject, who enters the life of the painting in much the same style as several Romantic critics entered the world of the poet, characterized by play and vivid imagination.[132] Diderot remarks of one painting, 'I actually find myself there . . . A painting . . . which puts you in the scene, and from which the soul receives a delicious sensation, is never a bad painting.'[133]

Only a few decades after Diderot, both Schleiermacher and the Romantics wanted to de-theatricalize reading through a hermeneutic which radically involved the reader in the inner meaning of text and author. This 'new sort of reader' gained such intimate access not by simply losing him/herself in the text, but through a heightened awareness of his/her own feeling as connected to the author's by virtue of a common humanity in which both participated as 'partners', to use Stewart's term. What we learn from Fried's study is that the belief that sympathetic participation in a work of art played a vital role in the creative process was widespread in Europe in the late eighteenth and early nineteenth centuries. His argument lends further support to our claim that English Romantic writers and readers shared a view of literature as an intimate dialogic encounter in which both active and receptive (or listening) faculties were required of the reader. This was fundamental to Schleiermacher's hermeneutics, which held that 'the mere passive spectator . . . will not attain, by those means alone, to a knowledge of the proper natures of the whole'.[134]

An understanding of the author's thoughts and feelings – 'the whole' – does not occur, contrary to what Stewart argues, at the expense of understanding the exchange, or communication, *between* the author and reader. It is this 'betweenness', or two-way sympathy, which makes understanding possible, for a hermeneutic of this kind is largely dependent on the author in the first place. Wordsworth explains in his 'Essay, Supplementary to the Preface [of 1815]' that 'every great poet . . . has to call forth and to communicate power . . . [The reader] is invigorated and inspirited by his leader, in order that he may exert himself; for he cannot proceed in quiescence, he cannot be carried like a dead weight'.[135] This is why, for instance, Diderot developed an aesthetic criteria for evaluating painting, based on the degree to which it invited sympathy through its qualities of natural expression as opposed to dislocating the beholder – that is, denying him/her a place in the painting and in the painter's inner life. Only when thus led can the reader exert 'a cooperating power'[136] in order to 'answer' – as in a dialogue – the creative process. The goal of an artist in such a hermeneutic climate, according to Schleiermacher, is therefore 'to exhibit vividly his own thought to others, and by that means to excite and awaken theirs'.[137]

The sympathetic relationship between reader and author, like any relationship, can be viewed in terms of how power is divided up or shared between the two parties. When he wrote that 'whoever is powerful becomes so by making others sympathize with him', Hazlitt identifies the abuse of power which sympathy can spawn. Marshall illustrates how sympathy, when pursued for its own end rather than as an effort to know and understand another, reifies both subject and object, sacrificing an interactive relationship for the sake of psychological domination. Aware of this potential in sympathy, Stewart seeks to avoid reifying the Other by focusing on the event rather than the psychology of it. However, by neglecting the psychological, ironically he threatens to lose the human beings for the event, making his interpretive listeners secondary to the spectacle of communication. As I have endeavoured to illustrate through examination of Romantic views of reading, only with a thorough understanding of sympathy are we able to recognize the listening element in Schleiermacher's hermeneutics and thus to fortify Stewart's idea of communication with the psychology of human relationship.

Notes

1. P. De Man (1982), introduction to H. R. Jauss, *Toward an Aesthetic of Reception*, T. Bahti (tr.), Minneapolis: University of Minnesota Press, ix.
2. W. Hazlitt (1934), *The Complete Works of William Hazlitt*, 21 vols, P. P. Howe (ed.), London: J. M. Dent, vol. 12, 360.
3. S. T. Coleridge (1956–59), (letter to Tom Poole, 23 March 1801), *Collected Letters of Samuel Taylor Coleridge*, 3 vols, E. L. Griggs (ed.), Oxford: Oxford University Press, vol. 2, 709.
4. M. Redeker (1973), *Schleiermacher: Life and Thought*, J. Wallhauser (tr.), Philadelphia: Fortress Press, 174.
5. E. S. Shaffer (1990), 'The Hermeneutic Community: Coleridge and Schleiermacher', in R. Gravil and M. Lefebure (eds), *The Coleridge Connection,* Basingstoke and London: Macmillan, 206.
6. Shaffer, 'The hermeneutic', 211.
7. K. F. Morrison (1988), *'I Am You': The Hermeneutics of Empathy in Western Literature, Theology, and Art,* Princeton, NJ: Princeton University Press, 260.
8. P. B. Shelley (1967), 'A Defence of Poetry', in D. Perkins (ed.), *English Romantic Writers,* New York: Harcourt, Brace and World, 1085.
9. Shelley, 'A Defence', 1072.
10. J. Duke (1977), 'Schleiermacher: On Hermeneutics', (translator's introduction) in F. D. E. Schleiermacher, *Hermeneutics: The Handwritten Manuscripts,* H. Kimmerle (ed.), J. Duke and J. Forstman (tr.), American Academy of Religion, Texts and Translations Series, Missoula, MT: Scholars Press, 2.
11. Duke, 'Schleiermacher', 1.
12. Shelley, 'A Defence', 1076.
13. Schleiermacher, *Hermeneutics*, 113.
14. R. Palmer (1969), *Hermeneutics: Interpretation Theory in Schleiermacher, Dilthey, Heidegger and Gadamer,* Evanston, IL: Northwestern University Press, 85.

15. H.-G. Gadamer (1975), *Truth and Method*, G. Barden and J. Cumming (tr. and eds), New York: Seabury Press, 162–3.
16. R. R. Niebuhr (1964), *Schleiermacher on Christ and Religion*, New York: Scribner's and Sons, 85 (quoting from Schleiermacher's *Werke* I/7, 'Hermeneutik and Kritik', p. 17).
17. Schleiermacher, as quoted in R. R. Niebuhr (1960), 'Schleiermacher on Language and Feeling', *Theology Today*, 17, (2), July, 151.
18. Schleiermacher, *Hermeneutics*, 109.
19. Gadamer, *Truth and Method*, 168.
20. T. F. Torrance (1968), 'Hermeneutics According to F. D. E. Schleiermacher', *Scottish Journal of Theology*, 21, (3), September, 258.
21. T. Torrance, 'Hermeneutics', 258.
22. Schleiermacher, *Hermeneutics*, 101.
23. Niebuhr, *Schleiermacher*, 79.
24. Ibid., 74–5.
25. T. Torrance, 'Hermeneutics', 258.
26. Palmer, *Hermeneutics: Interpretation*, 88.
27. J. B. Torrance (1968), 'Interpretation and Understanding in Schleiermacher's Theology: Some Critical Questions', *Scottish Journal of Theology*, 2, (3), September, 270–1.
28. J. Torrance, 'Interpretation', 272.
29. Gadamer, *Truth and Method*, 166.
30. Palmer, *Hermeneutics: Interpretation*, 131.
31. Duke, 'Schleiermacher', 5.
32. T. Torrance, 'Hermeneutics', 260.
33. Ibid., 261.
34. Morrison, *'I Am You'*, 255.
35. Palmer, *Hermeneutics: Interpretation*, 87.
36. Morrison, *'I Am You'*, 240.
37. Palmer, *Hermeneutics: Interpretation*, 87.
38. Schleiermacher, *Hermeneutics*, 112.
39. Niebuhr, *Schleiermacher*, 86.
40. Morrison, *'I Am You'*, 244.
41. Ibid., 239.
42. Ibid., 259.
43. Gadamer, *Truth and Method*, 262.
44. Schleiermacher, *Hermeneutics*, 112.
45. Ibid., 113.
46. Gadamer, *Truth and Method*, 164.
47. Morrison, *'I Am You'*, 238.
48. Schleiermacher, *Hermeneutics*, 98.
49. Gadamer, *Truth and Method*, 164.
50. J. Torrance, 'Interpretation', 270.
51. Ibid., 260.
52. Morrison, *'I Am You'*, 242–3.
53. Gadamer, *Truth and Method*, 173.
54. J. Torrance, 'Interpretation', 269.
55. W. Dilthey (1972), 'The Rise of Hermeneutics', F. Jameson (tr.), *New Literary History*, 3, (2), Winter, 241.
56. Morrison, *'I Am You'*, 241.
57. T. Torrance, 'Hermeneutics', 260.

58. F. D. E. Schleiermacher (1836), *Schleiermacher's Introductions to the Dialogues of Plato*, W. Dobson (tr.), London: J. and J. J. Deighton, 15.
59. Niebuhr, *Schleiermacher*, 87, (Schleiermacher's quote from *Friedrich Schleiermachers sammltliche Werke*, (1835–64), Berlin, sect. 6, p. 109).
60. Morrison, *'I Am You'*, 251.
61. Ibid., 250.
62. Niebuhr, 'Schleiermacher', 154.
63. Niebuhr, *Schleiermacher*, 80.
64. Morrison, *'I Am You'*, 251.
65. M. Butler (1981), *Romantics, Rebels and Reactionaries: English Literature and Its Background, 1760–1830*, Oxford: Oxford University Press, 31–2.
66. Hazlitt, *Complete Works*, vol. 1, 1–2.
67. Hazlitt, *Complete Works*, vol. 20, 168–9.
68. Hazlitt, *Complete Works*, vol. 12, 50, 247, 248.
69. Hazlitt, *Complete Works*, vol. 17, 57.
70. Ibid., 63.
71. Indeed, the degree to which Romantic readers valued language steeped in feeling is copiously illustrated throughout Romantic literary reviews. For instance, Wordsworth is praised by John Stoddart in a review of the *Lyrical Ballads* (1800) in the *British Critic* in 1801 because 'he has deeply studied human nature, in the book of human action; and he has adopted his language from the same sources as his feelings'. D. H. Reiman (ed.) (1972), *The Romantics Reviewed: Contemporary Reviews of British Romantic Writers*, 9 vols, New York: Garland, 1972, Part A, 'The Lake Poets', 2 vols, vol. I, 131.
72. Schleiermacher, *Hermeneutics*, 113.
73. Hazlitt, *Complete Works*, vol. 12, 356.
74. Ibid., 55.
75. Reiman, Part A, I, 139.
76. C. Siskin (1988), *The Historicity of Romantic Discourse*, New York: Oxford University Press, 67.
77. Reiman, ed., Part A, vol. I, 228.
78. Hazlitt, *Complete Works*, vol. 5, 47.
79. Hazlitt, *Complete Works*, vol. 12, 55.
80. Reiman, Part A, vol. I, 277.
81. Ibid., 140.
82. D. H. Reiman, (ed.) (1972), *The Romantics Reviewed: Contemporary Reviews of British Romantic Writers*, 9 vols, New York: Garland, Part C, 'Shelley, Keats, and London Radical Writers', 2 vols, vol. 2, 599.
83. Quoted in T. Torrance, 'Hermeneutics', 261.
84. Morrison, *'I Am You'*, 250.
85. D. M. Moir (1851), *Sketches of the Poetical Literature of the Past Half-Century*, Edinburgh: William Blackwood, 200.
86. Hazlitt, *Complete Works*, vol. 12, 55.
87. Hazlitt, *Complete Works*, vol. 5, 3.
88. Ibid., 12.
89. Ibid., 6.
90. Hazlitt, *Complete Works*, vol. 12, 249–50.
91. Hazlitt, *Complete Works*, vol. 5, 15.
92. Hazlitt, *Complete Works*, vol. 19, 60.

93. D. H. Reiman, (ed.) (1972), *The Romantics Reviewed: Contemporary Reviews of British Romantic Writers*, 9 vols, New York: Garland, Part B, 'Byron and Regency Society Poets', 5 vols, vol. I, 128.
94. Ibid.
95. Ibid.
96. Ibid., 129.
97. Butler, *Romantics*, 2.
98. Their keen interest in the author as a person was indeed remarkable, as evidenced by this passage from a review of *The Excursion* by James Montgomery which appeared in *Eclectic Review* in 1815, in which the critic is commenting on the poem being only a part of a longer autobiographical poem, *The Recluse*:

    > We love to pry curiously into the secrets of a human heart; and since no living Author affords such familiar and complete access to his heart as Mr. Wordsworth does, we rejoice in every opportunity of visiting and exploring its inexhaustible riches of thought, imagery, and sentiment. How these were originally discovered, and how they have been gradually accumulated, we are desirous of knowing (Reiman, Part A, vol. I, 357).

99. Reiman, Part B, vol. I, 128.
100. Ibid., 392.
101. Ibid., 144.
102. Ibid., 125.
103. Schleiermacher, *Hermeneutics*, 95.
104. W. Wordsworth (1806–11), *The Letters of William and Dorothy Wordsworth*, E. de Selincourt (ed.), 2nd edn, vol. I, 'The Middle Years', Part I, revised by M. Moorman (1969), Oxford: Oxford University Press, 148.
105. Wordsworth, *Letters*, vol. I, Part I, 149.
106. Reiman, Part A, vol. I, 334.
107. As an anonymous reviewer writes of Wordsworth's 'Peter Bell' in the *British Critic* in 1819, 'the poet ... seeks to communicate pleasure to others. The process by which he arrives at that object is the exciting feelings correspondent to those which he has himself experienced'. Reiman, Part A, vol. I, 168.
108. J. Stewart (1983), 'Interpretive Listening: An Alternative to Empathy', *Communication Education*, 32, October, 381.
109. Stewart, 'Interpretive Listening', 380.
110. Gadamer, as quoted by D. C. Hoy (1978), *The Critical Circle: Literature, History and Philosophical Hermeneutics*, Berkeley, CA: University of California Press, 62.
111. P. Ricoeur, as quoted by Stewart, 'Interpretive Listening', 382.
112. Ibid., 384.
113. Niebuhr, *Schleiermacher*, 89.
114. M. Buber (1965), *The Knowledge of Man*, M. Friedman and R. G. Smith (tr.), London: George Allen and Unwin, 75.
115. Stewart, 'Interpretive Listening', 385.
116. Schleiermacher, *Hermeneutics*, 97.
117. Niebuhr, 'Schleiermacher', 157.

118. Niebuhr, 'Schleiermacher', 153.
119. Hazlitt, *Complete Works*, vol. 12, 250.
120. Stewart, 'Interpretive Listening',387.
121. S. T. Coleridge (1983), *The Collected Works of Samuel Taylor Coleridge: Part 7, Biographia Literaria, or Biographical Sketches of My Literary life and Opinions*, 2 vols, J. Engell and W. J. Bate (eds), Princeton, NJ: Princeton University Press, vol. 2, 28.
122. S. T. Coleridge, *Coleridge's Shakespearean Criticism*, 2 vols, T. M. Raysor (ed.), Cambridge, MA: Harvard University Press, vol. 2, 344.
123. Hazlitt, *Complete Works*, vol. 1, 41.
124. Coleridge, *Shakespearean Criticism*, vol. 1, 212; vol. 2, 94; vol. 1, 132.
125. Stewart, 'Interpretive Listening', 389.
126. Coleridge, *Collected Works: Biographia Literaria*, vol. 2, 14.
127. D. Marshall (1988), *The Surprising Effects of Sympathy: Marivaux, Diderot, Rousseau and Mary Shelley*, Chicago: University of Chicago Press, 3, 2, 48, 5.
128. M. Fried (1980), *Absorption and Theatricality: Painting and the Beholder in the Age of Diderot*, Chicago: University of Chicago Press, 92.
129. Ibid., 101.
130. Ibid., 131.
131. Ibid., 104.
132. For example, in Diderot's discussion in his 'Salon de 1763' of Philippe-Jacques de Loutherbourg's 'Un Paysage avec figures et animaux', addressed (as his reviews often are) to Friedrich Grimm, he exclaims:

> Ah! My friend, how beautiful nature is in this little spot! Let us stop there. The heat of the day is beginning to be felt, let us lie down next to these animals. While we admire the work of the Creator, the conversation of this shepherd and this peasant woman will divert us. Our ears will not disdain the rustic sounds of the cowherd who charms the silence of this solitude and beguiles the tedium of his condition by playing the flute. Let us rest. You will be next to me, I will be at your feet, tranquil and safe, like this dog, diligent companion of his master's life and faithful keeper of his flock. And when the weight of the light has diminished we will go our way again, and at some remote time we will still remember this enchanted place and the delicious hour that we spent there (Fried, *Absorption*, 120).

133. Fried, *Absorption*, 121.
134. Schleiermacher, *Introductions to the Dialogues of Plato*, 14.
135. W. Wordsworth (1974), *The Prose Works of William Wordsworth*, J. B. Owen and J. W. Smyser (eds), 3 vols, Oxford: Oxford University Press, vol. 3, 82.
136. Wordsworth, *Prose Works*, vol. 3, 82.
137. Schleiermacher, *Introductions to the Dialogues of Plato*, 14.

CHAPTER TWO

Diaries and the sympathetic underworld

If you would know yourself, take heed of the practice of others; if you would understand others, look to your own heart within you.[1]

When you wish to be heard, you whisper.[2]

Diary-writing is a quintessentially solitary and independent enterprise, yet as a written form it assumes and implies a reader, if only the diarist him/herself at some future date. Arthur Ponsonby, who spent a good part of his lifetime reading English diaries, came to the conclusion that 'it is almost impossible for anyone to write [a diary] without imagining a reader, so to speak at the other end, however far off that other end may be – self in old age, family, a friend, the public or remote posterity'.[3]

Not only might the diarist imagine a reader as he/she gradually creates his/her 'book of the self',[4] but the diary itself gradually takes on a capacity to interact with the imagined reader, as well as with the writer him/herself. It assumes a life of its own. Robert Fothergill is a more recent chronicler of English diaries who recognizes this interactive, dialectic yearning which the diary can be said to engender and which sets it apart from other genres. According to Fothergill, 'the diary, unlike other forms of communication, creates its own reader as a projection of the impulse to write. The reader is literally a figment of the writer's mind, a completion of the circuit'.[5] The writer and the reader are seen as two parts of a whole, intertwined and complementary. The imagined listener/reader, much like the persona of the diarist him/herself, exists at the level of the writer's imagination or the subconscious, though it comes to life in the words on the page. Thus, although diary-writing is ostensibly a solitary activity, it cannot be fully appreciated except in the context of relationship.

The study of many diaries suggests two ways of understanding this relationship. First there is the relationship between the writer and the reader, both the imagined reader existing in the diarist's mind and the actual reader. Equally subtle and paradoxical is the relationship between the writer and the diarist, the historical figure and the person – or persona – who emerges in the pages of the diary. The identity of the diarist – that is, the one speaking – is as important to understanding the writer as is the identity of the reader, the one listening. In fact a diary is all about identity – conceiving one, achieving one and believing in one. The extent to which the diarist and the writer should be considered as one and the same has long been the subject of debate among psychologists and students of the genre. For some, such as Thomas Mallon, the diary is uniquely unmediated literature, the distance between reader and writer being as negligible as that between the writer and his/her text. Reading a diary, contends this school of thought, is the perfect way of knowing the writer's deepest personality. Unlike other genres, 'one cannot read a diary and feel unacquainted with its writer. No form of expression more emphatically embodies the expresser: diaries are the flesh made word'.[6] For Fothergill, the issue is not so straightforward. He argues that 'one must make a mental distinction between the first-person narrator who speaks in the diary and the historical personage who held the pen'.[7]

Awareness of cultural phenomena underlies this advice. In the beginning of the nineteenth century, there is a 'growing consciousness in the mind of the diarist of diary-writing as literary composition, a process in which the writer has an eye on himself writing'.[8] Not only is this a result of the fact that, as Fothergill observes, 'in the early nineteenth century personal diaries are beginning to appear in print' and therefore 'by this period few diarists any longer write in the certainty that they will *not* be published, posthumously at least'.[9] The manner of self-presentation was also affected by another connection between creative literature and other forms of writing, a consequence of 'the waning of the Augustan cultural ethos': Fothergill further states that 'creative literature tends increasingly to draw on the intimate emotional life of the writer as a primary resource; so, conversely, does that mode of writing whose substance has long been the personal life come to regard itself as "literary", and to adopt literary conventions'. The Romantic diary stresses both form and feeling. This chapter will show that its form actually gives rise to feeling and identity as well as providing them with an outlet and a shape.

This blurring of form and feeling parallels the relationship between the diarist and the reader. In both cases, intimacy is responsible for ambiguity. Determining the sincerity of emotional expression is not the primary task of the reader of diaries. In order to understand and know the diarist, one must invariably spend day after day alongside the diarist experiencing with him/her the mundane events and moments of his/her life. It is upon entries of this sort that the reader must base his/her understanding of the diarist. Far more private than in any other genre, the relationship between the reader and the diarist can be likened to that between the psychoanalyst and the patient, or 'analysand'. The latter is essentially a narrator relating stories and scenes from his/her life. As the relationship develops over time, the analyst learns better what to listen for, so that more is revealed than is consciously communicated by the analysand. Ponsonby found in his reading that 'it is not through their intentional and deliberate self-dissection that we really get to know people ... A diarist reveals himself or gives himself away by casual and quite unpremeditated entries far more than by laborious self-analysis'.[10] It is the reader who must make connections among passages, decipher language, and interpret feelings and mundane events based on his/her own personal response as well as in terms of the composite portrait which emerges. Seeing the parts in terms of the whole (unrecognized by the analysand) and the whole in terms of the parts (hidden to the analysand) is precisely the sort of hermeneutic circle[11] which psychoanalyst R. Greenson describes as his technique of listening to a patient he has come to know over time:

> I go back over the patient's utterances and transform her words into pictures and feelings in accordance with her personality. I let myself associate to these pictures *her* life experiences, *her* memories, *her* fantasies. As I have worked with this patient over the years I have built up a working model of the patient consisting of her physical appearance, her behavior, her ways of moving, her desires, feelings, defenses, values, attitudes, etc. It is this working model of the patient that I shift into the foreground as I try to capture what she was experiencing.[12]

Fothergill's term, 'imprint', strongly echoes Greenson's description. 'The word was chosen', he writes, 'in order to convey the dual power of a diary-passage to carry the writer's deliberate self-expression together with unintended and unconscious aspects of his personality.'[13] It is as if the diarist narrates his/her life story through daily entries, with the tacit awareness of a sympathetic reader who will 'complete' his/her 'book of life' by performing the function of a listening analyst. The reader, like the analyst, must actively involve his/her sympathetic imagination in the creative process, for it is not merely a book that is being created, but the very identity of the diarist. The paradoxically intimate nature of this genre stems from the fact that while the diary allows the reader to observe extraordinarily closely the details of the diarist's life, it often only hints at the nature of his/her inner life. As a result, only the active and sympathetic reader may resolve the puzzling riddle of identity. Ponsonby characterizes diary-writing as unusually revelatory because it is uniquely dependent on the process of identification:

> We can enter into the trivial pleasures and petty miseries of daily life – the rainy day, the blunt razor, the new suit, the domestic quarrel, the bad night, the twinge of toothache, the fall from a

horse, the newly purchased book, the good meal, the over-sharp criticism, the irritating relation, the child's maladies, the exasperating servant. We know them all. We have experienced many of them ourselves. Through these casual notes we are brought into a sort of familiar relationship and fellow-feeling with the writer which philosophic discourses or even collected correspondence cannot produce in quite the same way.[14]

'Fellow-feeling' is what links the reader of diaries to the psychoanalyst, and what distinguishes sympathetic reading of diaries from psychoanalytic literary interpretation, for both reader and analyst rely on a keen sense of relationship based on consistency and intimacy in seeking to identify themselves with the underlying humanity of the Other and thereby come to know intimately the Other's absolutely unique individuality. Greenson's process captures what Ponsonby has in mind for the reader: 'I shift from listening from the outside to listening from the inside. I have to let a part of me become the patient, and I have to go through her experiences as if I were the patient and to introspect what is going on in me as they occur.'[15]

A text becomes a context for working out identities and relationships, a text characterized by the surprise and wonder of day-to-day events and experiences, the diary is defined by its unfinished quality. This very incompleteness might be expected to reflect the state of the diarist him/ herself: identifiable, yet somehow without identity. Sympathy alone can make sense of this underlying paradox and 'complete the circuit' begun by the diarist, for sympathy is itself a phenomenon rooted in paradox. According to psychologists and sociologists, it centres around the inextricable interrelationship between knowing oneself and knowing another.

I will examine in detail the diaries of William Jones, a country clergyman in the early nineteenth century, Dorothy Wordsworth, Byron, Amelia Opie, a novelist and poet of strong religious conviction, and James Woodforde, a late eighteenth-century country parson, applying to each certain recent theories of sympathy and empathy which shed light on our understanding of the diary, the diarist and the reading of diaries. Although the idea of sympathy first attracted me because it was important in personality and aesthetic theory in the late eighteenth century, reading Romantic diaries in conjunction with twentieth-century theories about the ways in which one person can know another has made sympathy and diaries seem an utterly natural marriage.

Reverend William Jones

On 7 April 1798, just after his son has embarked on his first naval
voyage, Reverend William Jones records the following entry in his
journal:

> My dear son, Wm, occupies very much of my thoughts. I knew not
> the strength of my love & attachment to the dear fellow, till I
> parted with him. It is now drawing towards one o'clock Monday
> morning. I trust he is comfortably asleep on board the *Wm. &*
> *Mary*. Perhaps he is now dreaming of myself, his dear Mother &
> his Broxbn. home (pp. 107–8).[16]

At once utterly plain and deeply moving, this passage illuminates and
typifies the tenor of Jones's diary in several ways. Though brief, the
detail and sensitivity with which he imagines William's experience illustrate his tendency to see a relationship between his understanding of
others and his own inner experience, and to regard his own self as a
being standing in radical need of a home – that is, a more permanent
sense of connectedness and belonging. Determining what this home is
for Jones depends to a great extent upon the reader's own willingness to
read with sympathetic imagination, to experience Jones's world as he
did, in all its mundane detail, and to contemplate imaginatively his
response based on what is and is not said in the pages of his journal –
both what they tell and what they reveal. His irrepressible need for
privacy stems from the same nature which defines itself in elemental
relationship to others. We will first examine this elemental relationship
and then see what it can tell us about Jones's inner identity.

As a clergyman, Jones places the utmost importance upon sympathy
of a certain kind, namely, self-effacement before God. Total denial of
self and participation in the divine Other is Jones's goal as a man of
God, and the earlier portions of the journal are typically self-flagellat-
ing in the tradition of Methodist diaries. Along with travelogues and
historical records, self-improvement diaries were virtually the only kind
of diary to have thrived up to the late eighteenth century.[17] Yet it soon
becomes clear that Jones's journal does not fit easily into this or any
category. In a noteworthy passage written as an Oxford undergraduate,
Jones illustrates his tendency to understand others in terms of his own
experience and feelings; far from denying the other's uniqueness, however, the level of self-involvement entailed in this phenomenon actually
allows Jones to extend his understanding beyond the bounds of his own
experience and to know that person more fully. He is speaking of the
elderly Mrs Crutch, a woman whom he visited regularly and came to
know while at Oxford:

How admirable is her habitual Frame of Mind! Her heart is almost (I had almost said altogether) swallowed up in the Love of God. She walks in that well-nigh forsaken Path of humble Dependence on her God & chearful Resignation to His Will ... The happiest state is when she is nothing, & Xt is all. Her whole Delight is in conversing about the things of God; indeed her knowledge as well as her converse about worldly things is very circumscribed (p. 7).

Note that while he admires her largely because she embodies the religious values he espouses, his understanding of her – her feelings as well as her knowledge – surpasses the confines of his own experience. She is a model of what he would like to be. Thus the passage shows Jones entering into her experience as he imagines it to be for her; and while he is able to do this precisely because he shares with her a very basic set of beliefs, he maintains a detachment from her – referring, for instance, to '*her* God' rather than simply 'God'. Awareness of what he feels and believes allows him a more complete picture of his friend; moreover, particularly in light of his other fond diary references to her while in Oxford – a place where he felt generally alienated – his awareness of her feelings and beliefs, in turn, reaffirms for him basic elements of his own self.

Like the reader, whose knowledge of the diarist is based on what can aptly be described as 'daily' encounters, Jones here bases his awareness and analysis of Mrs Crutch on a sympathetic response made possible by regular interaction with her. Participating (as personal friend, observer or reader) in the mundane life-routine of another engages and intertwines the natural quests for self-knowledge and knowledge of the other. This constitutes the unique connection between sympathy, self and the diary.

For Max Scheler, a philosopher writing in the early part of the twentieth century, sympathy is crucial to the connection between our capacity to know others and our capacity to know our own self. Sympathy, Scheler asserts in his seminal work, *The Nature of Sympathy*, 'is a genuine out-reaching and entry into the other person and his individual situation, a true and authentic transcendence of one's self'. It is characterized by 'an awareness of distance between selves'[18] precisely because of an act of self-transcendence on the part of the sympathizer. Significantly, this act allows one not to escape oneself but rather to understand oneself more fully, precisely through one's simultaneous understanding of the other in all his uniqueness. Scheler explains:

Understanding is not confined to the understanding of others (on the strength of what I have already perceived in myself). It is equally ultimate as an understanding of oneself. Understanding ... is a basic type of participation, distinct from and in no way based upon perception, whereby one essentially spiritual being can enter into the life of another one.[19]

Scheler's use of the word 'perception' suggests the link between the reader of the diary and the diarist himself. In this case, our knowledge of Jones is based not on his physical presence, but rather, I would argue, on the 'interaction' that goes on – in place of actual physical encounter – between his responses to his experience, as recorded in his journal, and our full and sympathetic response to those entries. His words are not his inner self but signs of that self, just as they are not his experience itself but his recorded response to it. The mediation between physical reality and individual (psychological) response which occurs in both cases – first Jones's, then the reader's – is actually a process of understanding (sympathy).

Another passage in Jones's journal depicts a different sort of sympathy, for it involves Jamaican slaves with whom Jones apparently has nothing in common. Nevertheless, note how he seems to have reached outside himself in order to imagine concretely the experience of these men who have exchanged one kind of bondage for another. He is speaking of a regiment of negro and mulatto soldiers whom he has observed daily from his window and while walking:

> Were Jamaica to be reduc'd, either by French or Spaniards, these wretches wou'd no longer enjoy their Liberty unmolested, whose sweets, once tasted, they wou'd give up with greater reluctance & more regret than Life itself. Their Officers, who are always whites, are perpetually sounding alarms in their ears, & representing to their imaginations Servitude attended with every conceivable horror. There is little reason to apprehend that they will ever flinch when put to the test (p. 40).

In Scheler's terms, this passage exemplifies Jones's refusal to be confined to the 'prison of [his] own casual experiences'.[20] In addition to being generally sympathetic toward their plight, Jones's imagination takes him beyond the immediately perceived and into the realm of conjecture and wonder, where the limitations of one's own experience hold little sway. No doubt his sense of their 'reluctance', 'regret' and perpetual fear are based, to a certain extent, upon his own imagined feelings, as we saw in the previous passage. This does not mean he has failed to transcend himself, however; on the contrary, Scheler makes emphatically clear the connection between self-understanding and understanding others.[21] The former does not precede the latter, but rather the two work in conjunction. While Jones knows what fear and reluctance feel like to him, in order to imagine the 'horror' in the slaves' imagination he must go outside himself and experience the 'enlargement of [himself] by participation in another's experience'.[22]

This image of enlargement aptly points to the way in which the phenomenon of sympathy is a true meeting of minds; it can occur neither in the confines of one's own self, nor in the immediately perceived physical evidence. For the reader, this evidence is the words on a page; for Jones (or anyone else) it is people and actions within sensual reach. The sympathetic phenomenon demands feeling and reflection upon what is immediately given in the Other. Only thus, according to Scheler, can one truly know any person, whether oneself or another: 'The more deeply we penetrate into a human being, through knowledge and understanding ... the more unmistakable, individual, unique, irreplaceable and indispensable does he become in our mind.'[23] Perception, or the physical presence of the Other, is not what determines our knowledge or understanding of that person any more than our knowledge of ourselves is limited to our bodies. What enables sympathetic union between Jones and both a dear, inspired friend as well as a group of desperate strangers, and likewise what links the reader with Jones – through the survival of his journal – is not so much particular coincidence of experience as a disposition and desire to know and feel human nature more completely.

What, then, is the connection between Jones's sympathetic imagination and the feeling of discontent which pervades the journal? To begin to find an answer, we turn to the early pages of the journal, which reveal his unhappiness as an Oxford undergraduate – 'Alone within the dismal College-walls, & very discontented' (p. 5) – and although such feelings are not uncommon to a young man away from home, in Jones's case the feeling never really leaves him. So when he identifies (in the initial passage cited) with what he imagines must be his son William's feelings soon after leaving home, in a very real sense he is identifying with a part of himself. Imagining his son's dream recalls a certain dream which Jones had while living in Jamaica, where he worked for the British government for two years immediately after leaving Oxford. Although he later writes that those two years were the happiest of his life, his journal entries during his stay paint the picture of a sad and lonely young man who longs to return home. A few months after arriving he writes, 'Out of my room window I view the Harbour I entered, & cast many a wishful Look over the Seas I have lately cross'd. Oft as I do it, I spread a Gloom over many successive Moments. Every repeated Look adds keenness to my Anguish' (p. 28). Upon leaving at the end of his assignment, he writes, 'To my very great satisfaction, on Frid. the 28th. we lost sight of the Island; & I never desire to see it any more' (p. 68). It is not surprising to find that he records the following in 1779:

> Sund. 2nd May. I almost forgot to note the happy night I passed on Frid. Methought I was at [home in] Abergavenny saluting my friends, particularly my mother, with whom, in chief, I held a long Conversation; recounting the mercies of my various deliverances, &c. Much of what we said, or seemed to be said, I well recollected, after I awoke; & I must confess the image was so lively and striking, & my Enjoyment so exquisite, that my disappointment was not small, when I found it was a dream (p. 53).

The image of the dream, which recalls the passage cited above when his son leaves home, serves to connect him and his son, and exemplifies a capacity for sympathetic identification. As there is no indication on 7 April 1798 that Jones at that moment consciously recalls his earlier dream, the reader can only assume that he imagines his son dreaming of home for the obvious reason that any young man may do so shortly after departing. Yet, longing is a recurrent feeling in this journal, and the fact that Jones imagines his son's experience in the form of a dream similar to his own during a time when he longed for home, suggests that his longing for home has never completely left him.

The diary bears this out in the number of ways in which Jones reveals his unfulfilled desire for rest and repose. After serving as curate of Broxbourne for 20 years, he is finally made vicar, a post he has long and passionately hoped for because of the leisure time and greater financial security it would provide him. But one misfortune seems to follow another, making him continually unhappy. Accompanying Jones day after day, the reader experiences the impact of it all: 'Sunday 20th Feby 1791. With what astonishment should I have been struck, had any one assured me 7 or 10, or still rather 12, years ago, that the time would come, when I should be circumstanced as I feel myself at this present moment!!' (p. 98). Many entries simply record his daily routine of tutoring, preparing sermons, walking many miles to visit the sick, worrying over financial woes and soliciting contributions, a drudgery he particularly dislikes: 'I am at a loss for words to express the meanness & grudging illiberality with which many of my parishioners pay me a trifle in lieu of my tithes, &c; & the scandalous injustice of many others, who refuse to pay me at all' (p. 187). However, usually it is in our imagining the situation itself, rather than in any overt expression of emotion, that the nature of Jones's experience emerges for the reader:

> On Friday last I lost two very fine calves – the next morning I received a letter referred to, respecting the loss of the Warrens [family friends]. Yesterday a very valuable cow died. Not many days ago I heard for a certainty that the Jamaica Pacquet is taken, which contained a remittance of some considerable amount from Mr. Parke for the education of his two sons [whom Jones tutored for income]. These, & other less considerable ills have seemed to

tread on each other's heels like Job's messengers of evil (pp. 103–4).

Even after becoming Vicar of Broxbourne (in September 1801), tranquillity eludes him and he is haunted by the dream, a longing for a home he seems never to reach. Although initially ecstatic – 'Blessed be Heaven! I now enjoy what my soul has long wished for, a considerable share of *otium* – time at my disposal . . . I know not the human being with whom I would exchange situation' (p. 127) – his journal confirms what Jones himself observes at one point, that he is 'neither more nor less than a paradox!' (p. 175). In May 1806 he writes the following:

> the sun shines, I hear the birds singing, & all nature looks gay; but not to me, my cup of life is embittered, my mind is unsettled & beclouded: &, instead of actually enjoying any thing round me, I seem like a sentinel, longing impatiently, & looking out, for relief (pp. 186–7).

At times the reader feels that Jones is attempting to disguise his unhappiness, or to suppress it. On 1 October 1804, he writes: 'A stranger, who might chance to read some of these dolorous scrawls, would imagine me to be one of the most miserable of all miserable, unhappy beings – but is it so? – no – no such thing' (p. 175). His very insistence on his being happy despite regular evidence to the contrary betrays the restless, discontented undercurrent in the journal, the fear that he is a failure and that his life is irrelevant.

Throughout the journal Jones expresses a sense of powerlessness to ameliorate his situation. On 30 March 1800, he writes: 'My dear wife is a lawyer's daughter, & possesses a wonderful volubility of speech, such a miraculous power of twirling & twisting every argument to her interests, that I am no match for her High Mightiness' (p. 113). The problematic nature of his relationship with his wife, a constant theme in the journal, points to his general feeling of frustration and inefficacy. He learns, for instance, of a college friend who has been very successful and achieved some renown through his preaching and teaching in Wales, news which prompts this response (27 April 1799): 'Different indeed, far different is my lot! My school-employment, my private reading, my compilation of extracts, &c, in short my whole life, (to describe it as favourably as I can), seems scarce anything but a course of laborious trifling' (p. 108). It is as if the home he has made satisfies the simple needs of the humble clergyman, but fails to answer some persistent longing. Hence his admission, long after being made vicar, of high hopes for his son George's success – success in worldly terms, success which implies not only the leisure which Jones himself finally does attain, but along with it recognition and respect, which he clearly feels the lack of. On 2 September 1805 he muses: 'Shall I ever live to see my George a lieutenant, – a Captain, – shall I say – an Admiral?' (p. 182). Indeed, his sons' fortunes are an abiding concern, and he frequently indicates his desire for them to satisfy their ambitions and achieve success. This is a perfectly natural paternal desire. But Jones feels trapped and unhappy, and this deep-seated feeling is what connects his dream long ago to his sons, who represent, among other things, the possibilities he himself never realized. An entry in April 1797 sums up the sense which continues to haunt him in various manifestations throughout the diary: 'I seem overpowered by the largeness of my family, & am continually dinned by my wife's complaints of the dearness of the times, & the absolute impossibility of our living on our present income' (p. 104). Neither money nor financial security, nor even domestic control, is the issue here; what eludes and 'overpowers' him seems to be an ideal notion he has of happiness and success to which no reality can ever compare.

As a result, his sole source of solace, particularly as he gets older, becomes the one symbol of his success and independence – his room. His journal is replete with simple and straightforward statements proclaiming the prominent and vital place of his private room in his life: 'With the greatest reluctance do I ever quit my Cell' (p. 258). Indeed, this 'nest' (p. 270) takes on the qualities of an ideal home environment, a reflection of his idiosyncratic self:

> How happy, how very happy, do I feel myself in my dear little room, which some delicate folks would, perhaps, rudely call a hog-sty! I am undisturbed, I have my cheerful little fire, my books & in short every comfort which I can reasonably desire. I read, I reflect, I write, & endeavour to enjoy, as far as I can, that blessed leisure & absence of care ... (p. 147).

Like the journal itself, his 'cell' is vitally close to his heart and to his sense of self. He says of his journal, 'I don't know what I should do, were I deny'd pen, ink & paper' (p. 34). It is characteristically expressed in the negative, like 'reluctance' and 'overpowered' above, suggestive of the way he lives – constant fear of loss. Perhaps by virtue of this pervasive dread, when in his private space he spends much of his time writing in his journal; indeed, shortly before his death, while confined to his bed, he writes: 'When I awoke, this morning, before day-light, I seemed to be uttering these words, – "Let me take to my Journal again"' (p. 278). Indeed, the analogy between the journal and his 'cell' is clear: both represent an escape into self, into the freedom to reflect upon and express himself. He writes (7 November 1787), 'How ardently do I wish that I could spend more time in retirement & in converse with my own soul! This would teach me many useful lessons of self-knowledge . . . ' (p. 96). Ostensibly, at least, what draws him so powerfully to seek the privacy of his journal is a desire for self-knowledge. Yet clearly he also simply sought an escape from his unpleasant home situation and the tedium of his job. In both cases, what the journal provides him is an arena in which to express himself, or if it is not exactly cathartic (as, for instance, Benjamin Haydon's diary was), he has the opportunity to speak and do as he likes, a freedom denied him in his public roles as father, husband and vicar.

In a book entitled, *Between Public and Private: The Lost Boundaries of the Self*, sociologists Joseph Bensman and Robert Lilienfeld argue that the self is split between its public and private halves. The basic assumption behind the need for privacy, they posit, is:

> that the individual possesses a self and a history that is broader and deeper than any role he plays; that 'normal' role performance involves a projection of only part of the self; and that the role performer selects from the total selves that constitute his personal history the responses that are appropriate to a given situation, as defined by his official role or position at a given time and place.[24]

We see an example of the tension Jones feels in an entry dated 10 April 1805. Of an evening spent with 'men of taste' and high society, he writes: 'I have very seldom attended such grand dining-matches, without saying many things, which, in the first moment of reflection, I have felt reason to be ashamed of, & doing too many things, which have given me pain, though, perhaps, they have escaped the observation of my fellow-worms' (p. 178). When writing in the journal he feels liberated from the fear of such falseness and self-betrayal, for it provides for him a forum in which both to unearth and create the self he wishes to be.

This process, which he himself describes as 'converse with my own soul' and in which he feels transformed through 'lessons of self-knowledge', is what psychiatrist Alfred Margulies describes as 'empathy with oneself'. Through the persona of the diarist, however 'accurate' or incomplete a depiction of the writer that persona may be, Jones establishes an Other with whom he develops a relationship over time, the very interactive setting most conducive, as both Greenson and Scheler have argued, to self-understanding. The basic assumption of Margulies's study is that empathy is ultimately a search for self, not for the other. 'The self,' he argues, 'can be defined as that psychic structure that comes into being with the enigmatic process of self-reflection – that is, the self as simultaneously both subject and object.'[25] The diarist persona becomes the object with whom Jones can (subjectively, feelingly) identify. It is thus that the creation of the diary and its narrator serves Jones's own self-discovery: 'empathy . . . is a process which creates the self, either through the other or through empathy with oneself. That is, the self defines itself through empathy'.[26]

Sitting in his 'cell' and writing in his journal is, put simply, Jones's way of discovering who he is by gaining distance and perspective on the mundane demands of his life. What must be understood is that this cannot and does not take place through self-absorption. On the contrary, by its very nature, sympathy ensures that this search for self is not self-absorbing, for it depends on one's self-transcendence: 'in looking for you, I must identify my own reflection and continually put myself aside'.[27] Nor is Jones the kind of man who revels in his own discontent. Nevertheless, that he was discontented and needed some way to simultaneously get outside himself and understand himself, he could not deny. One may say he turned to his diary in lieu of a confidant, for, as Margulies puts it, 'telling one's narrative to another helps one find and constitute oneself'.[28] Moreover, this twofold phenomenon of self-transcendence and heightened self-awareness is what transforms Jones's diarist from a disembodied voice to an intimate Other – for Jones as well as for the reader. Bensman and Lilienfeld explain how sympathy transforms privacy into intimacy: 'Intimate relations consist in the attempt to escape the burdens of privacy by finding social supports for a private, intimate self that are short of the demands of public and official norms.'[29] As previous passages illustrate, Jones clearly felt little or no such support outside his room, either in high society or with his wife or parishioners.

The 'burdens of privacy' refer to the total self-absorption mentioned above, while social supports – which Jones creates for himself in the form of his diary – constitute the sympathy one either knows or imagines to exist in some listening Other. In one entry he remarks: 'I have just observed that I ended the last sentence with "I assure you". I suppose I may have frequently used the same form of expression, as if appealing to some listening friend, some person at least attentive to my lamentations & woes' (p. 113). Whether it be the imagined reader whose sympathy 'completes the circuit' of his journal or the narrative persona with whom Jones the writer acts as sympathetic Other (sympathy with his own diarist-self), Jones creates a dynamic of interaction – of telling one's story, as the analysand does, and of listening actively and sympathetically to that story, as the analyst does.

On some intuitive level, as well as out of the basic human need for both solitude and solace, for self-awareness and relationship, Jones understood the paradoxical interconnection between privacy and intimacy, sympathy and self-discovery. Margulies has studied this paradoxical dynamic and describes it thus: 'In projecting a self onto the other in the interpersonal dialectic, I participate in the creation of a self that I now empathize with. In its very process empathy actualizes its object of contemplation.'[30] Although on the one hand I agree with Ponsonby's description of Jones as a 'simple-hearted sort of man',[31] on the other hand I disagree emphatically. The events of his life were only as simple as our reading of his diary is superficial and passive. His inner life, as revealed by diary entries, suggests complexity and depth no one, including himself, could fathom. With sympathy, however, we can try.

Dorothy Wordsworth

The nature of Dorothy's sympathetic imagination is illustrated by her journal's prodigious use of metaphor. Her metaphorical use of language indicates not only an imaginative way of seeing the world, but a particular way of experiencing one's 'being-in-the-world'.[32] While she and William were on a boat on Rydale:

> we heard a strange sound in the Bainriggs wood, as we were floating on the water; it seemed in the wood, but it must have been above it, for presently we saw a raven very high above us. It called out, and the dome of the sky seemed to echo the sound. It called again and again as it flew onwards, and the mountains gave back the sound, seeming as if from their centre; a musical bell-like answering to the bird's hoarse voice (vol. I, p. 52).[33]

In metaphorical language which penetrates the landscape, she takes pathetic fallacy to new depths. Aware that she is merely imagining, she nevertheless invests her language and description with a sense of deeper awareness founded on belief. Though the sky could not literally produce an echo of the raven's cry, her persistence with the image of bird and sky in symbiotic relationship charges her image with greater impact, if not a sense of actuality. Indeed, the relationship she depicts parallels the interactive phenomenon underlying her imaginative description. Her frequent and apparently spontaneous use of metaphor shows how she implicitly analyses objects and events around her for their hidden significance, venturing into the realm of the unknown Other.

Philosopher Martin Buber was intensely concerned with understanding what it means to be a person, an experiencing 'I', and how the Self comes to know the Other. A process central to achieving this profound understanding is what he calls 'imagining the real', his account of which is strikingly similar to what Dorothy's use of metaphor reveals about her active, searching mind and her relationship with nature:

> Imagining the real ... is not a looking at the other, but a bold swinging – demanding the most intensive stirring of one's being –

into the life of the other. This is the nature of all genuine imagining, only that here the realm of my action is not the all-possible,
but the particular.[34]

Far from merely responding 'feelingly' to the world around her, as
Fothergill claims, Dorothy involves herself in interactive relationship
with it by imagining its own deeper life. As a result she becomes aware
of what Buber calls the 'dynamic centre' of the external world; its
uniqueness, unperceived by – because foreign to – the casual observer, is
made known to her through her sympathetic imagination. For awareness of the other's unique nature 'is only possible when I step into an
elemental relation with the other, that is, when [it] becomes present to
me'.[35]

The words 'still' and 'quiet', which occur remarkably often in the
journal, suggest the most consistent and important way in which Dorothy
conceives of this fundamental, sympathetic encounter and the reason
why her journal evokes the reader's active sympathy. Throughout the
journal stillness and quietness characterize her most valued time spent
and are instrumental to her 'making present' the world around her. In a
typical day's description, she writes: 'a sweet evening as it had been a
sweet day, a grey evening, and I walked quietly along the side of Rydale
Lake with quiet thoughts – the hills and lake were still – the Owls had
not begun to hoot, and the little birds had given over singing' (vol. I, p.
125). There is an absolute communion of stillness between the silent,
contemplative Dorothy and the natural world – hills, lake, owls and
little birds are all quiet. And it is within Dorothy's sympathetic imagination that this communion of stillness and quietness has been consum-
mated, for it is only by virtue of making this connection between herself
and the external world that her reflective consciousness is able successfully to complete the process of self-reflection.

As Theodor Reik explains in *Listening with the Third Ear*, 'the deepest and most vital region of the self is inaccessible to its own contemplative and inquiring consciousness. In order to comprehend it psychologically, it needs to be reflected in another'.[36] Relationship – connection
through sympathy – is the key to self-understanding. This is the function which the reader's presence performs. Dorothy leaves a 'silence' for
the reader to fill. For Dorothy silence is conducive to inner stillness. The
abundance of description in her journal of the stillness and quiet of
natural objects and scenes is a reflection of her sensitive powers of
observation, but more important it points to her own inner need for the
silence which allows profound thought. Her accounts of the natural
world around her indicate more than passive observation. Dorothy
interacts with her surroundings as a way of moulding her identity from
nature's own images.

The emotion evoked by quiet thought varies. At times the stillness stirs sadness: 'I strolled on, gathered mosses etc. The quietness and still seclusion of the valley affected me even to producing the deepest melancholy. I forced myself from it. The wind rose before I went to bed' (vol. I, p. 40). 'It' seems to me crucial to our accurate understanding of the diarist. Under the assumption that 'it' refers to 'the quietness and still seclusion', Gittings and Manton comment that sometimes 'the lack of sound was almost too much'[37] for Dorothy to bear. If we learn anything from her journal, however, it is that she relishes quiet. As her grammar would imply, therefore, she forces herself from the melancholy, not from the secluded valley. The range of emotions she experiences during her daily rounds within those silent environs testifies to her utterly instinctive ability to 'be' – happy or sad – 'quiet'. She frequently identifies her own emotional state with that of her surroundings. For instance three days after William's departure she records, 'incessant rain from morning till night ... The Skobby [finch] sate quietly in its nest, rocked by the wind, and beaten by the rain' (vol. I, p. 39). Surely Dorothy sees herself in the fragile little bird, as she remains faithfully home at Grasmere, a sort of silent sufferer enduring the trials of awaiting her beloved's return.

Often nature, even in its most solemn state, has a salutary effect. On 16 May, two days after William's departure, she writes:

> Grasmere was very solemn in the last glimpse of twilight; it calls home the heart to quietness. I had been very melancholy in my walk back. I had many of my saddest thoughts, and I could not keep the tears within me. But when I came to Grasmere I felt it did me good (vol. I, p. 39).

Here Grasmere's 'solemn' stillness lifts Dorothy from sadness precisely by acting as a reminder to her of the inner 'quietness' which she equates with 'home'. The role of the sympathetic imagination is crucial to transforming this external sign (that is, Grasmere) available to the senses, into an Other with which Dorothy sees herself in relationship. This process is what Buber has in mind when he says that imagining the real 'completes the findings of the senses'.[38] Only by engaging herself in her environment can she respond in a way fruitful to her inner self, a response completed by writing it in the journal. Psychologist Robert Katz attributes to empathy a similar healing, recovering capacity for the self. Empathy, he posits, 'is motivated by the human need to communicate, to share in the emotions of others, to affiliate and overcome loneliness, to recover lost ties, and to apprehend by techniques of dramatic imagination'.[39] The cumulative effect is to invite a similar activity on the reader's part.

As these passages illustrate, particularly the last one, Dorothy not only empathizes with the natural world, understanding nature by projecting on to it her own feelings; equally important, in understanding (creating, defining) herself in terms of nature, she clearly also envisions herself on the receiving side of the empathic process. Her constant companion, nature, acts for her as a listening, sympathetic confidant with whom she finds herself – literally 'finds (discovers) herself' – in relationship. It seems that important to these moments of quiet thought is her lying or sitting down. In fact the journal leaves one with a vivid image of Dorothy reclining in thought beside a lake, for virtually every entry describes herself as having 'sate a long time' or 'lay in stillness'. It is as if Dorothy has an intuitive sense that one's physical posture, and literal stillness, is necessary to establishing the inner quiet necessary for the sympathetic relationship and thus for self-understanding: 'after dinner we both lay on the floor – Mary slept. I could not for I was thinking of so many things' (vol. I, pp. 184–5). Lying still is closely linked to deep thought. It likewise opens the door to extraordinary experiences. She records the following on 1 June 1800:

> after tea, went to Ambleside, round the lakes – a very fine warm evening. I lay upon the steep of Loughrigg, my heart dissolved in what I saw, when I was not startled but recalled from my reverie by a noise as of a child paddling without shoes. I looked up and saw a lamb close to me. It approached nearer and nearer, as if to examine me, and stood a long time. I did not move. At last it ran past me, and went bleating along the pathway, seeming to be seeking its mother (vol. I, p. 43).

Only through the medium of physical stillness, and its concomitant inner quiet, is she granted the privileged encounter with the Other.

The uniqueness of the journal itself similarly hinges on its being a medium rooted in the paradoxical marriage of self-transcendence and self-understanding. The reader, like Dorothy, in order to know and understand the Other – in the reader's case, the narrative 'I' – must 'complete the findings of the senses', venturing beyond the words on the page to reproduce the thought and experience behind the words. This is what we call sympathetic reading. What Katz sees as the creative element in empathy, then, unites the reader with Dorothy in the search for meaning: 'the qualities of the good empathizer in human relations are similar in many respects to the qualities of the gifted artist. There is the same need to involve the emotions, to relax conscious controls, and to permit oneself to be projected into other objects'.[40] Just as Dorothy's characteristic posture is reclining on the ground, physically still but listening with an active imagination, so the reader must be absorbed into Dorothy's tranquillity while responding with his own feeling.

Dorothy commonly envisions this elemental relationship as a melting. She describes a walk with William:

> Earth and sky were so lovely that they melted our very hearts. The
> sky to the north was of a chastened yet rich yellow, fading into pale
> blue, and streaked and scattered over with steady islands of purple,
> melting away into shades of pink. It made my heart almost feel like
> a vision to me (vol. I, p. 161).

The entire passage creates and imparts a sense of profound and all-embracing harmony. William's and Dorothy's 'melting hearts' seem to blend not only together but likewise into the 'fading' and 'melting' elements of the sky. In both cases, (Dorothy's) imagination obliterates difference. Recounting her trip with William and Mary shortly after their wedding, she records: 'when we passed through the village of Wensley my heart was melted away with dear recollections – the bridge, the little water-spout, the steep hill, the church. They are among the most vivid of my own inner visions' (vol. I, p. 180). The objects are so closely associated with the precious emotions she experienced in that place that those objects themselves have become inextricably one with her innermost spirit. In other words, during that initial visit Dorothy so closely attends to and engages in the concrete world around her that its very identity 'melts' into her own.

The journal, as the intimate record giving flesh to the initial conjunction of object and feeling – self and other – is the vehicle for her artistic creation. Thus to Susan Levin's assertion that the 'characteristic mode of viewing [which] helps shape the journal' is Dorothy's naming a thing as 'distinct from yet defined by its surroundings'[41] I would add only that it is Dorothy herself that achieves the coherence in things around her by virtue of what William called the 'plastic power' and 'auxiliar light',[42] her sympathetic imagination. After a walk with her new sister-in-law, Mary, she records the following:

> The lake was perfectly still, the sun shone on hill and vale, the
> distant birch trees looked like large golden flowers. Nothing else in
> colour was distinct and separate, but all the beautiful colours
> seemed to be melted into one another, and joined together in one
> mass, so that there were no differences, though an endless variety,
> when one tried to find it out. The fields were of one sober yellow
> brown (vol. I, pp. 184–5).

Whether or not such a perfect melting together actually occurred in the natural scene on that day is ultimately unimportant. What matters is that Dorothy's journal, the surviving remnant of that moment, enacts a relationship so complete as to suggest indistinguishability not merely of colour, tree, flower, etc., but of the diarist and the world around her.

Her sympathy with other people likewise illustrates this phenomenon of the diarist's losing herself in the Other. On 8 February 1802 she records:

We met our patient bow-bent Friend, with his little wooden box at his back. Poor fellow, he straddled and pushed on with all his might; but we soon outstripped him far away when we had turned our back with our letters. We were very thankful that we had not to go on, for we should have been sadly tired. In thinking this I could not help comparing lots with him! He goes at that slow pace every morning, and after having wrought a hard day's work returns at night, however weary he may be, takes it all quietly, and, though perhaps he neither feels thankfulness nor pleasure, when he eats his supper, and has no luxury to look forward to but falling asleep in bed, yet I daresay he neither murmurs nor thinks it hard. He seems mechanized to labour (vol. I, p. 108).

Engaging herself feelingly and sympathetically in others' experience, she transforms the mundane into the extraordinary. Moreover, by 'making present' the other person's emotional state, she breaks down the barriers dividing self and other and contributes to the formation of community in its truest sense. 'Molly says folks thinks of their mothers. Poor body, she has been little thought of by any body else' (vol. I, pp. 109–10). Even using Molly's grammar is indicative of her commitment to imagining and recreating others' experience of the world. The loss of self in the Other implied by the 'melting' metaphor is at once tempered and made complete in the journal-writing itself, Dorothy's means of giving coherence to her world and to her own search for self.

Byron, Amelia Opie and James Woodforde

The relationship between what a diarist says and what he reveals represents a quintessential part of any reader's experience and understanding of that diary. Of Benjamin Haydon's diary, Fothergill observes, 'Haydon is surprising for how much he reveals yet fails to see.'[43] Byron's journals, by contrast, are remarkable for how much they apparently see and reflect into the diarist himself, yet how much they fail to reveal. His journals are as explicitly self-revelatory and self-absorbed as any in the period.

Similarly, Amelia Opie's diary engages in overt self-analysis, in her case motivated by religious fervour; yet in the end the reader does not know the diarist any more intimately. Because every such passage contains its own neat conclusion, any sense of uncertainty or spontaneous self-exposure seems undermined by a perfectly phrased resolution. Reik's thesis is that 'the decisive factor in understanding the meaning and the motives of human emotions and thoughts is something in the person of the observer, of the psychologist himself'.[44] Taking the reader as the attentive observer and the text of the diary as the 'text' of the analysand's narrative, then one may say that if the reader is to achieve a valid understanding, as opposed to a detached psychoanalytic 'reading', the text must reflect its inner source, its author. Sympathy, in other words, requires a minimum of reciprocity. Thus, if these two diaries whose narrative personae are ostensibly engaged in intense self-searching, paradoxically leave the reader without a genuine awareness of the diarist's unique self, then it suggests that self-analysis is inadequate to establishing intimacy between diarist and reader.

James Woodforde, a late eighteenth-century country parson, by contrast, says next to nothing about his inner life, yet his entries disclose an enormous amount about him, such that the cumulative effect of his diary is to create an intimate bond with the reader, who feels he has known this simple parson for years. While Amelia Opie sought eloquent resolution in her diary, and Byron sought to portray in his journals a self in profound internal conflict, Woodforde seems to have wanted little else from his diary than the solace of keeping a daily record of his life.

Byron's journals are characterized by three principal elements: his expressing his opinion about every subject and literary figure that comes to mind; accounts of his extensive social life; and his revelation of nagging internal angst. The last two features may be described respectively as the public and the private Byron. Indeed, he frequently indicates the chasm dividing the two worlds and his deep dissatisfaction with the social events he attended famously. On 27 February 1814 he writes, 'here I am, alone, instead of dining at Lord H.'s, where I was asked, – but not inclined to go anywhere. Hobhouse says I am growing a *loup garou*, – a solitary hobgoblin. True; – "I am myself alone"' (Byron, vol. 1, p. 247).[45] He repeatedly claims to desire solitude over company: 'all the world are to be at the Stael's to-night, and I am not sorry to escape any part of it. I only go out to get me a fresh appetite for being alone' (Byron, vol. 1, p. 239). He suggests a reason for this desire on 10 April 1814: 'I do not know that I am the happiest when alone; but this I am sure of, that I never am long in the society even of her I love ... without a yearning for the company of my lamp and my utterly confused and tumbled-over library' (Ibid., p. 257). However, the journals are filled with detailed accounts of socializing, as well as learned, self-conscious bravado with which the diarist opines prodigiously, so that the personality which finally emerges is by no means that of a loner, as is overtly suggested by regular moments of self-revelation.

Instead of making Byron appear subtle and complex, this discontinuity gives the journals a contrived quality. Because the diarist's personality becomes not so much a mystery as a deliberate contradiction, the writer appears invisible behind the narrator and remains impenetrable to the reader's sympathy. In Bensman's terms, it represents a private as opposed to an intimate relationship – between the reader and the narrator as well as between Byron and his persona:

> intimacy refers to the individual in close, continuous, and relatively deep association with others . . . Privacy refers to the individual in relation to himself: his sense of his own uniqueness and apartness, and his sense of having a historical (ontogenetic) continuity that transcends both the intimacy which is in part continuously defined in close association with others and the public performances which exhaust only a portion of his total self.[46]

One wonders whether Byron experienced intimacy of this nature, but it is clear from the journals that he felt the tension between public and private. Nevertheless, the private remains private as long as the individual refuses to allow the sympathetic Other to understand him. In this case, the journals' narrator is so consciously concerned to establish 'his own uniqueness and apartness' that the reader is allowed only a crafted portrait which reveals not the painter but his technique. I agree with Fothergill's assessment of Byron's journal: 'he avails himself of the diary's waiting page to exercise a role, to strike attitudes as though for an impressed audience rather than a sympathetic friend'. Ironically, it is by this very role-playing that he actually reveals something of the self within, for 'even in their disguises, evasions, and lies diarists are responding to the pressure of first-hand experience; they are being, for better or worse, themselves'.[47]

An entry dated 31 January 1821 may help us begin to understand the motive behind the studied contradiction. Byron writes:

> I have been reading Grimm's *Correspondences*. He repeats frequently, in speaking of a poet, or a man of genius in any department . . . that he must have *une ame qui se tourmente, un esprit violent*. How far this may be true, I know not; but if it were, I should be a poet 'per excellenza'; for I have always had *une ame*, which not only tormented itself but every body else in contact with it; and an *esprit violent*, which has almost left me without any *esprit* at all (Byron, vol. 2, p. 580).

It seems from his journals that Byron modelled his diarist persona after this image of a poet. From the events of his life we know that his tormented spirit was not wholly fictitious. Nevertheless, the close affinity between the 'ideal' poet and the personality that emerges in the journals undercuts the unmediated experiential quality which a diary can possess. The narrator is so concerned and insistent about his identity that he becomes predictably inconsistent; self-contradiction and spontaneity become his conscious trade mark rather than a means to genuine self-discovery:

This journal is a relief. When I am tired – as I generally am – out comes this, and down goes every thing. But I can't read it over; and God knows what contradictions it may contain. If I am sincere with myself (but I fear one lies more to one's self than to any one else), every page should confute, refute, and utterly abjure its predecessor (Byron, vol. 1, p. 234).

Not nearly so ingenuous as he would have us believe, his journal becomes a creative outlet for avoiding himself: 'to withdraw myself from myself (oh that cursed selfishness!) has ever been my sole, my entire, my sincere motive in scribbling at all' (Ibid., p. 226). The diarist's malaise, 'ennuye' (Ibid., p. 237; vol. 2, p. 555), and angst, while part of a self-conscious self-fashioning, actually suggest an underlying self-consciousness in Byron himself. This quote, in consciously purporting a wish to divert attention from 'myself', unintentionally points the sympathetic reader – the listening Other attentive to the narrative quality of unconscious self-revelation – to the man holding the pen.

From the standpoint of the reader, this approach to journal-writing makes it difficult to know or understand the writer, for we do not get any sense of how the diarist experiences any given moment. The entries are either intellectual discourse, flippant opinion, or an autobiographic portraiture of the 'Byronic' hero. This portraiture is epitomized by the entry in which he composes his own epitaph, a literal encapsulation symbolic of the way in which Byron treats the journal's persona throughout. His perfect summation of the perfect tormented figure reads thus:

1821
Here lies
interred in the Eternity
of the Past,
from whence there is no
Resurrection
for the Days – Whatever there may be
for the Dust –
the Thirty-Third Year
of an ill-spent Life,
Which, after
a lingering disease of many months
sunk into a lethargy,
and expired,
January 22d, 1821, A.D.
Leaving a successor
Inconsolable
for the very loss which
occasioned its
Existence (Byron, vol. 2, p. 571).

Here as elsewhere the tone is more than half ironic, making it even more difficult simply to understand the diarist's self in any concrete sense. In Buber's terms the reader is unable to 'imagine the real' and 'make present' the particular person, precisely because the particularity is obscured in what seems a crafted identity. In this case, the task is made more difficult by his having buried the diarist altogether. 'Relation', according to Buber,

> is fulfilled in a full making present when I think of the other not merely as this very one, but experience, in the particular approximation of the given moment, the experience belonging to him as this very one. Here and now for the first time does the other become a self for me.[48]

To engage sympathetically in the diarist's experience the reader must feel capable of identifying with him as an individual. By so blatantly trying to create a distinct persona, however, Byron remains hidden in the very ways he sought to reveal himself, and in the process ironically exposes a self-consciousness he desperately sought to obviate and conceal.

Like Byron, Amelia Opie was an extremely well-known and well-travelled literary figure in England and on the Continent. Her diary reflected her literary style and copious output, just as Byron's journals embodied the mixture of styles seen in the verse tales and dramas, on the one hand, and the *ottava rima* of *Don Juan* on the other. And like Byron, the nature of her diary is coloured by an ideal: Byron's was the 'romantic' hero, while hers was the Christian of unquestioning faith. A fervent Quaker, she measures the relative success of her day by her performance of religious duty and whether she made any progress in self-improvement. A typical entry occurs on 4 January 1827:

> A very unprofitable day, meeting time excepted; I grow worse, I fear, rather than better. I am so dissatisfied with myself, that I dare hardly ask or expect a blessing on my labours. How cold and dead in the spirit I feel to-night; but I know 'we have an Advocate with the Father, Jesus Christ, the righteous', and how I need one! (Opie, p. 202).[49]

Self-flagellation and a sense of unworthiness characterize much of her diary. Although she often expresses a melancholy associated with this, as she does here, it is just as frequently dismissed by a deference to the faith that will overcome all adversity, internal or external. In most cases the word 'but' signals this dismissal, serving to contradict and undercut what precedes it – usually an expression of inadequacy or a more subtle indication of discontent. Everything considered, the 'but' phrase acts as the appropriate corrective to the appropriate religious self-effacement, thus completing the proper circuit of spiritual struggle and harmony. The reader is distanced from the diarist because he/she is unable to discern any genuine uncertainty or mundane foibles on the part of the diarist. Every experience is made to fit into a pattern, which the narrator fulfils, rather than gradually emerging as a distinct individual experiencing life one day at a time: 'had, at morning meeting, one of my paroxysms of regret for ill-fulfilled duties, and was brought very low; "but He helped me", and all is peace again, and I shall lie down in quiet' (Ibid., p. 206). Instead of exploring the nature of this feeling of regret and being 'brought very low', or recording her response to it, the diarist allows it to be swallowed up in the peace which prevails, merely using her own feelings as a foil to the ideal resolution of those feelings. Completeness, harmony and polish are inimical to sympathetic reading.

Mrs Opie's diary is particularly unsatisfying to the sympathetic reader because she leaves nothing incomplete. Though unlike Byron in obvious ways, this is where their journals coincide. She regards the diary, along with the self that is presented in it, as a finished product. Although Byron's narrator asked different questions and did not always have an answer, both diarists seem consciously to 'present' an inner life, and in so doing actually – paradoxically – erect a barrier to (a reader's) sympathy or (their own) self-discovery, two inextricable phenomena. By having already analysed and completed the self, thereby denying the diary its function as a crucible for self-confrontation and self-discovery, the diarist seems to preclude the reader from psycho-emotional engagement in the existential dynamic. Needless to say, the diarist is free to write whatever kind of diary he or she wishes. Nor is it the point to berate either diarist for having approached the diary as a literary creation or historical document: the point is to note that in these two diaries, written by extremely high-profile literary figures, we are given a very different aspect of their personality. Yet despite the explicit glimpses of inner life and apparent inner conflict, no necessary connection exists between a diary's language of self-revelation and its actual capacity to make the diarist known to a sympathetic reader. In fact, the greater the degree of overt self-analysis the smaller the reader's capacity to involve himself in the spontaneous, daily experience of life and hence to understand the diarist in sympathetic terms.

Two passages from Amelia Opie's travels which centre around a response to a scene of natural beauty help to illustrate this point. The night before returning home from a trip along the Rhine she writes:

> I rose in the night to look at the river, &c., and for the last time gazed on its beauty from the spot where I first saw it. How much had I undergone of trial, in many ways, since I saw it last! I felt humbled, but resigned and contented, and, I trust, taught (Ibid., p. 331).

It is the perfect response to the ideal scene. Though it is natural to be reminded by nature of an earlier time in one's life (for example, Wordsworth in 'Tintern Abbey'), her actual experience at that moment is distanced not only by the deliberately vague and understated exclamation, but also by the past tense of 'had' rather than 'have' which creates the impression of an authorial voice far removed from the person who stood near the river. After suggesting an emotional response, albeit vague and perfunctory, she neatly provides closure and harmony in her self-analysis with the assumption of self-improvement over time, an all-important clause introduced with the characteristic 'but'. During a trip to Scotland she writes:

> It was a lovely afternoon, the sky was blue, and the clouds floated in silvery brightness above the mountains, and even the lofty head of Ben Lomond was unveiled! As I gazed upon his grandeur, and listened to the gentle ripplings of the waters of the lake as they broke against the shore, I felt a soothing calm and a devotional enjoyment (Ibid., p. 312).

Once again, her response is so perfect and ideal that it denies any mark of individuality.[50] Her abundance of natural descriptions are much the same, providing the opportunity to affirm her properly imperfect faith and God's inspiringly perfect grandeur.

When sympathy is present, according to Scheler, 'the shadowy figures around us come again to life and fill anew with flesh and blood'.[51] Perhaps this 'fleshy' quality is precisely what distinguishes the diary of James Woodforde from those of Byron and Amelia Opie. The contrasts between diary styles as well as between historical personages abound. The record of an obscure, unworldly and provincial man, Woodforde's diary is preoccupied with the mundane, physical details of life. There is neither introspection nor self-referentiality. Its pages are filled with accounts of nagging ill health, seasonal planting and harvesting, and a peremptory appetite for food. Routine is the fabric of his diary and, we gather, of his life, as illustrated in this passage in which news of his sister's death is (as it were) sandwiched between accounts of the meals he had that day: 'We breakfasted, dined, &c. again at home ... The melancholy News of the Death of poor dear Sister Pounsett made me very miserable indeed. It is our great Loss ... Dinner to day, a Turkey rosted etc.' (Woodforde, pp. 571–2).[52] Woodforde experiences all things purely in relation to his own continuous routine. The daily flow of his simple life is able to absorb and temper all events: illness, death, political upheaval, etc.

Food, the eating of meals, is the most basic human need and symbolizes the importance of routine to simple, daily survival. Not a day passes without Woodforde's diary mentioning what he ate. He measures his health according to his appetite: 'I eat five times a day – at breakfast, abt. Noon, Dinner, Afternoon at Tea, and at Supper – and at all times with a proper relish' (Ibid., p. 579). 'Proper relish' is no small understatement. In fact, throughout the diary what he eats acts as a frame around which all else takes place, as food literally surrounds more serious and affecting events. For instance, his entry for 31 May 1799 begins, as usual, with his breakfast and proceeds thus: ' . . . I was but poorly to day, a great weakness inwardly which I take proceeds from too great depression of Spirits from many divers Family Losses and the unpleasnt Prospect of things on that Account. Dinner to day, Part of a Rump of Beef boiled &c.' (Ibid., p. 585). Framing the diary entry with meals is not a way of suppressing deeper feelings or stronger responses to experience, but of taking and regarding all things – particularly unexpected and uncontrollable circumstances – in the context of something continuous, if not more permanent. This feature strikes the reader as utterly natural and indicates the ingenuous and unmediated nature of this diary, a product of this earthy man.

Woodforde's world is only as large as his physical experience and his immediate consciousness. He remarks in only a passing and ill-informed way about the storming of the Bastille two weeks after the fact. The following entry illustrates his handling of 'great events':

> Dinner to day, Neck of Pork rosted, &c. By the publick Papers every thing appears on them the most alarming not only respecting Great Briton but every other State in Europe, and beyond it – Oh Tempora oh Mores. I hope my Strength is increasing as I feel better to day (Ibid., p. 563).

While he displays sincere concern for the condition of the world beyond his community, his boundaries and his consciousness are defined by local and personal news:

> We breakfasted, dined, &c. again at home. My Brother & Wife breakfasted, dined &c. here again. My Brother had a Letter from our Sister Pounsett this Morn'. It came by a Norwich Carrier to Taylor Cary's. All Friends tolerably well in Somersett – upon the whole a pleasing Letter. Mr. Corbould read Prayers & Preached at Weston Ch. this Afternoon. Mrs. Woodforde and Nancy were at Church to day. Dinner to day, fryed Soals again and Pigs Fry &c. Not quite so well again to day – very much blown up (Ibid., p. 553).

He frequently mentions his ill health which obviously concerns him and affects his daily life. On 15 October 1797 he writes, 'for the last two days I have been very bad indeed not able to put on some of my Cloaths or pull them off' (Ibid., p. 556) and the following March, 'I made a very good dinner today considering my State' (Ibid., p. 561). Nevertheless he treats what are clearly ongoing health problems in as perfunctory a fashion as his meals.

His regular habit and conscientious manner of measuring the growth of his crops and trees is similar to his way of treating every other event in his life. He writes, 'a stalk of Wheat (from a field that was formerly a Furze-Cover) I measured this Morning, and it was in Length six feet seven inches and about a barley corn' (Ibid., pp. 419–20). It is not that the smallest details are equal in significance to greater events, still less that the diarist blows up small things into great ones; rather, his diary suggests simply that there are no great events, but only significant mundane details which fill his life. Thus his health, the French Revolution, small plants, meals, relatives, the weather, and the amount he pays each day for butter – all receive equal attention and exist side by side in the pages of his diary:

> I measured a Scotch Fir Tree of my Planting in the Shrubbery near the Pond by me about twenty Years ago, and it was fifty four inches in Circumference at the largest Girt. Dinner to day, a fore-Quarter of a small Pig rosted &c. Busy in plowing and sowing Turnip-Seed (Ibid., p. 566).

Like the corn and tree over which he labours meticulously, all the various events mentioned in his diary are like life components which he carefully measures at regular intervals, all in the context of their cumulative presence in his life.

To say that his world is small is not to say he is self-absorbed. As mentioned, he does not dwell on his own feelings or responses in the diary, but refers to them in a characteristically understated manner. For example, after a fitful night's sleep he laconically records, 'Last night I had but indifferent Night of Sleep, having very hurrying & frightful Dreams at times. Dinner to day, Peas Soup & some Beef Steaks' (Ibid., p. 546). While suggesting a great deal with 'hurrying & frightful', he does not really describe his emotional response. He merely reports it to the diary alongside and in similar detail as his account of dinner. An entry in response to local family conflicts in his parish, which no doubt affected his work and daily life enormously, is similarly reserved: 'Rather low-spirited to day, all Family Affairs in the Country contrary to my desire or wish and those People which ought to be Friends by blood turn out the greatest Enemies on Earth' (Ibid., p. 584). The diary suggests that Woodforde's inner life is on a par with his physical circumstances; he experiences both in what can only be interpreted as a straightforward, measured way. The reader must supply the rest. Or perhaps he uses the diary as a means of providing order to it all. The latter theory, however, is made implausible by virtue of the fact that his diary suggests neither repression of emotion nor a contrived identity overlaid on the events as they actually occurred. Woodforde seems not to express his feelings in a manner appropriate either to the situation he is recording – like Amelia Opie – or to the self he is fashioning – like Byron – but rather to record the situation and his experience of the situation as equal parts of the truth and hence of the diary entry. Woodforde writes during the exceedingly cold winter of 1798–99, 'Scarce ever known such severe Weather for the last forty Years and still likely to continue. It affects me extremely indeed, have scarce any feeling, am almost benumbed both in Mind & Body' (Ibid., pp. 575–6).

This unpremeditated technique on Woodforde's part provides the reader with a far more powerful sense of engagement in his life than either Mrs Opie's or Byron's diary. Its very emphasis on physicality enhances the concrete individuality of the diarist and as a consequence the reader's desire to become sympathetically involved in Woodforde's daily routine. In an extensive diary the cumulative effect of physical aspects of daily experience is to create a concrete connection between reader and narrator. The sympathetic reader's attempts at such a relationship, as we saw, are thwarted in Byron's diary by the histrionic self-consciousness. The reader of Woodforde's diary is constantly reminded of the 'unfinished' nature of the diarist, who experiences each day's entry as an implicit moment of immediate self-awareness and self-discovery. The entry for 20 February 1802 embodies a blunt simplicity with which every person can identify: 'Very low, faint and very unwell all the Morn'. I don't know that I ever felt myself so depressed and so spiritless as this very day' (Ibid., p. 611).

His awareness of others' feelings is equally laconic and an essential part of the context in which he records each day's experience. Without dwelling on it, he conveys a deep sympathetic capacity for a poor widow whom he visits: 'I found her spinning by the fire tho' she is almost blind. I gave her to buy Tobacco as she smokes 0.1.0' (Ibid., p. 430). Similarly, a parishioner visits him one day and Woodforde's remark in the diary, 'He looked very sadly, I thought' (Ibid., p. 605), indicates an awareness of feeling without the need, or capacity, to elaborate. It is this very preference in this diary for the raw and unadorned over explicit or dramatic expressions of feeling which allows the reader to sympathize with the diarist. It invites wonder and speculation and spurs the imagination. As Hazlitt describes in his 'On Imitation', and Coleridge throughout his Shakespeare criticism, suggestiveness of something incomplete draws the Other into the object – in this case the diary – and allows him to complete the creative act.

Reik asserts that 'the greatest hindrance to the advance of knowledge is ... that people think they have long been in the possession of the truth, the whole truth'.[53] While Byron and Opie present in their diaries self-conscious personae who have plumbed the depths of self-analysis and know where their weaknesses lie, Woodforde, by contrast, appears to have comprehended little of himself; indeed he appears not to be concerned with this at all. He presents himself, to the extent that he does present himself, as knowing each day's events and how they affect him. For him writing is a daily routine whose fruits remain unknown to all except the sympathetic reader. The relationship thus established was not a conscious creation of Woodforde's, but rather part of the great mass of unknown toward which he staunchly, daily proceeded in the pages of his diary.

Notes

1. J. C. F. von Schiller, as quoted in T. Reik (1949), *Listening with the Third Ear: The Inner Experience of a Psychoanalyst*, New York: Farrar, Straus, 250.
2. T. Reik (1949), *Listening with the Third Ear: The Inner Experience of a Psychoanalyst*, New York: Farrar, Straus, 144.
3. A. Ponsonby (1923), *English Diaries: A Review of English Diaries from the Sixteenth to the Twentieth Century with an Introduction on Diary Writing*, Freeport, NY: Books for Libraries Press, 8.
4. R. Fothergill (1974), *Private Chronicles: A Study of English Diaries*, London: Oxford University Press, 52.
5. Fothergill, *Private Chronicles*, 95–6.
6. T. Mallon (1984), *A Book of One's Own: People and Their Diaries*, New York: Ticknor and Fields, xvii.
7. Fothergill, *Private Chronicles*, 48.
8. Ibid., 32.
9. Ibid., 33.
10. Ponsonby, *English Diaries*, 10.
11. For a useful description of the 'hermeneutic circle' see R. Palmer (1969), *Hermeneutics: Interpretation Theory in Schleiermacher, Dilthey, Heidegger, and Gadamer*, Evanston, IL: Northwestern University Press, 87–8. See also, K. F. Morrison (1988), *'I Am You': The Hermeneutics of Empathy in Western Literature, Theology, and Art*, Princeton: Princeton University Press, 250 ff.
12. R. Greenson (1967), *The Technique and Practice of Psychoanalysis*, New York: International Universities Press, 367–8, as quoted in J. D. Lichtenberg (1984), 'The Empathic Mode of Perception and Alternative Vantage Points for Psychoanalytic Work', in J. D. Lichtenberg, *Empathy II*, Hillsdale, NJ: Analytic Press, 115.
13. Fothergill, *Private Chronicles*, 55.
14. Ponsonby, *English Diaries*, 32.
15. Greenson, *Empathy II*, 115.
16. W. Jones (1929), *The Diary of the Rev'd William Jones*, O. F. Christie (ed.), London: Brentano. All subsequent references are from this edition.
17. 'Self-assessment in the light of a personal ideal of individual development

is a dominant preoccupation of diaries prior to the end of the eighteenth century', Fothergill, *Private Chronicles*, 68.

18. M. Scheler (1971), *The Nature of Sympathy*, Hamden, CT: Archon Books, originally published in German (1913), 46, 23.

19. Scheler, *The Nature*, 224. One of Scheler's main objectives in his book is to refute those who believe that others' minds are impenetrable and that therefore our knowledge of others is based solely on inferences we make about them.

20. Scheler, *The Nature*, 49.

21. In another passage, Jones imagines what his long-time personal enemy and fiend within the Broxbourne community must be feeling inside, based on his behaviour:

> I doubt not but if one knew the history of his secret hours, poor Rogers passes many very uncomfortably, not to say wretchedly. He must be very ill at ease, for he has war in his own heart. When he lies down, his pillow must often seem planted with thorns, & the gloom of night must feed the dark melancholy of his wretched mind. He is better able to dissipate the clouds which hover around him by the bustle of the day, & when the friendly alehouse is open to admit him; but even here he is always an unwelcome guest both to the landlord, & to his customers (1 May 1801, p. 118).

Although we cannot know whether Jones's imaginative understanding of Rogers's internal state actually betrays something about Jones's own secret anguish, the circumstances do suggest a parallel. This is precisely the period during which a vacancy in the Broxbourne vicarage has occurred and Jones's thoughts are consumed with worrying over whether anything – particularly the influence Rogers could exercise with the bishop – will keep him from being appointed to the spot. More than this, however, it shows us another example of his tendency toward sympathy in circumstances which would seem hostile to such a phenomenon.

22. Scheler, *The Nature*, 52.

23. Ibid., 121.

24. J. Bensman and R. Lilienfeld (1979), *Between Public and Private: The Lost Boundaries of the Self*, New York: Free Press, 9.

25. A. Margulies (1989), *The Empathic Imagination*, New York and London: W. W. Norton, 133, 109.

26. Margulies, *The Empathic*, 142–3.

27. Ibid., 58.

28. Ibid., 142.

29. Bensman and Lilienfeld, *Between Public*, 157.

30. Margulies, *The Empathic*, 142.

31. Ponsonby, *English Diaries*, 109.

32. Margulies, *The Empathic*, 34.

33. D. Wordsworth (1959), *Journals of Dorothy Wordsworth*, E. de Selincourt (ed.), 2 vols, London: Macmillan. All subsequent references are from this edition.

34. M. Buber (1965), *The Knowledge of Man*, M. Friedman and R. G. Smith (tr.), London: Allen and Unwin, 81.

35. Buber, *The Knowledge*, 80.

36. Reik, *Listening*, 464.
37. R. Gittings and J. Manton (1985), *Dorothy Wordsworth*, Oxford: Clarendon Press, 100.
38. Buber, *The Knowledge*, 85.
39. R. Katz (1963), *Empathy: Its Nature and Uses*, New York: Free Press, 97.
40. Katz, *Empathy*, 135.
41. S. Levin (1987), *Dorothy Wordsworth and Romanticism*, New Brunswick, NJ: Rutgers, The State University, 20.
42. W. Wordsworth (1966), *The Prelude, or Growth of a Poet's Mind* (1805), Ernest de Selincourt (ed.), London: Oxford University Press, book II, lines 381, 387.
43. Fothergill, *Private Chronicles*, 156.
44. Reik, *Listening*, 18.
45. Byron, L. G. G. (1950), *Byron: A Self-Portrait, Letters and Diaries 1798 to 1824*, Peter Quennell (ed.), 2 vols, London: John Murray. All subsequent references are from this edition.
46. Bensman and Lilienfeld, *Between Public*, 28.
47. Fothergill, *Private Chronicles*, 115–16, 10.
48. Buber, *The Knowledge*, 71.
49. A. Opie (1854), *Memorials of the Life of Amelia Opie, Selected and Arranged from Her Letters, Diaries, and Other Manuscripts*, C. L. Brightwell (ed.), Norwich: Fletcher and Alexander. All subsequent references are from this edition.
50. On a Swiss tour with Hobhouse, Byron records a response to natural beauty which, though the exact opposite of Mrs Opie's, illustrates the same phenomenon. In this case, the diarist is perfectly, ideally inconsolable and impenetrable. He writes:

    > I was disposed to be pleased. I am a lover of Nature and an admirer of Beauty. I can bear fatigue and welcome privation, and have seen some of the noblest views in the world. But in all this – the recollections of bitterness, and more especially of recent and more home desolation, which must accompany me through life, have preyed upon me here; and neither the music of the Shepherd, the crashing of the Avalanche, nor the torrent, the mountain, the Glacier, the Forest, nor the Cloud, have for one moment lightened the weight upon my heart, nor enabled me to lose my own wretched identity in the majesty, and the power, and the Glory, around, above, and beneath me (Byron, vol. 1, p. 356).

51. Scheler, *The Nature*, xl.
52. J. Woodforde (1978), *The Diary of a Country Parson, 1758–1802*, J. Beresford (ed.), Oxford: Oxford University Press. All subsequent references are from this edition.
53. Reik, *Listening*, 512.

CHAPTER THREE

'Epistolary intercourse': sympathy and the English Romantic letter

> Your letters are like angels sent from heaven on missions of peace; they assure me that existence is not valueless, they point out the path which it is Paradise to tread.[1]

'An obvious difference between reading and all forms of social interaction', according to Wolfgang Iser, 'is the fact that with reading there is no face-to-face situation. A text cannot adapt itself to each reader it comes into contact with.' With respect to Romantic letters, his assertion is only half correct. While the ongoing exchange of personal letters is not 'face-to-face', what he calls the 'dyadic' nature of personal interaction is precisely the quality that endows Romantic correspondence with its characteristically intense mutual intimacy and identification.[2] This chapter will demonstrate how sympathy inspires and influences the way letters between friends are written and read in the English Romantic period. Using recent psychology of sympathy, I analyse the blurring of the demarcation between the roles of reader and writer in four correspondences: Mrs Dunlop's letters to Robert Burns, Charles Lamb's letters to Coleridge, and the letters between Shelley and Elizabeth Hitchener and Coleridge and Thomas Poole. This dissolution of boundaries between correspondents, I will argue, results from an active, intimate kind of reading, grounded in sympathy.

Sympathy, paramount among the virtues espoused by English Romantic readers and writers, is what propels Romantic correspondents into each other's lives, at least the life as it is conveyed in letters. According to W. J. Bate, sympathy, 'which is achieved through the imagination, characterizes the highest moral and aesthetic exertion' for the Romantics.[3] That this is true explains the Romantics' belief that the act of reading was and should be creative. Writing in 1816, critic Josiah Conder asserted that 'The only converse to be held with a poet's mind, is that of sympathy. The feelings of the reader must be strung to a pitch in unison with those of the poet himself, or they will not vibrate in reply.'[4] It is not enough for the reader to be sensitive to the words; 'converse', 'vibrate' and 'reply' suggest that the reader must engage in an interactive relationship with the writer him/herself. Coleridge believed that such reading is achieved only by 'an active creative being', a condition which must 'come from within – from the moved and sympathetic imagination'.[5] According to Wordsworth, the reader must 'exert himself; for he cannot proceed in quiescence, he cannot be carried like a dead weight'. In response to the poet's self-expression, he must exercise 'a co-operating power' in order to complete the work.[6]

Twentieth-century psychology has confirmed and extended Romantic beliefs about sympathy. The pioneering work of Carl Rogers showed sympathy to be a process of 'entering the private perceptual world of the other and becoming thoroughly at home in it. It involves being sensitive ... to the changing felt meanings which flow in this other person ... It means temporarily living his/her life, moving about in it ... '.[7] 'Entering', 'becoming', 'changing' and 'moving' graphically capture the active, dynamic workings of sympathy. In a book which has striking, if unacknowledged affinities with Romantic beliefs about reading, psychiatrist Alfred Margulies argues for an appreciation of sympathy as 'not merely a resonating with the other, but an act of will and creativity'.[8] According to Martin Buber, in any sympathetic interchange 'the meaning is to be found neither in one of the two partners nor in both together, but only in their dialogue itself, in this "between" which they live together'.[9] Far from being a static or unilateral phenomenon, sympathy hinges on the dynamism of interpersonal psychology and emotion.

In the course of their fervid 12-month correspondence, Shelley and Elizabeth Hitchener both explicitly extol sympathy as the inspiration behind their letters. Hitchener indicates that with Shelley she has found a sympathy she despaired of ever knowing:

> The world severely & very early taught me, that my soul was fraught with sentiments visionary to them, they pronounced me romantic, eccentric & conceited, & compelled me to live without sympathy for I seem'd created to awaken in them, only surprise, vacancy, & stupidity; yet is this sympathy the charm of life, a balance which outweighs its evils, a sacred gift which amply compensates the ills of life, its sweetest solace, mysterious cement of the soul, soother of life, oh lovely sympathy I owe thee much & the few months I have drank of thy reanimating cup atones for the blank of years I had endur'd.[10]

Not only is sympathy necessary to understanding her particular character, but it is implicitly identified with the creative imagination in general. Only one inspired by sympathy can recognize and appreciate the 'visionary', 'romantic' and 'reanimating' nuances of human personality. Those who do not possess it, by contrast, are characterized as lacking in insight and emotional depth ('vacancy', 'stupidity'). In addition to being a practical antidote to loneliness and melancholy, sympathy is given a distinctly spiritual cast ('sacred gift', 'mysterious cement of the soul').

Sympathy as formulated in this exchange pervades Romantic correspondences. Generated by a mutual process of self-emptying and identification, Romantic letters enact a process by which the reader must fill
not only textual gaps but also psychological and emotional needs. The
act of reading a letter anticipates, and is the basis for, the reader's
written reply: the internal (emotional and psychological) response is in
this way literally creative. Similarly, in his/her written response each
correspondent gives expression to the sympathetic activity which he/she
engages in as reader. Letters, therefore, epitomize the Romantic belief in
the reader as co-creator, for each correspondent fulfils a dual role of
writer and reader. The sympathetic reader whose presence is inherent in
every act of letter-writing becomes the one person able to 'complete' the
letter. While ultimately the reader's co-creative function is to write, it is
first simply to understand.

One of the most striking features of Romantic correspondence is the
expression of isolation and concomitant sense of exclusiveness between
correspondents: 'only we two sympathize with each other in an otherwise unsympathetic world'. Robert Burns's long-time correspondent
Mrs Dunlop tells him, 'When worldly advantages forsake and worldly
disappointments distress me, when Heaven deprives me of friends I love
. . . my mind is driven to seek its last hold of existence, and there alone
it finds something to make that existence sufferable.'[11] Feeling 'forsaken' and 'distressed', she 'is driven' by the instinct for psychological
survival to her 'last hold of existence'. The correspondence is a sort of
sacred vessel into which she pours herself and from which she receives
refreshment and strength. For Mrs Dunlop – who 'at the time the
Correspondence opens . . . was suffering an accumulation of distresses',
including her husband's recent death and her estrangement from her
eldest son – the letters to Burns represent a refuge from a life perceived
as hostile and hard.[12] She writes:

> Deprived as I am of all the friends of my former life, the notice of
> the Bard has been almost the only foreign circumstance of pleasure
> that has helped to gild the bloom of a long train of domestic
> misfortunes, and reconcile me to the world and myself . . . When
> reflection becomes intolerable, I lose it in writing to you . . . what I
> would commit to no other eyes.[13]

The passage conveys the sense that, her 'former life' being gone, the
emotional parameters of her life are shaped by the correspondence with
Burns. He represents her exclusive ('the only', 'no other') human connection. It is not merely that she perceives the world around her as
hostile; she is at odds with her own self. The correspondence – contact
with a sympathetic Other – both provides an escape from herself 'when
reflection becomes intolerable' and 'reconciles' her 'to the world and

[her]self'. She can 'lose' herself and find it in the sympathetic gaze of another.

Lamb, too, was exclusively reliant on a sympathetic outsider. Between 27 May 1796 and the end of 1797, during which time Lamb's sister Mary killed their mother in a fit of madness and he was trying to care for her and his aged father, Lamb writes to no one except Coleridge. His only source of consolation, the correspondence likewise serves as a stark record of his despair and utter isolation. He tells Coleridge, 'you are the only correspondent & I might add the only friend I have in the world'. Into his letters to Coleridge he can pour his deepest self, even if that self seems empty: 'I am ashamed of what I write. But I have no topic to talk of. I see nobody, and sit, and read or walk, alone, and hear nothing. I am quite lost to conversation from disuse.' He perceives himself as a misfit ('lost to conversation') so isolated that he seems to exist in a sensual vacuum ('see nobody . . . hear nothing'). 'Ashamed' of his letters and the state they describe, he nevertheless writes out of sheer desperation for meaningful human contact.

Lamb's letters illustrate the extreme of the Romantic concept of the self as absolutely unique: Lamb feels himself a being set apart, and so feels cut off from the rest of the world, which does not know and cannot understand him. His identity cannot survive in the suffocating vacuum which is his own weary spirit, and he feels impelled both to express his emptiness and to have it validated in the sympathetic consciousness of another: 'My letter is full of nothingness. I talk of nothing. But I must talk. I love to write to you . . . It makes me think myself not totally disconnected from the better part of Mankind.'[14] The contradiction which marks this passage is typical of his letters. His letter is *full* of nothingness'; moreover, he *'must* talk' 'of nothing'. He feels at once full and empty, just as he feels the need to converse though his words strike a hollow note in his own psyche. The sympathy of a friend makes sense of the contradictions: only in these letters to Coleridge, Lamb feels, does his 'disconnected' self find relationship. Quintessentially Romantic, the letters illustrate that what matters most is not the subject-matter but the feeling which imbues them.

The letters between Shelley and Elizabeth Hitchener dramatize how the desire for affirmation and fulfilment through a correspondence manifests itself as the idealizing of one's reader. Shelley imagines Hitchener as the perfect complement to his personality. If they were together, he tells her, 'the resources of your powerful intellect would mature schemes, and organize those of mine which yet are immature'. Despite little evidence in Hitchener's letters to support this image of her as a 'profound intellect', he envisions her as his 'better genius, the judge of my reasonings the guide of my actions the influencer of my usefulness'. He repeatedly seeks her advice, imploring her, 'do you be my mentor my guide my counsellor the half of my soul'. As evident in the lack of punctuation, there is a desperation about the copious and highly implausible roles he imagines her to fulfil. For both – but especially for Shelley – the imagination is what gives life to the correspondence: Hitchener's actual identity is virtually absorbed into his image of her as his ideal comrade. This accounts for the fact that he can say to her (whom he has met only once or twice and corresponded with for a total of 12 months): 'it seems to me you know me better than I do myself'. 'Let us', he exhorts, 'in the great pursuit in which we are engaged consider ourselves as little as possible in the light of individuals who have separate interests to gratify and separate ends to answer.'[15] The perfect friend with boundless sympathy and bound to him by sympathy, she is one with him even as she is quintessentially apart from him.

For Shelley and Hitchener the correspondence is not simply a refuge from an unsympathetic world, but springs from their common pursuit of an idealized virtuous life. They are, in Shelley's words, 'two hearts panting for the happiness and liberty of mankind'. For both, the correspondence comes to represent their social ideal in microcosm. But even more important, 'panting' captures the impassioned urgency with which they appeal to and encourage one another in their mutual belief. Hitchener's reference in her first letter to Shelley to the 'degenerate times' they live in indicates the link between their feverish intimacy as friends and a larger goal. The huge disparity between the world and their idealized relationship with one another is something which Shelley and Hitchener thrive on in their letters, even as they bewail it. By making their position seem more dire and embattled, their relationship becomes all the more exclusive and intensely interdependent. Hitchener repeatedly extols Shelley for being her last best hope for friendship and camaraderie: 'whom but you could understand me ... the congeniality of soul which I had despair'd of ever meeting with'. In response to her expressions of insecurity regarding society's disparaging attitude toward her as Shelley's social inferior and because she was black, Shelley constantly affirms his commitment to her and repudiates the world's prejudice and inequality. He expresses his confidence that 'you would share with me the high delight of awakening a noble nation from the lethargy of its bondage'. Having recently experienced a falling out with his close friend Hogg, Shelley wanted a soul mate with whom to share his social vision. 'Your letters', he writes, 'resuscitate my slumbering hopes.'[16] It is the 'us versus them' mentality which fires their relationship and makes the correspondence a world unto itself, governed by an idealized sympathy which eradicates all distance between the two correspondents as it separates them from the outside world.

Ironically, it is the physical distance between Romantic correspondents which makes possible the establishment of such a heterocosm.[17] Their separation is the context for sympathy, which is the psychological and emotional means of bridging distance. Distance between correspondents allows each writer free reign both to foreground certain aspects of his circumstances and to maintain an idealized image of his reader. The passage cited earlier in which Mrs Dunlop identifies Burns with a 'foreign circumstance' illustrates this aspect of Romantic letters. Because Burns is distant, she can depict events as she wants – as her feelings and imagination shape them to be – not necessarily as they are. She is free to write how and what she wishes because accuracy is subordinate to subjective feeling. Yet at the same time the correspondence is an escape from subjectivity and self-reflection. The decisive role which her letters play in Mrs Dunlop's psychological survival depends on her belief that her distant reader's sympathy will spur him to identify with her grief. In this way she hopes he will be apart from ('foreign circumstance') and yet a tangible and intimate part of ('to gild the bloom'; 'what I would commit to no other eyes') her experience. Thus, however bitter the Romantic correspondents' complaints over their separation – 'How I could tell to you a thousand feelings and thoughts to which letters are inadequate'[18] – the energy and vitality they share is contingent on physical separation.[19]

Although sympathetic reading generates an interchange which may produce the sense of oneness between correspondents, without distance between the two there can be no sympathy. Carl Rogers believes that sympathy is feeling the other's 'private world as if it were your own without ever losing the "as if" quality'.[20] In sympathy, as David Woodruff Smith describes the process, 'I "identify" with the other, appreciating her experience *as if* I were going through it, but the boundaries between myself and the other, between my own experience and hers, remain clear to me.'[21] What makes these letters so fascinating is that while they are concrete evidence of the distance separating the two correspondents, the emotion and intimacy which they manifest demonstrate a collapsing of boundaries. According to psychoanalyst Theodor Reik, in sympathy one must enter into the other person's emotional state 'and yet be capable of grasping it as something outside himself and comprehending it psychologically, sharing the other person's experience and yet remaining above the struggle'.[22] Romantic correspondents graphically enact this paradox. Hazlitt himself recognized that however profound my sympathy, 'I always remain perfectly distinct from others.'[23]

As Shelley tells Hitchener, it is by virtue of being apart that they are 'joined . . . by friendship and sympathy': 'our souls can meet, for these become embodied on paper'.[24] Letters are not merely an expression of the writer's thoughts and emotions; in so far as they are the physical object which both correspondents touch and continually exchange, they incarnate the ideal of a perfectly sympathetic relationship in which the unknown and distinct is transformed into the known and shared. Because each correspondent's response to a letter takes the form of another letter, these correspondences dramatize the creative and interactive nature of Romantic reading. Moreover, the quintessential materiality of the correspondence – distinct texts written by distinct individuals – serves as a reminder that the sympathy between them is contingent upon their binary (self–Other) relationship. In so far as each letter in an ongoing correspondence must be seen as both a text and a reader's response, the emotional response becomes indistinguishable from the governing mode of creativity – writing. In this light, Romantic correspondence is a more graphic and (literally) literal precursor to what Jane Tompkins describes as reader-response criticism, in which 'reading and writing join hands, change places, and finally become indistinguishable only as two names for the same activity'.[25]

This interchangeability comes about in these correspondences as a result of their conversational quality. For the Romantics, formality in expression implies pose and reserve. Filled with spontaneous outpourings of emotion, these letters dramatize the fact that there is no constraint or formality and indicate the correspondents' shared view of letter-writing as a form of thinking aloud in the presence of the Other: 'not a thought shall arise which shall not seek its responsion [*sic*] in your bosom', Shelley writes to Hitchener, illustrating his view of the letters as segments in an ongoing conversation.[26] Repeatedly the letters both express and convey a sense of uninhibited communion with what Shelley calls a 'second self', with whom he can 'speak' 'with truth sincerity & unreserve'.[27] Hitchener's letters are steeped in this conversational spontaneity: 'all my feelings all my ideas as they arise are thus yours'; 'I shall write to you with all the freedom of thought;' 'it is my custom to communicate to you my dearest friend to that brain of sympathetic sensibility every idea as it arises, as I do to my own'; 'to *you* I tell everything that passes in my soul, even the secret thoughts sacred alone to sympathy'.[28] Theirs is a shared 'secrecy' not merely in that they conceal it from others, but more important because they utilize the correspondence as an engine of unedited evocation and revelation. Imagining a reader's 'sympathetic sensibility' frees the letter-writer to be vulnerable, to 'tell everything' as if 'to my own' self. Mrs Dunlop describes the 'ease with which I feel myself encouraged to say whatever my mind prompts' as a result of being able 'to indulge myself in believing' that Burns will read it 'with the sympathy of a friend'. Assured of Burns's sympathetic reading, she can concentrate on revealing her inmost self without having to worry about decorum or exactness of expression. Formality, she implies, is inversely related to sincerity and truth. As she tells him, 'you will read the woman in it, however incoherently exprest'.[29]

Moreover, 'conversing' by letter produces a new kind of text – one wholly dependent on the *context* in which it is written and read. During the heyday of their correspondence – between 1796 and 1803 – Poole and Coleridge create a seamless record of emotions and events generated by 'the unrestrained familiar interchange of thought and sympathy'.[30] The conversational quality of their letters points to a sympathetic exchange in which the distant friend creates at once the need and the opportunity to express one's innermost feelings. Coleridge tells Poole, 'write to me all things about yourself – where I can not advise, I can console – and communication, which doubles joy, halves Sorrow'.[31] Self-revelation to a sympathetic friend, Coleridge is saying, eases pain. In particular, sharing with a distant friend through letters creates a unique context for communicating anxiety or grief. For as we have seen, physical separation is not a hindrance to sympathy, but rather its prerequisite. In this way, writing letters is a way of coping with worldly and personal concerns by allowing the writer to distance him/herself from his/her anxieties even while expressing them. By giving them over to a 'second self' he/she can feel he/she is not ignoring them but simultaneously relieve him/herself of their immediate burden. Coleridge urges Poole to write for the sake of writing, then, because he believes that the context of their communication – a correspondence based in sympathy – is more important than its content.

In their effort to achieve the effect of raw, unfiltered self-revelation, Romantic correspondences are the lyric poetry of personal relationships. According to Henry Crabb Robinson, the lyric is that genre 'in which the poet gives mainly objects as they are reflected in the mirror of his own individuality'.[32] Similarly, correspondents' self-conscious reflections and professions of emotion show their letters to be 'the spontaneous overflow of powerful feelings' in a more exclusive context.[33] Indeed, Romantic definitions of poetry, especially lyric, are strikingly accurate descriptions of the letters we have been examining. Mill viewed poetry as 'feeling confessing itself ... bodying itself forth ... in representations of the feeling in the exact shape in which it exists in the poet's mind'.[34] In his essay, 'The Philosophy of Poetry' (1835), Alexander Smith argues that poetry, as the expression of emotion, must 'transmit that feeling from one mind to another ... creating a sympathetic participation of it in the mind of the hearer'.[35] In both cases, the poet's success is measured by his ability not merely to express his own feelings, but to stimulate analogous emotional and psychological activity in his reader.

Hegel's account of the lyric is particularly informative with respect to the letter because both are quintessentially First Person texts. Works 'are the more lyrical', he posits, 'the more they emphasize . . . the inner state of soul in which the poet tells his story and give us the whole circumstance in such a way that the poet's mood itself has a living echo out of them in us'.[36] By his criteria, Romantic letters are highly lyrical: they are an (at least ostensibly) unmediated sharing of one's private self ('inner state of soul'). Moreover, over time a correspondence becomes a type of narrative of the correspondent's life ('his story'), in which the details ('whole circumstance') are less important than the manner of the telling and their impact on the reader ('a living echo . . . in us'). This is what Wordsworth means in the 'Preface' to the *Lyrical Ballads* when he argues that 'the feeling . . . gives importance to the action and situation, and not the action and situation to the feeling'.[37] The significance of the lyric, then, like Romantic correspondence, hinges as much on the reader as on the writer. Accordingly, Hegel asserts, readers must 'be inwardly conscious of the heart which has put itself into [the text] and . . . be moved by that consciousness to have the same mode of feeling or meditation'.[38] The exchange of letters, I would argue, gives graphic expression to the Romantic connection between lyric and sympathy. The reader is 'moved' physically as well as emotionally: he/she puts his/ her response in writing, thereby enacting not only the same 'mode of feeling' but also the same mode of behaviour.

By virtue of this kind of thoroughgoing sympathy, correspondents develop a language which is *sui generis*. This is why Lamb feels compelled to share with Coleridge what no one else will understand. He indicates that Coleridge supplies in his letters the compassion and acuity which his 'society' would give if they were together: 'I have no one to talk all these matters about too – I lack friends, I lack books to supply their absence . . . O my friend . . . talk seriously with me when you do write.'[39] The correspondence with Coleridge decidedly fills a 'lack' and represents Lamb's only refuge from a workaday world unsympathetic to his peculiar trials and passions. Even more important, the letters give voice to a part of himself which seems inaccessible *except* within the context of this written dialogue with his friend. In the 'talk' exchanged with Coleridge, what I would call Lamb's 'lyric' self – discernible only to a sympathetic reader – finds expression and communion. By contrast, the people around Lamb 'talk a language I understand not: I conceal sentiments that would be a puzzle to them. I can only converse with you by letter and with the dead in their books'.[40] For Lamb, the physical presence of a kindred spirit is less important than the capacity to feel emotionally connected with one of like sensibilities. The written word, when infused with powerful feeling, can engender a fellowship between author and reader which more than compensates for physical absence. Coleridge, like the dead poets Lamb loves, is 'alive' to Lamb by virtue of their sympathetic intercourse in written texts.

Any Romantic text, whether lyric or letter, achieves its fullest potential meaning only when a subtle and passionate kind of reading is brought to bear on it. In a letter of 11 April 1796 Coleridge expresses his confidence in Poole's ability to read in such a manner: 'My very dear Friend! I send these poems to you with better heart than I should to most others, because I know that you will read them with affection however little you may admire them.'[41] The clear distinction he makes between affection and aesthetic judgement illustrates that for Coleridge and Poole, as for Romantic readers in general, to 'read with affection' is to go beyond grasping the meaning of a text toward immersing oneself in the consciousness of the author. Far from being purely emotional or internal, reading 'with affection' entails vigorous and even physically taxing involvement in the text. In direct reply to Shelley's anxiety and grief over losing Hogg's friendship, Hitchener offers a vivid account of her reading: 'my heart bleeds in sympathy with yours . . . had you seen me as I read your Ltr., so far from reading fast, I seem'd almost depriv'd of breath & sight, & after having read a few lines, could not for a length of time finish it'. She describes an extremely deliberate, self-conscious reading, akin to the agonizing process by which the letter was no doubt written. In genuine fellow-feeling, she suffers with him: she 'bleeds', nearly blacks out ('depriv'd of breath and sight') and is virtually paralysed ('could not . . . finish it'). When a long-time friend abandons her several weeks later, Shelley expresses his uncompromising desire to know and share in her experience: 'do not feel – yes, do, feel, that I may feel with you, that every vibration of your nerves may be assimilated to mine, mine to your's'.[42] His language evokes physical images of 'vibration' and 'assimilation', again suggesting the all-consuming nature of their sympathy. Coleridge gives a similar account of his response to a letter from Poole: 'Two Hours have past, since I received your Letter – it was so frightfully long since I received one!! – My body is weak and faint with the Beating of my Heart.'[43]

One reason why sympathy was so important to English Romantic writers and readers was that having or imagining a kindred spirit was central to their conception of self. Romantic letters share with sympathy an emphasis on the self as a primary source of meaning and understanding. Shelley's letters to Hitchener reveal the profound degree to which his idealized image of her was a reflection of an idealized component of his own identity. To understand their correspondence, it is not enough to agree with Frederick Jones that Hitchener 'was the creation of his imagination'.[44] Shelley's letters, as Richard Holmes observes, became 'an arena . . . for his attempts at emotional self-analysis'.[45] When he calls her 'my second self',[46] one cannot help but recall his description, written several years later, of the 'antitype' as 'a soul within our soul . . . the ideal prototype of everything excellent or lovely that we are capable of conceiving . . . an imagination which should enter into and seize upon the subtle and delicate peculiarities which we have delighted to cherish and unfold in secret'.[47] Not an autonomous being, the antitype is completely encompassed by and contained within Shelley himself ('*within* our soul', 'everything . . . *we* are capable of conceiving'). It is characterized by its capacity to 'enter into' *his* personality, not to reveal its own. He similarly identifies Hitchener as one who not only 'understand[s] my motives to action', but 'whose views are mine'. He refers in his letters to '*our* identity' and calls her 'the sister of my soul', 'the partner of my thoughts'.[48] The processes of corresponding and of self-reflection have become indistinguishable.

The sympathy in which Shelley – and the rest of these correspondents – are steeped is as much a process of self-discovery as it is a quest to understand and affirm the other person. This leads us to a consideration of sympathy's dual nature in both Romantic and twentieth-century theory. On one hand there is sympathy understood as identification with another. When, for instance, Shelley praises Hitchener as 'the shrine of sympathy',[49] he refers to her active and searching identification with his feelings. According to psychologist Robert Katz, in sympathy 'we seem to be fused with and absorbed in the inner experience of the other person'.[50] On the other hand, Shelley's image of Hitchener as a sort of antitype points to what Margulies calls sympathy's 'projective nature'. Margulies believes that when we sympathize we 'unavoidably find ourselves reflected within our gaze toward the other. I look for you and see myself'.[51] Similarly, Katz views sympathy as 'a source for our own self-understanding, a mirror in which we are reflected'.[52] Romantic notions of sympathy, too, ranged from self-abnegating identification with the Other, such as Keats's 'negative capability' – in which one 'let[s] the mind be a thoroughfare for all thoughts'[53] – to using oneself as a gauge with which to understand others, such as Hazlitt describes in his 'Essay on the Principles of Human Action'. Hazlitt argues that the sympathetic imagination 'must carry me outside myself into the feelings of others by one and the same process by which I am thrown forward as it were into my own future being, and interested in it'.[54]

Whether sympathy is primarily projection or identification, the crucial component common to both is the profound intermingling of self and Other. Margulies believes that sympathy 'leads to the irreducible paradox of the self – which defines and finds itself through the other in its own reflective and interpersonal spiral'.[55] The key here is 'interpersonal', for Margulies finds an essential balance between the affirmation which sympathy generates both in oneself and in the object of one's sympathy. 'Invariably', he writes, 'in searching for the other in an active fashion, we come to our own reflection.' It is the 'active' searching which prevents mere self-absorption and lends to sympathy 'the dialectical quality of finding and creating meaning'.[56] When Coleridge refers in a letter to Poole to 'that sympathy, in which Friendship has it's Being', his meaning depends less on discerning precisely how 'that sympathy' operates than on his belief in the capacity for their correspondence to create out of two distinct individuals one shared 'being'.[57]

Profound involvement in another person's inner life, sympathy theory tells us, inevitably engages one in self-analysis. Romantic correspondents knew implicitly that the self is affirmed by sympathizing *with* another as much as it is by the sympathy *of* another. When Lamb confidently tells Coleridge, 'you have a view of what my situation demands of me like my own view', the subtleties of their symbiosis can only be grasped within the larger context of the correspondence as a process of creating at once a personal and a shared identity.[58] For the Romantic letter is less about communication than about dramatizing the primacy of feeling and the individual psyche. Time and again these letters show that they are as much about the search for personal solace as they are about relationship. In so far as they believed that giving sympathy to the Other is an essential component of their own personal happiness, Romantic correspondents demonstrate an innate recognition of the 'paradox of the self'. Hence Coleridge to Poole: 'a few lines in your last letter betokened, I thought, a wounded spirit. Let me know the particulars, my beloved Friend! – I shall forget & lose my own anxieties, while I am healing your's with cheerings of Sympathy'.[59] Their correspondence is rooted in the mutual desire for concrete 'particulars' of the other's life. Moreover, this passage testifies to a belief in sympathy not only as a 'healing' balm to Poole's 'wounded spirit', but also as an anodyne to Coleridge's 'own anxieties'.[60]

Voicing and meeting interdependent needs is what their correspondence is all about. Throughout 1796, while living with his mother-in-law in Bristol, Coleridge came to regard Poole's house in Nether Stowey as 'a haven of rest and sympathy' and 'a harbour of refuge'.[61] Coleridge, like a ship drifting at sea, was drawn to the solid dependability of Poole's character and life. This same sense of sanctuary and freedom becomes closely linked in Coleridge's imagination with the feelings he entrusts to Poole in his letters. The correspondence becomes the incarnation of the stable world which Coleridge associates with Poole's house. In the view of Mrs Sandford, editor of Poole's papers, Coleridge admired 'Poole's calm, well-ordered life' at Stowey, and so came to regard it as 'the one happy resting-place where he might be safe from all his cares amongst those who loved him'.[62] Poole seemed to Coleridge to possess precisely what he himself most longed for: the ideal home and a 'high degree of practical vigour and utility'.[63] According to W. J. Bate, after pantisocracy died, Coleridge discovered in Poole (seven years his senior) 'a moral leader' who 'was all that Coleridge would himself wish to be: respectable and firm . . . and yet . . . tolerant and open-minded'.[64]

For Poole, by contrast, Coleridge provided constant intellectual stimulation. Moreover, he made Poole feel indispensable. The emotionally intense and reciprocal nature of their correspondence was the result of a mutual need and capacity for sympathy. Poole exclaims in a letter to another friend, 'happy is the genius who has a friend ever near of good sense, a quality distinct from genius, to fill up by his advice the vacuity of his character'. Mrs Sandford observes that for Poole 'the mere contact with Coleridge's genius, the delight and stimulation of intercourse with one so highly gifted, was as a draught of clear spring water to a man whose energies were paralysed by thirst'.[65] More significantly, in seeking to 'fill up' a certain 'vacuity' in the Other, Poole is enacting an important component of sympathy: recognizing and responding to another's emotional need while in the process answering a need in himself.

When in the summer of 1796 Coleridge writes to Poole of his disappointment at losing a teaching position which had been promised him, Poole responds in a letter not only exemplifying his capacity to enter into his friend's situation, but also suggesting Poole's strong desire to provide sympathy:

> My dear fellow, you are schooled to disappointment. I hope you bear this with steadiness. You say you do, *and never tell me what is not true.* The delusion, however painful the discovery that it was a delusion, has produced solid advantages . . . I write immediately, to ease my own heart, for it fears that you may be impatient to be sure that it feels as you feel, and I am in hopes also that it will reach you before you leave Darley.[66]

This passage demonstrates how carefully Poole reads and responds to Coleridge's letter and how vividly he imagines his friend's reaction to the bad news. In saying, 'you are schooled to disappointment', Poole recognizes Coleridge's cumulative sense of his own ill fortune. He plainly refuses to render or accept a sugar-coated version of the truth, either about the circumstances or about Coleridge's state of mind. His sympathy takes the form of an enlightened realism, as he offers encouragement where he feels it is warranted: while acknowledging his friend's pain, he also points out the 'solid advantages'. Not only does Poole know what his friend needs to hear; these needs are deeply interconnected with his own. Poole's admission that he writes partly 'to ease my own heart' illustrates that assuring Coleridge that he 'feels as you feel' likewise gives comfort to Poole himself.

The correspondence is characterized by an extraordinary emotional pitch, as evidenced by Coleridge's recurrent hypersensitivity to Poole's every word and omission. He is at once conscious of and controlled by a deep-seated sense of vulnerability, as the following passage reveals:

> Since we last parted I have been gloomily dreaming, that you did not leave me so affectionately as you were wont to do. – Pardon this littleness of Heart – & do not think the worse of me for it. Indeed my Soul seems so mantled & wrapped round by your Love & Esteem, that even a dream of losing but the smallest fragment of it makes me shiver – as tho' some tender part of my Nature were left uncovered & in nakedness.[67]

Coleridge images himself as a vulnerable child utterly dependent on Poole's 'Love & Esteem'. So 'tender' is he that the very 'dream' of losing the warmth of that affection which makes him feel safely 'mantled & wrapped' causes him to 'shiver' as if 'uncovered & in nakedness'. The reference to his 'littleness of Heart', which indicates that he is conscious of the extraordinary nature of his insecurity, further evokes a sense of his childlike dependence: 'my Nature', in particular, suggests that his anxiety at the thought of any diminution of Poole's affection stems from the profound degree to which he views Poole – and the correspondence – as integral to his self-identity. Especially considering Coleridge's anxiety at this period (1796) due to financial insecurity, his self-image as a vulnerable child testifies to his desperate desire to believe in Poole as a source of comfort and support.

Poole's response characteristically addresses his friend's concerns in direct and unequivocal language: 'By you, Coleridge, I will always stand, in sickness and health, in prosperity and misfortune.'[68] More than merely providing the ideal reassurance to Coleridge, however, Poole's reply demonstrates the advantage of the letter over actual conversation. Poole's response is purged of any adverse reaction he may have had to reading of Coleridge's disappointment in him. Moreover, the time to reflect before responding allows his written reply to go beyond simply showing an awareness of his friend's need for affirmation; he is able to anticipate the unspoken thoughts which he imagines Coleridge to entertain.

Analysis of several letters pertaining to Coleridge's desire to move to Stowey reveals how his dependence on Poole's friendship, even as it can be the catalyst for sympathy, can at times be an impediment to understanding. Coleridge asks his friend to find him a house in Stowey. Poole is happy to do so, but later suggests that Coleridge reconsider because he is concerned about the potential incompatibility between the quiet, provincial village and Coleridge's gregarious personality and controversial politics. Coleridge's long and frantic reply attests to his desperation:

> My friend! while I opened your letter, my heart was glowing with enthusiasm towards you – how little did I expect that I should find you earnestly & vehemently persuading me to prefer Acton to Stowey ... Surely, my beloved Friend! there must be some reason, which you have not yet told me, which urged You to send this hasty and heart-chilling Letter![69]

Coleridge's sense of self is so intertwined with Poole's affection that he has read into his friend's letter feelings and motives which are not present, in the process failing to see Poole's caution for what it was – the desire for Coleridge's happiness.

When Coleridge continues his reply in a second letter the following day, admitting, 'I meant to have written calmly; but Bitterness of Soul came upon me', his tone is all the more raw and frank: 'I am indeed perplex'd and cast down.' His feelings are his guide, and so the word 'heart', which appears twice in the previous passage as a gauge for his state of mind ('my heart was glowing', 'heart-chilling'), is again used as a measure of the authenticity and primacy of feeling: 'As the sentiments over Leaf came from the Heart, I will not suppress them.' Whatever the consequences, he seems to say, feelings must be given voice – in many ways the credo of Romantic correspondence. He concludes with an impassioned plea for the same openness from Poole:

> if any circumstances have occurred that have lessened your Love, or Esteem, or Confidence, or if there be objections to my settling at Stowey on your own account, or any other objections than what you have urged, I doubt not, you will declare them openly & unreservedly to me, in your answer to this, which I shall expect with a total incapability of doing or thinking of, any thing, till I have received it.

Interestingly, the feelings which spur him to write these letters – a profound insecurity and the desire for complete communion with Poole – likewise prevent him from recognizing the reasons for his friend's behaviour. The same feelings, in other words, which usually produce sympathetic fellowship between the two are responsible for a sort of paralysis of understanding. Hence Coleridge's blunt declaration that until he receives Poole's explanation – or at least an explanation which will assuage Coleridge 's anxiety – he will have 'a total incapability of doing or thinking of, any thing'.[70]

The confusion in this interchange between Poole and Coleridge dramatizes a danger with sympathy – namely, that the subjective element in the reading/listening process will become over-emphasized at the ex-

pense of accurate understanding. Nevertheless, Coleridge's volatile sensitivity should not be regarded as an unfortunate aberration; the correspondence is all the more lively and genuine for its emotional outbursts
and miscues. This is part of what gives Romantic letters their lyrical
quality: interpretation plays a crucial role. The reader's response is
necessarily uncertain because the text itself is infused with emotion and
personality.

Just as Romanticism was a movement which defined itself over against
science, sympathy can be understood as the opposite of scientific inquiry. Psychologist David Stewart believes sympathy, as a means of
knowing another person, is fundamentally *un*scientific. While the scientist and his object of study constantly remain 'distinct and clearly
independent of one another', when one sympathizes with another person 'the neat dichotomy ... is no longer present'. The sympathizer,
Stewart explains:

> knows the other by identification with himself, he projects or
> introjects, not sure at first whether he has mistakenly identified,
> either in one direction or another. Still, his feelings are essential in
> understanding the feelings of the other, though he can never be
> completely sure either of his feelings as belonging independently to
> himself, or, of the other's as belonging independently to the other.[71]

A knowing which is based on feelings is not inferior to one based on the
clarity of fact, but altogether different. Unlike scientific investigation,
sympathy demands an investment of self and has as its goal understanding, which entails the concomitant danger of *mis*understanding.

Although reader-response criticism rarely employs the term sympathy, it shares with contemporary sympathy theory an awareness that
there is no such thing as purely objective understanding: meaning re-
sides in relationship and demands, in Hazlitt's terms, that one be 'carried outside [one]self'. According to Georges Poulet, the reader acti-
vates and shares the consciousness which lies behind the text: 'I encounter ... [a] consciousness [which] is open to me, welcomes me, lets me
look deep inside itself, and even allows me, with unheard-of license, to
think what it thinks and feel what it feels.'[72] Poulet's conception of
reading as an intimate exchange sheds light on the remarkably interactive nature of Romantic correspondence. For instance, Coleridge tells
Poole that he wishes to live in Nether Stowey in order 'to be mingling
identities with you'.[73] Poole, in turn, declares that 'I have never for a
moment, since I first knew you, ceased to feel that sort of affection for
you which ... makes the person for whom it is felt a part of yourself.'
Whatever befalls the other, he writes, 'you feel that it is yourself acted
upon'.[74] This con/fusion of identity in reading – in which, in Poulet's
words, 'my consciousness behaves as though it were the consciousness

of another'[75] – resembles contemporary accounts of sympathy. David Woodruff Smith, for instance, argues that in sympathy, 'I see "her" as another "I" . . . As self-awareness in consciousness is a direct awareness of oneself as "I", so other-awareness in empathic perception is a direct awareness of another person as "her" or "him" or "you", understood as if "I".'[76]

Coleridge's notion of 'mingling identities' aptly captures both the dangers and the opportunities generated by sympathetic reading. In *The Implied Reader*, Iser explains that 'if reading removes the subject-object division that constitutes all perception, it follows that the reader will be "occupied" by the thoughts of the author, and these in their turn will cause the drawing of new "boundaries"'. Studying these letters reveals that as both correspondents assume the dual role of reader and writer, their feelings and even identities overlap and interact. While a source of comfort and reassurance, this process can also produce confusion and misunderstanding. For, as reader-response theory shows, meaning cannot be located in the letter (text) itself, nor in the one who wrote it. By nature the letter is intended for a specific reader, and its meaning therefore lies in its encounter with that reader – in what Buber calls the 'between' and Poulet identifies as the reader's 'innermost self'. As that reader translates his response into a text of his own, then he becomes an author, completing the process whereby the two correspondents participate equally in the creative act. In this way, as Iser asserts, 'text and reader no longer confront each other as object and subject'.[77] Instead, through the correspondence they attempt to share an intertextual, interpersonal identity.

In so far as it simulates interior monologue, while at the same time dramatizing the sympathetic and symbiotic relationship between author and reader, the letter is the consummate Romantic form. No less than Coleridge's conversation poems or Wordsworth's greater lyrics, the letter asserts that formality in expression is inimical to sympathetic reading. More important, these correspondences graphically illustrate the dual desire to evoke sympathy and to give it, to express one's innermost self and to see feelingly into another's.

Notes

1. P. B. Shelley to Elizabeth Hitchener, 26 November 1811. F. L. Jones (ed.) (1964), *The Letters of Percy Bysshe Shelley*, vol. 1, *Shelley in England*, Oxford: Oxford University Press, 193.
2. W. Iser (1980), 'Interaction Between Text and Reader', in S. R. Suleiman and I. Crosman (eds), *The Reader in the Text*, Princeton: Princeton University Press, 108–9.

3. W. J. Bate (1945), 'The Sympathetic Imagination in Eighteenth-Century Criticism', *Journal of English Literary History*, 12, 159.
4. J. Conder (1816), *Eclectic Review*, 2nd series, 5, January, 33.
5. S. T. Coleridge (1987), *The Collected Works of Samuel Taylor Coleridge*, vol. 5, *Lectures 1808–1819 On Literature*, 2 vols, R. A. Foakes (ed.), Princeton: Princeton University Press, vol. 1, 251; vol. 2, 268–9.
6. W. Wordsworth (1974), *The Prose Works of William Wordsworth*, 3 vols, J. B. Owen and J. W. Smyser (eds), Oxford: Oxford University Press, vol. 3, 82.
7. C. R. Rogers (1975), 'Empathic: An Unappreciated Way of Being', *The Counseling Psychologist*, 2, 4.
8. A. Margulies (1989), *The Empathic Imagination*, New York: W. W. Norton, 18.
9. M. Buber (1965), *The Knowledge of Man*, M. Friedman and R. G. Smith (tr.), London: George Allen and Unwin, 75.
10. Jones, *Shelley in England*, 187.
11. W. Wallace (ed.) (1898), *Robert Burns and Mrs. Dunlop*, 2 vols, New York: Dodd, Mead, vol. 2, 81–2.
12. Wallace, *Robert Burns*, vol. 1, xxv, xxvi.
13. Wallace, *Robert Burns*, vol. 2, 175.
14. C. Lamb (1975), *The Letters of Charles and Mary Anne Lamb*, vol. 1, *Letters of Charles Lamb, 1796–1801*, E. W. Marss, Jr (ed.), Ithaca: Cornell University Press, 17, 112, 89.
15. Jones, *Shelley in England*, 263, 196, 214, 99.
16. Ibid., 234, 160, 263, 191.
17. For an account of the heterocosmic analogy, see M. H. Abrams (1958), *The Mirror and the Lamp: Romantic Theory and the Critical Tradition*, New York: W. W. Norton, 35, 327.
18. Jones, *Shelley in England*, 234.
19. The idealized union is preferable to the actual one, as illustrated by the disillusionment and falling out between the two which occurs within weeks after Hitchener does finally move in with the Shelleys. Shortly after she moves out, Shelley refers to her in a letter to Hogg as 'The Brown Demon . . . our late tormentor', Jones, *Shelley in England*, 336.
20. C. R. Rogers (1958), 'Characteristics of a Helping Relationship', *Personality Guidance Journal*, 37, 13.
21. D. W. Smith (1989), *The Circle of Acquaintance: Perception, Consciousness and Empathy*, Dordrecht: Kluwer Academic, 117.
22. T. Reik (1949), *Listening with the Third Ear: The Inner Experience of a Psychoanalyst*, New York: Farrar, Straus, 468.
23. W. Hazlitt, 'Essay on the Principles of Human Action', *The Complete Works of William Hazlitt*, 21 vols, P. P. Howe (ed.), London: J. M. Dent, vol. 1, 141.
24. Jones, *Shelley in England*, 234, 152.
25. J. Tompkins (1989), 'Introduction', in J. W. Tompkins (ed.), *Reader-Response Criticism: From Formalism to Post-Structuralism*, Baltimore: Johns Hopkins University Press, x.
26. Jones, *Shelley in England*, 149.
27. Ibid., 189, 149.
28. Ibid., 189, 193, 160, 207, 213.
29. Wallace, *Robert Burns*, vol. 2, 83, 85.

30. Mrs H. Sandford (1888), *Thomas Poole and His Friends*, 2 vols, with illuminations by Mrs H. Sandford (ed.), London: Macmillan, vol. 2, 175.
31. E. L. Griggs (ed.) (1956–71), *Collected Letters of Samuel Taylor Coleridge*, 6 vols, Oxford: Oxford University Press, vol. 1, 251.
32. As quoted in Abrams, *The Mirror*, 243.
33. W. Wordsworth (1967), 'Preface' to the 2nd edn of the *Lyrical Ballads* (1800), in D. Perkins (ed.), *English Romantic Writers*, New York: Harcourt, Brace and World, 321.
34. J. S. Mill (1976), 'What Is Poetry?', in F. M. Sharpless (ed.), *Essays On Poetry by John Stuart Mill*, Columbia, SC: University of South Carolina Press, 12.
35. A. Smith (1835), 'The Philosophy of Poetry', *Blackwood's Edinburgh Magazine*, 38, 829.
36. G. W. F. Hegel (1975), *Aesthetics: Lectures on Fine Art*, 2 vols, T. M. Knox (tr.), Oxford: Oxford University Press, vol. 2, 1134.
37. 'Preface' to *Lyrical Ballads*, in Perkins, *English Romantic Writers*, 322.
38. Hegel, *Aesthetics*, 2, 1134.
39. Lamb, *Letters of*, 66.
40. Ibid., 79.
41. Griggs, *Collected Letters*, vol. 1, 644, 204.
42. Jones, *Shelley in England*, 170, 187, 240.
43. Griggs, *Collected Letters*, vol. 1, 453.
44. Jones, *Shelley in England*, (fn) 97.
45. R. Holmes (1975), *Shelley: The Pursuit*, New York: E. P. Dutton, 72.
46. Jones, *Shelley in England*, 189.
47. 'On Love', in Perkins, *English Romantic Writers*, 1071.
48. Jones, *Shelley in England*, 149, 173, 161, 232.
49. Ibid., 187, 191.
50. R. Katz (1963), *Empathy: Its Nature and Uses*, New York: Free Press, 5.
51. Margulies, *The Empathic*, 58.
52. Katz, *Empathy*, 79.
53. J. Keats (1958), *The Letters of John Keats, 1814–1821*, H. Rollins (ed.), 2 vols, Cambridge, MA: Harvard University Press, vol. 2, 213.
54. *The Complete Works of William Hazlitt*, vol. 1, 1–2.
55. Margulies, *The Empathic*, xii.
56. Ibid.
57. Griggs, *Collected Letters*, vol. 1, 249.
58. Lamb, *Letters of*, 51.
59. Griggs, *Collected Letters*, vol. 1, 252.
60. As if to confirm this concept, psychologist David Stewart calls sympathy 'the therapeutic corrective of self-pity and pain'. D. Stewart (1956), *A Preface to Empathy*, New York: Philosophical Library, 13.
61. Sandford, *Thomas Poole*, vol. 1, 130, 146.
62. Ibid., 173–4. Coleridge's wife had something to do with the strong need Coleridge felt for refuge and a sympathetic ear. Sandford puts it thus:

> A young and untrained wife, fond of him indeed, but perplexed by ways and gifts entirely beyond her small experience, and no doubt tempted to feel both irritated and alarmed at the total absence of what commonplace people call 'prospect', is more to be pitied than blamed if she clung and cried when she ought to have encouraged and comforted, and could

neither be very hopeful nor very helpful in the desperate
condition of her husband's affairs. To keep out of debt, and
to make such small sums of money as drifted irregularly into
her hands last as long as possible, must have been to her the
one subject of absorbing interest and difficulty (Sandford,
vol. 1, 149).

Moreover, beginning now and for the remainder of his life – even after
receiving the Wedgwood annuity, Coleridge could never escape feeling
'the gnawing pressure of straightened means' (Sandford, vol. 1, 262).

63. Ibid., 172.
64. W. J. Bate (1987), *Coleridge,* Cambridge, MA: Harvard University Press, 28.
65. Sandford, *Thomas Poole,* vol. 1, 134, 163.
66. Ibid., 152–3, (original emphasis).
67. Griggs, *Collected Letters,* vol. 1, 235.
68. Sandford, *Thomas Poole,* vol. 1, 161.
69. Griggs, *Collected Letters,* vol. 1, 271.
70. Ibid., vol. 1, 273, 276.
71. Stewart, *A Preface,* 136–7.
72. G. Poulet, 'Criticism and the Experience of Interiority', in J. W. Tompkins (ed.), *Reader-Response Criticism: From Formalism to Post-Structuralism,* Baltimore: Johns Hopkins University Press, 42.
73. Griggs, *Collected Letters,* vol. 1, 249.
74. Sandford, *Thomas Poole,* vol. 2, 256.
75. Poulet, 'Criticism', 44.
76. D. W. Smith (1989), *The Circle of Acquaintance: Perception, Consciousness and Empathy,* Dordrecht: Kluwer Academic, 112.
77. W. Iser (1974), *The Implied Reader,* Baltimore: Johns Hopkins University Press, 293.

CHAPTER FOUR

Co-creating a life: sympathetic autobiography

I am made unlike any one I have ever met; I will even venture to say that I am like no one in the whole world. I may be no better, but at least I am different.[1]

... it seems a contemptible thing, and certainly is a criminal and dangerous thing, for a man in mature life to allow himself [the] thoughtless escape from self-examination.[2]

Autobiography and Romanticism

Sympathy implies human relationship. When a person says or writes something in a context in which he or she knows it will be heard or read sympathetically, this activity embodies a defiance of any notion of the self as solipsistic, self-sustaining or ontologically private. Thus sympathy must be understood as a historical, communicative and linguistic event. It is the intention of this chapter to demonstrate the symbiotic relationship between sympathy and autobiography in the Romantic period. Both are phenomena which serve to unlock the most intimate, hidden aspects of the self, and in the process reveal the inherent search for relationship with and understanding from the Other. They are less about being-in-relation-to-itself than being-in-relation-to-the-world. A fresh approach to current autobiography criticism shows a critical connection with the psychology of sympathy and empathy. By applying twentieth-century theory to three autobiographies from the late eighteenth and early nineteenth centuries, I will illustrate how autobiographers of this period employed a variety of textual strategies in order to enlist the reader's support in their task of self-creation.

Donald Stauffer has written about the way in which 'the English attitude toward the life of the ordinary man changed' in the late eighteenth century. This increased interest corresponds to 'the cult of eccentricity in English biography' at that time.[3] While the autobiographers I have chosen – Daniel Mendoza, Mary Robinson and Olaudah Equiano – were by no means ordinary, neither were they as dazzling and beloved as Byron or Scott. In fact, none was primarily a literary figure, and all were known – to the extent that they were known at all – for other feats or pursuits. This literary marginality is crucial to my intent here: each of these autobiographies in its own way represented a challenge to readers' capacity to reach psychologically and emotionally beyond their own individual experience – including their experience as readers – and enter into the unfamiliar, often bizarre world of another.

The transition from neo-classical to Romantic values was character-ized by a rising interest in the uniqueness of personality. In his book, *Identity: Cultural Change and the Struggle for Self* (1986), Roy Baumeister explains how it was that 'personality came to be taken more seriously as a vital and central feature of each person's identity':

> In the eighteenth century the basic assumption was that ideal de-velopment would reveal human nature to be a constant. In other words, everyone would turn out pretty much the same if permitted to grow up under optimal conditions. People would all be kind, generous, honest, true, loyal, friendly, and so forth. The nineteenth century, however, rejected the idea that everyone would be the same, espousing instead the belief that optimal conditions for de-velopment would produce unique individuals.[4]

According to Stauffer, the concomitant growth in emphasis on the imagination meant that 'the individual becomes increasingly important for his own sake . . . not only for his significant thoughts and actions, but for his tears and velleities, his slightest movements, his daydreams'.[5]

The aesthetic consequences of this heightened psychological and emotional interest can be seen in both the popularity and conception of biography. 'Because each man came to be considered as an unpre-dictable bundle of mysterious forces, in which infinite permutations and combinations were possible, the growth of genuine biography was natural enough.' Moreover, 'with the dominance of the imagination' it is natural that writing lives shifts from exemplification of virtue to presenting the unique and idiosyncratic variety of human beings.[6] Biographies came to be written as intimate profiles of the whole person rather than purely exemplary portraits.[7] As such, according to Stauffer, they 'provided means of freeing the imagination and the heart, transporting the sensitive soul into expansive regions of gener-ous emotion or mysterious realms of melancholy'. As 'the capacity to enter imaginatively into the lives of others, touched the writing of lives with a new beauty and a new nobility', the effect of the account of one's life on readers gave readers a greater role in the conception of biographical writing. In autobiography and biography alike, writers became increasingly aware of their relationship to the reader, whose capacity to feel and understand the subtlest features of the subject's personality was, in turn, instrumental in determining the level of intimacy assumed in the written Life. As a result, 'autobiographers themselves became increasingly aware of their own minds and of the complexity of human consciousness'.[8]

Sympathy and autobiography

Sympathy, then, was at the centre of autobiography (a term coined by Southey in 1809). In fact, David Marshall has written that 'autobiography ... presupposes at least the possibility of an act of sympathy in which the reader could enter into the author's sentiments ... the possibility that one person could know another'.[9] Nevertheless much current autobiography theory questions the nature and the very existence of the authorial self as something to be known. In *Imagining a Self: Autobiography and Novel in Eighteenth-Century England* (1976), Patricia Spacks posits that the novel and autobiography both use narrative to create the 'illusion of substantiality' with respect to the individuals depicted.[10] In the eighteenth century, people wanted life to make sense, and these two genres met this desire by appealing to the imagination. 'Man's need to understand his life as a story and his need to tell that story suggest that the subjective faith in continuous personal identity depends on the explanations provided by the imaginative process of story-telling as well as the bare recollections of memory.' It is the need to 'read' one's life like a carefully designed story which drives autobiography, not a desire simply to report one's life as one remembers it. Identity is created in the activities of writing and reading autobiography. 'The heroes and heroines of autobiography achieve identity as objects of their own imagination. Both assume new life in the imagination of the reader.'[11] Although 'the narrative mode that novel and autobiography share is in this sense a mode of fantasy', because fantasy is what people (autobiographer and reader) really want, 'it may provide the best – or even the only – way to express the real'.[12]

In denying the simple referentiality of autobiography, Spacks shifts the locus of meaning from the self to the imagination. In his 1979 article, 'Autobiography as De-facement', Paul De Man takes the argument one step further. De Man rejects the notion that the self exists outside of language, asserting instead that autobiography produces the self:

> Are we so certain that autobiography depends on reference, as a photograph depends on its subject or a (realistic) picture on its model? We assume that life *produces* the autobiography as an act produces consequences, but can we not suggest, with equal justice, that the autobiographical project may itself produce and determine the life and that whatever the writer *does* is in fact governed by the

technical demands of self-portraiture and thus determined, in all its aspects, by the resources of his medium?[13]

To consider autobiography as a person's true life story, De Man suggests, is not only to falsely privilege the self, but thereby to perpetuate a distorted conception of the way in which meaning comes into being. That is, being – or the autobiographical self – has meaning, not prior to, but by virtue of, 'the autobiographical project'.

De Man is reacting against what Janet Gunn calls 'classical autobiography theory', epitomized by Georges Gusdorf. In his seminal 1956 article, 'Conditions and Limits of Autobiography', Gusdorf makes explicit the belief that the self is the only source of self-knowledge: 'no one can know better than I what I have thought, what I have wished'.[14] For theorists who thus privilege the self, according to Gunn, the 'act of unsituating the self from the world' becomes 'a condition of the self's authentic nature'. They hold that 'the true self is not only private and hidden . . . it is also timeless and unchanging'. In this view, 'autobiography has . . . to be understood as a form of "transcendental voyeurism" – as though the reader were getting a second-hand account of what the self, watching and overhearing itself, has seen and heard'.[15]

In offering an alternative to this view, Gunn argues that 'the question of the self's identity becomes a question of the self's location in the world'.[16] Her goal is to ward off what she sees as a threat from the 'right' and to restore autobiography to the world of time and relationship: 'Rather than starting from the private act of a self writing, I begin from the cultural act of a self reading.' This act takes place in 'the autobiographical situation', which consists of a twofold activity of reading – the autobiographer 'reading' his life and the reader similarly participating in and interpreting the autobiographical text: 'As the reader of his or her life, the autobiographer inhabits the hermeneutic universe where all understanding takes place. The autobiographer serves, by this habitation, as the paradigmatic reader; and the autobiographical text, embodying this reading, becomes, in turn, a model of the possibilities and problems of all interpretive activity.'[17] The self who thus engages in this hermeneutic activity – the 'displayed self' – 'is the self who speaks', 'lives in time, and participates in depth and thus can experience the inter- and transpersonal grounds by which personal identity becomes possible'.[18]

Gunn's use of the term 'understanding' reinforces her conception of autobiography as an *inter*active event. She goes on to explain that the 'inter- and transpersonal' experience of reading, undertaken on both sides of the text, happens in two ways – 'participatory' and 'distantiating'. Both these modes allow the reader to experience the autobiographical Other without losing the distance between distinct selves, allowing 'the reader to look at the universe of common experience from a perspective different from his or her own'.[19] This dual activity entailed in Gunn's notion of reading can be seen as a sort of sympathetic catalyst or prerequisite. Indeed it is similar to many conceptions of sympathy and empathy as activities which involve participation in the other's experience while maintaining awareness of distinct identities.[20] True understanding of the text, according to Gunn, calls for 'neither assimilation (the reader's takeover of the text) nor accommodation (the text's takeover of the reader). Autobiographical response requires, instead, an integration – what Hans-Georg Gadamer calls a "fusion of horizons"'.[21]

For Gunn the notion of linguisticality is key to establishing autobiography firmly in the world of relationship and experience. 'It is by means of language (*graphie*) that self both displays itself and has access to depth; it is also through language that self achieves and acknowledges its *bios*.'[22] Language implies history, relationship (hence: self and Other), culture and communication. Paul Eakin shares Gunn's desire to demonstrate the link between self and language by removing autobiography from the realm of private, self-absorbed act and situating it in the context of history – particularly its relationship with the reader. According to Eakin, 'pursuit of the origins of the self, both as entity and idea, has led us not inward, as one might expect, into some cul-de-sac of solipsism but always outward into a social dimension, to others, to culture, to language and literature'.[23]

In the concluding chapter of his *Fictions in Autobiography: Studies in the Art of Self-Invention* (1985), Eakin first provides an overview of the current debate within autobiography theory regarding 'the nature of the self and its relation to language' ('Is the self autonomous and transcendent, or is it contingent and provisional, dependent on language and others for its very existence?').[24] While accepting De Man's (along with Derrida, Sprinker et al.'s) critique of the traditional position in autobiographical discourse 'that there is ... such a thing as the self, and that language, following after, is sufficiently transparent to express it', Eakin goes on to propose that this illusion is fundamental to autobiography because it is likewise fundamental to human be-ing. 'If the metaphor of the self can be said finally to be only a metaphor', claims Eakin, then

> we should acquiesce precisely in the power of language to create one of the most enduring of human illusions: if autobiographical discourse encourages us to place the self before language ... the fact of our readiness to do so suggests that the power of language to fashion selfhood is not only successful but life-sustaining ... Some such belief as this seems to me to be intrinsic to the performance of the autobiographical act.[25]

If the goal of autobiography is self-presence, then to those who say that self-presence is illusory Eakin replies that however illusory, the self as present in the autobiographical text communicates truth and meaning, if only by conveying – or 'displaying', to borrow Gunn's term – that the self is an illusion. For 'the enduring autobiographers' introduce 'us into the illusion of presence even as they make us know it for the illusion it is'.[26]

Communication, therefore, is a central component in determining autobiography's intention and efficacy. Eakin's argument highlights this, as it hinges on 'the moment of language' – that is, the belief that the self comes into being at the moment a person discovers language.[27] 'In this perspective the writing of autobiography emerges as a symbolic ana-logue of the initial coming together of the individual and language that marks the origins of self-awareness; both are attempts, as it were, to pronounce the name of the self.'[28] The autobiographer's re-enactment of the initial moment of self-awareness necessarily coincides with an act of communication between one self and another. In 'pronouncing' his/her self, the autobiographer implicitly acknowledges that the success of his autobiographical endeavour depends on the reader's capacity to 'listen' and understand. His own and the reader's 'presence' encounter one another in the text: If we accept the writing of autobiography as a kind of speech, and if we posit that it is the 'intention' of such a text to communicate the nature of the author's self ... then we may entertain the possibility that autobiography, like speech, could afford a medium in which for both the autobiographer and his or her reader the self might be apprehended in its living presence.[29]

Eakin's assertion that 'interpersonal experience is the *sine qua non* of selfhood'[30] suggests significant parallels between his communication-based autobiography theory and recent sympathy and empathy theory. Psychologists point to the fact that empathy plays a crucial role in the achievement of both identity and communication. In his book, *Preface to Empathy* (1956), David Stewart's thesis is that 'empathy is the basic action of human behavior'. As such, it 'not only preserves and clarifies personal identity, and interpersonal knowledge with it, but also ... without it, communication, the basis of human relations, would be impossible'.[31] Like the notion of autobiography as an interpersonal, *con*textual activity, empathy preserves the self from isolation and solip-sism and allows it to 'pronounce' itself to the Other. Stewart's concept of empathy is implicitly linguistic in so far as personal identity and the communication between self and Other are seen as virtually indistin-guishable phenomena. According to linguist Emile Beneviste, the self cannot be considered in a vacuum: 'the speaker's being depends upon the audience'.[32] 'It is in a dialectical reality that will incorporate the two terms ["I" and "other"] and define them by mutual relationship that the linguistic basis of subjectivity is discovered.'[33]

Empathy is instrumental to the constitution of self and to communication by virtue of its hermeneutical quality. In his innovative exploration of empathy, John Stewart uses empathy's kinship with 'interpretive listening' to explain how texts are the site of dialogue and relationship. Echoing Eakin's 'moment of language', he posits that 'since human being happens in speaking', the self is not a static object but an ongoing creation in which the empathic listener participates. Moreover, 'rather than primarily listening "behind" or "beyond" the words for clues to covert intentions or psychological states, each listener attends to the happening-now of the communicators' verbal and non-verbal language'.[34] Understanding 'begins not with a psychological event but with a communication event. The focus is not on what is happening "inside" the communicators but on what transpires between them'.[35] Citing Gadamer, Stewart applies this concept to written texts: 'interpretation or understanding is developed in a mutual process between historically contextualized subjects ... an "I" and "Thou"'.[36] Just as the listener in a communication event participates in the 'moment of language' and thus by his/her very presence makes the utterance meaningful, so does the reader provide the 'context' which prevents the text (and the self) from remaining a solipsistic and pre-linguistic phenomenon.

Stewart attempts to redefine understanding as 'a participation in a shared meaning'. His description of hermeneutics as 'the explication of the being-in-the-world displayed by the text' recalls Gunn's 'displayed self'.[37] Moreover, in characterizing his hermeneutics as 'open to continuing development and change' he suggests a post-structuralist view of the autobiographical self, such as that articulated by Robert Elbaz in *The Changing Nature of the Self: A Critical Study of the Autobiographical Discourse* (1988): 'if the self is created in and through language, it can never be a finished product'.[38] Stewart's focus on context rather than text presents a particular challenge to autobiography, a kind of writing generally viewed from a psychological, rather than a communication standpoint.

Although Stewart never once addresses autobiographical writing, his argument illustrates the need to introduce empathy into contemporary autobiographical discourse. One can infer from his discussion that what empathy (or sympathy) brings to autobiography theory is a sort of reader-response approach to the whole idea of self-writing. For Stewart, the reader does not recreate the author's text (or self); he co-creates it. This accounts for the prominence of the terms 'context' and 'between' in Stewart. In an effort to achieve a rethinking of empathy, Ronald

Arnett and Gordon Nakagawa argue for a similar shift away from the privileged self toward a participatory relationship with the reader/listener. They identify empathy as a communicative phenomenon and attempt to reorient communication theory away from 'self' and toward 'selves'. Because of the 'internal bias' of empathy undue attention has been placed on the self, and 'the pursuit of the self results in a shift from self as "being-in-the-world" to self as "being-attempting-to-possess-the-world"'. They recommend instead 'a shift of attention from the internal self to a dialogical or hermeneutical transaction "between" persons and the importance of contextual demands on our listening'.[39]

In suggesting a shift 'from psyche to the linguisticality of human relationships', Arnett and Nakagawa hope to establish that meaning lies not in some false notion of self *qua* self, but in the discourse by which every self achieves membership in the human community. Empathy and sympathy facilitate this discourse by loosing the exclusive bonds a person feels to his/her own self and enabling him/her to feel communion with others. According to Robert Katz in *Empathy: Its Nature and Uses* (1963), empathy 'is motivated by the human need to communicate, to share in the emotions of others, to affiliate'. The empathizer 'has a sense of being connected to the other person, of participating in his experience with a temporary loss of self-consciousness, and of a relaxation of his own focus of attention. Into his empathic response enter[s] . . . a sense of belonging in a common ego'.[40] One autobiography critic has similarly described the experience of reading certain autobiographies as a participation in 'shared truths (embodied by language) larger than ourselves'.[41]

Although not a psychological phenomenon as much as a communication event, the therapy setting is a useful metaphor for conceptualizing the co-creative potential of empathic listening. Particularly in light of the fact that autobiography is a narrative of one's life, a situation in which one tells one's story to a sympathetic listener serves to highlight the connection between communication and creation. In *Being in the Text: Self-Representation from Wordsworth to Roland Barthes* (1984), Paul Jay draws a connection between Freud's 'talking cure' and the writing of autobiography. This link suggests the therapist's sympathetic presence as a metaphor for the reader's participation in autobiographical writing: 'it is both the linguistic ground and the creative potential of such a retrospective process of introspection that connects the narrativizing in an autobiographical text . . . with the narrativizing at the very heart of the psychoanalytic process'.[42]

It is no coincidence that autobiography theory and sympathy theory share such terms as 'participation', 'context', 'being-in-the-world' and 'linguisticality'. These all describe the mutuality inherent in written self-creation, an ongoing process that implies self–Other interrelationship. In what Eakin refers to as a 'reader-based poetics of autobiography', Philippe Lejeune has characterized autobiography as 'a mode of reading as much as it is a type of writing'.[43] According to Lejeune, the reader plays an essential role in the creative process instituted by the autobiographer. Like the analysand whose 'cure' depends on telling his story, the autobiographer has a 'fundamental poverty of needing to tell it to someone in order for it to exist in his own eyes. He needs me: it is in my expression that he looks for proof of existence, certificate of worth, response of love'.[44] It is as if the reader is in league with the autobiographer, whose work of self-creation exists only in the context of that reader's sympathetic presence. Lejeune's use of 'love' underscores the intimacy of the reader–autobiographer relationship. In a similar vein, Elizabeth Bruss envisions the reader as 'a sympathetic peer throughout the interchange, a full participant to whose sympathy and belief [the autobiographer] may appeal'.[45]

James Olney has written that 'the study of how autobiographers have ... discovered, asserted, created a self in the process of writing it out – requires the reader or the student of autobiography to participate fully in the process, so that the created self becomes, at one remove, almost as much the reader's as the author's'.[46] Sympathy and empathy theory suggests the possibility of profound connections between persons. David Stewart made explicit empathy's instrumental role in the creation of personal identity. Psychiatrist Alfred Margulies likewise affirms that self-creation is an ongoing process in which the sympathetic reader/listener has a crucial part: 'in projecting a self onto the other in the interpersonal dialectic, I participate in the creation of a self that I now empathize with. In its very process empathy actualizes its object of contemplation'. For such a reader, the autobiographer becomes more than an Other. The autobiographer, too, regards the sympathetic reader as confidant and co-creator in so far as he/she envisions his/her life as generated by dialogue and relationship. In this way, Margulies explains, 'telling one's narrative helps one find and constitute oneself ... The self defines itself through empathy'.[47]

What I have called the reader-response theory of autobiography suggested by Lejeune is amplified and made more explicit in an essay by Barrett Mandel entitled, 'Full of Life Now' (1980). Lejeune focused on 'the autobiographical pact' – that 'the name of the author on the cover' establishes the referentiality of all autobiographical texts – as the verification of truth and reality.[48] Like Lejeune, Mandel is concerned with identifying the qualities in autobiography which enable the reader to distinguish it from fiction; and like Lejeune he believes that 'autobiographies ... are experiential'.[49] For Mandel, however, the ultimate basis of autobiography's 'truth' and ability to reflect reality rests solely on the reader's active, sympathetic response to the text: 'The *content* of an autobiography is not alone sufficient to create truth. What actually transforms content into truth of life is the *context* that contains the content . . . I would argue that it is the reader's willingness to experience and cocreate this context that allows autobiography to speak the truth.'[50] 'Context' – that is, relationship, history, linguisticality – ensures that the autobiographer's experience is not merely private and self-absorbed because it is not based in a conception of the self as absolute. Instead, it is based on the dialectic and communication between self and Other made possible by language.

Mandel's notion of reader-response is less scientific than Lejeune's. He conceives of understanding autobiography as a sympathetic and symbiotic process rooted in emotion. Thus 'reality' and 'truth' in autobiography make sense only if the reader approaches the text as at once a profoundly personal narrative and an invitation to exercise imagination and creativity. Mandel describes the moments when he as a reader experiences the full 'pleasure' and 'truth' of autobiography as a sympathetic intercourse:

> These profound moments body forth a sense of my sharing life – being – with the author, no matter how remote he or she may be from me in some ways. The autobiographer springs open a door and gives me a glance into his or her deepest reality, at the same time casting my mind into a state of reverie or speculation. The being of the author is felt to merge with my own.[51]

As in a personal relationship, meaning in autobiography is forged out of give and take. The phrase 'body forth' suggests the image often applied to sympathy and empathy of temporarily losing oneself and entering fully into the experience of another. Thus self-transcendence characterizes both the autobiographer and the sympathetic reader of autobiography, for the privileged and solipsistic self no longer pertains. It is replaced by a fresh understanding of autobiography as co-creation.[52]

Eakin has suggested that the only way to understand autobiography is to submit to the illusion it creates. This in no way compromises understanding or the 'truth'/'reality' quality of the text because the autobiographer is still communicating him/her-self to the reader, who in turn assists in the communication by his/her own self-presence. If the reader knows as well as the author that the self is not a static, possessable entity, then far from 'breaking the spell' of authenticity or referentiality, this awareness frees him/her to enter all the more fully and potently into the creative process. As an illustration of the inherently sympathetic nature of this reader–autobiographer relationship, note Carl Rogers's description of empathy's 'as if' quality. Because in any communication event there is still the self and the Other, 'it becomes necessary to ground this theoretical and cognitive behavioral construct [i.e. empathy] on a fiction. I cannot actually "put myself in your place" or "see the world through your eyes", but, according to the empathic paradigm, I am to communicate *as if* I could'.[53] In this sense Roy Pascal got it wrong when, in one of the early monuments of autobiography theory, *Design and Truth in Autobiography* (1960), he said that 'the object [of autobiography] is not so much to tell others about oneself as to come to terms with oneself . . . by grasping oneself as a whole'.[54] As Margulies demonstrates through examination of empathy, the self can only be understood in terms of relationship. It is artificial to think of the self as a definable, 'graspable whole', for 'the self can never apprehend all of itself simultaneously'. On the contrary, 'the self . . . finds itself through the other in its own reflective and interpersonal spiral'.[55]

Rhythms of sympathetic autobiography

In a culture in which sympathy is prominent, the autobiographer is relieved of the burden of 'explaining' or 'revealing' himself before the reader, since the reader actively, willingly (to use Mandel's term) participates in the self-constitution. The Romantic period in England was just such a culture. During the late eighteenth and early nineteenth centuries, as we have seen, readers engaged in sympathetic relationship with texts and authors. Elizabeth Bruss captures this active quality in her account of autobiography as an 'act', or activity, as opposed to merely a kind of writing. What makes her analysis truly interesting and relevant to our discussion is the remarkably intimate level at which she views the reader's co-participation in the autobiographical act. 'To write or read any piece of literature', she argues,

> is to engage in action. The excitement and the potential aesthetic ambiguity of autobiography stem from how closely the literary act borders on the literal, how immediately the decisions of the autobiographer and his reader reflect traits and habits of an intellectual and social life beyond the pages of the text.[56]

Perhaps more than in any other period in literary history, in the Romantic era readers read with 'excitement' and relished the 'ambiguity' between fact and fiction, text and flesh, persona and person.

If, as Eakin posits, the autobiographical act is 'the culminating phase in a history of self-consciousness which originates in the acquisition of language', then it should be possible for the sympathetic reader to identify patterns of meaning which express and symbolize the author's interrelationship with the larger culture. Romantic autobiography is more than a memory or re-enactment; it embodies and expresses the author's personal history – that is, the interpersonal dynamic made possible by the 'language' of sympathy prevalent at the time. According to Eakin, 'the psychological rhythms of identity formation that pattern the autobiographical text' point to the way the author understands his/her relationship to the world in which he/she has lived.[57] Bruss describes in similar terms the need to recognize underlying patterns in the text, patterns which are not only human but 'interhuman'.[58] 'The meaning or rhythm', she explains, 'becomes clear only when we look for the person and the personality which holds it all together.' 'Rhythms' can be identified in every autobiography because every autobiographer undertakes his/her project out of a particular set of experiences, relationships, self-images and goals, all of which Bruss puts under the heading 'strategies'. According to Olney, in *Metaphors of Self: The Meaning of Autobiography* (1972), the 'strategy' corresponds to the way each autobiographer supplies the 'meaning-pattern' through language and imagination. Human experience, Olney summarizes, 'is void of meaning' without this 'design or pattern'.[59]

In the autobiographies examined in this chapter, the 'rhythm' or 'meaning-pattern' is profoundly connected to the author's desire for sympathetic relationship with his or her readers. The success of his or her 'life' depends on the reader's co-operation, through sympathetic response, in co-creating the meaning-pattern itself. In this sense the 'rhythm', like the self it reflects, is linguistic in nature: achieved not simply within the text itself, but in the reciprocal intercourse between autobiographer and reader. Such mutuality, rooted in sympathy, thrived in the Romantic climate. Understanding the texts in this chapter entails not only exploring the strategies involved in writing, but also recognizing the implicit relationship sympathy makes possible between creating and reading a life.

Daniel Mendoza

> I have been induced . . . to offer to the public a faithful narrative of the most material events of my own life, in the course of which I have endeavoured to trace the means by which I acquired a degree of public estimation and celebrity, which perhaps few men of my rank in life ever attained (p. 14).[60]

This passage from the opening paragraph of *The Memoirs of the Life of Daniel Mendoza* (1815) offers an illustration of the principal strategy as well as the underlying irony of this autobiography. Mendoza made his living as a boxer for most of his life, later essaying a miscellany of other vocations to stave off financial disaster. Throughout his narrative he uses the word 'induced' to describe the way he became involved in the countless fights which characterize his account of his life. As the above passage suggests, Mendoza conceives of the autobiographical undertaking itself as another prize fight: an act thrust upon him by others and by circumstances. Just as most of his fights are portrayed as acts of self-defence, so are his memoirs presented as the only natural response to a public desirous to hear from such a singular celebrity. In either case, by shirking the role of agent and initiator in activities – fighting and writing one's memoirs – which inherently demand agency and initiation by the subject, Mendoza reveals the book's primary 'meaning-pattern'. Casting himself as defender rather than aggressor, as reluctant autobiographer, he all but ensures his readers' sympathy, which will in turn make them co-creators of the gentlemanly hero who emerges in these pages.

From early youth fighting was a natural mode of self-expression for Mendoza. Indeed, he identifies this pugilistic penchant as an outgrowth of outstanding health and a mark of superior character:

> Being blessed with a robust and vigorous constitution, and enjoying excellent health and spirits, I engaged at this early period of my life in several contests with boys, considerably older than myself, till I at length attained such a reputation for courage, activity and strength, that none would venture to contend with me. I was acknowledged by all of them to be their master (p. 14).

Mendoza consistently makes the connection between fighting and character, in both of which he is 'master'. In recounting a victory over a man named Dennis – a fight he engaged in 'to punish Dennis for his insolence' (p. 27) – he says that 'though my opponent possessed great strength, he wanted courage and resolution as well as skill to maintain a long contest' (p. 28).

He is the unfailing defender of the underdog, and likewise is himself nearly always the underdog. His first job was working for a nearby greengrocer, of whose family Mendoza grew very fond. The job afforded Mendoza the opportunity to hone both his skills as a boxer and his good character:

> I was here frequently drawn into contests with butchers and others in the neighbourhood, who, on account of my mistress being of Jewish religion, were frequently disposed to insult her. In a short time, however, I became the terror of the gentry, and when they found, that young as I was, I was always ready to come forward in her defence, they forbore to molest her (p. 16).

During this same period, Mendoza gets into a fight with a porter who treated the greengrocer with 'impropriety' and 'abusive' behaviour. His extraordinary 'spirit and resolution' against 'an antagonist of such superior strength' illustrates how throughout the narrative, his moral strength outweighs his disadvantage in size.

In his introduction, Paul Magriel writes that Mendoza 'loved to play the knight errant, and whenever distress was recognisable – the other fellow's, not his own – Mendoza was ready to intervene, rescuing injured innocence, outraged virtue, or whatever needed his championing' (p. 10). That Mendoza was concerned to convince the reader of his virtue can be seen in the language he uses to 'set the stage' – much like the ring was erected for a prize fight – for one of his many encounters with a bully or thug. He prefaces one such incident, arising just after he had 'determined to avoid engaging in pugilistic contests', in the following way:

> There are circumstances and situations ... which would make any man not devoid of the feelings of human nature, lose sight of prudence at the moment, and at all risks stand forward to punish barbarity, and protect, if he were able, the infirm and defenceless against the attacks they are sometimes compelled to suffer from those, who, on account of their superior strength, seem to imagine they have a right to conduct themselves with as much brutality as they please (p. 85).

Consummately Romantic, the passage appeals to the reader's *feelings*, particularly his sense of upholding justice to the *individual*. Whether or not Mendoza exaggerates is less important than the fact that he consistently makes bold appeals to the reader's sensibilities, implicitly placing himself and the reader in the same camp as defenders against the unfeeling and uncompassionate. After another victory over 'the terror of the surrounding country' – not surprisingly, 'an uncommonly athletic man' (p. 87) superior in size to the author – Mendoza notes the sympathetic support he received from the spectators. They were the man's 'neighbours, and many of them having at different times received very ill treatment from him, were consequently highly gratified at beholding him at last vanquished, and his pride and haughtiness completely humbled' (p. 88).

Individualism in the Romantic period is a decided virtue, as Baumeister and Stauffer have shown. And Mendoza's memoir is a paean to the singularity of his character, a self-image achieved largely through constantly casting himself as a victim of circumstances. 'Mendoza was always the injured party', Magriel writes, 'the fights just seemed to seek him out' (p. 3). On one day no less than three fights sought him out, and he acquiesced reluctantly, if passionately. In one instance he recounts in detail how he was the 'victim of a conspiracy' (pp. 36–7). Mendoza sets himself apart from his 'rude' and 'aggressive' adversaries not only by emphasizing his disadvantage in size, but more importantly by indicating his rare combination of fiery temperament and powerful sense of justice and compassion. Being Jewish adds to his singularity and sense of victimization and makes Mendoza unusually vulnerable and sensitive to insults and maltreatment. At one point he remarks that his creditors 'were determined on my ruin' (p. 108) and compares himself to Shylock: 'but here the scene was reversed; the Christian was the unfeeling persecutor, – the Jew the unfortunate debtor' (p. 109). Magriel comments in the introduction that 'all his life [Mendoza] was dominated by his willingness to be Jewish and his pugnacity to defend Jewishness' (p. 1). Indeed, 'his identification, his billing, his presentation, always was under the label, "Mendoza the Jew"' (p. 4).

In one particular incident, he and a companion were accosted while innocently walking by a man 'considered as the bully of the place, who, observing two Jewish lads', remarked 'that he supposed "we were after no good", that "he hated to see such fellows strolling about the place", that "it was a pity we were not sent to Jerusalem"' (p. 23). After a heated exchange, Mendoza says that, 'boy as I was' and despite the man's 'superior strength and size', he offered to 'fight him on the spot'. Once again, Mendoza cites an extremely favourable public response – that the man's 'conduct had drawn on him a proper and deserved punishment' (p. 24). In fact his adversary's own father expressed gratitude to Mendoza, who 'he conceived had rendered an essential service to him and his family'. Making this kind of public reaction a vital part of these incidents goes far beyond 'excusing' violent behaviour; it is a strategy designed to enlist the sympathy of any self-respecting Romantic reader toward one whose character was as much defined by beneficence as by self-defence. Indeed, his refinement was of truly noble proportions. When Mendoza has occasion to go fox-hunting with the Duke of Oxford, and nearly gets into a fight with him, he tells the reader that it was the Duke who apologized afterward, admitting 'that the impetuosity of his temper often drew him into an intemperance of behaviour by no means becoming' (p. 38).

Besides portraying himself as heroic victim, then, Mendoza creates the image of himself as a genteel man of feeling as a means of evoking his readers' understanding and admiration. According to Magriel, 'in [Mendoza's] own estimate, never was there such a mild mannered man as he' (p. 3). His greatest adversary in and out of the ring was a man named Humphreys, whom Mendoza defeated once in an informal brawl. Mendoza's account of their next encounter illustrates his typical mode of self-presentation in the *Memoirs*: the virtuous man assailed. In a chance meeting at a pub, Humphreys used 'scurrilous and abusive language ... seized me by the collar, and tore my shirt with great

violence' (p. 30). Mendoza's measured response is calculated to evince
his reason and refinement:

> I, of course, felt much surprised and irritated at his behaviour, but
> ... suppressing my indignation as much as possible, contented
> myself with telling him that though I did not choose to resent the
> insult just then ... I doubted not, the time would come, when it
> would be in my power to requite him.

After each man had won one contest over the other, the two exchanged a series of letters in the newspaper in an attempt to arrange the
terms for their next fight. Mendoza's reproduction of the letters underscores the differences in character between the two. While Humphreys's
letters are abusive, accusatory and cocksure, Mendoza is the perfect
gentleman. Ever aware of his reputation, in one reply Mendoza writes:
'I regard my own duty to the publick too much, Sir, to disgust them by
retaliating in the same coarse language, and attempting to vie with my
antagonist in rudeness' (p. 53). He aligns himself with 'scholars' and
says he has no need to fight again, though he will do so 'merely as a
point of honour'. Characteristically, Mendoza is induced into one last
fight for moral reasons. Despite his temperate and civilized nature, he
must defend his own and the 'publick's' honour.

As Mendoza had suffered serious internal injuries as a result of their
latest bout, he needed time to recover fully before fighting again. During his convalescence Humphreys at one point publicly (at Mendoza's
own boxing academy) insulted Mendoza as a coward in order to induce
him to fight prematurely. He describes the event in terms clearly aimed
at producing pathos for him and disdain for Humphreys:

> at the moment when this illness was at its greatest height, and a
> circumstance happened which rendered my situation doubly dis-
> tressing, and would have wounded the feelings of any father, but
> particularly one whose youth is only liable to render him fonder of
> his children (I had only then lately lost an only child), at that
> moment, when I was incapable of resenting an injury, Mr.
> Humphreys took the opportunity of treating me in a manner which
> whatever might have been his previous expectations was felt by the
> publick as well as myself, to be as destitute of spirit as of humanity
> (p. 48).

Regardless of whether or not they actually felt so, his imputing feelings
of disgust to 'the publick' all but co-opts his Romantic readers into
sharing the feeling and embracing compassion as the only natural response toward him. In thus leaving the reader with very little choice but
to sympathize with him, Mendoza performs on the reader the same
'inducement' which he himself so often claims as his reason for fighting.
In this way the reader's sympathetic response not only helps to create

the autobiographer's self, but the reader's own identity is simultaneously shaped and defined by the autobiographer.

Throughout the *Memoirs* Mendoza defines himself in terms of his relationship to others. Whether as victim or as object of praise, his sense of self hinges on confrontation with those around him, self-defence amidst hostile circumstances, and the approval of 'spectators' and the general 'publick'.[61] Never shy about singing his own praises – when he goes on tour later in life to exhibit his boxing theories, he repeatedly tells the reader that he 'experienced considerable success' – he equally unabashedly reports others' good opinion of him. At one point he quotes from 'testimonials of approbation from . . . most distinguished citizens', who praise Mendoza's 'propriety and decorum' (pp. 98, 99) on the stage. To illustrate the success of a benefit held in his honour in Edinburgh, he tells the reader: 'if the benefit night of any public character ought to be considered as the criterion of his merit, or his popularity, I had ample reason to be gratified, as mine was the most productive of any ever known there' (p. 74). In his account of the time he spent as a sheriff's officer, after 'improvidence' (p. 8) during his boxing career had left him heavily in debt, Mendoza cites incidents which call attention to his extraordinary selflessness and compassion.

According to Olney, 'the self expresses itself by the metaphors it creates and projects, and we know it by those metaphors . . . We do not see or touch the self, but we do see and touch its metaphors'.[62] Another way of expressing this is that language creates both 'self' and 'other' – autobiographer and reader – at the same moment, the moment when the reader encounters the autobiographer's 'characteristic way of perceiving, of organizing, of understanding'. Conceiving of his life as an ineluctable hostile encounter with others, Mendoza attempts to counteract this by creating a self with which his readers would have to feel sympathy. If he could not fully determine his relationships in life, then he could at least create a lasting affection with readers. The *Memoirs* would have us believe that sympathy has the power to bridge the gap Olney describes between metaphor and self. In the Romantic period in England, it no doubt did.

Mary Robinson

Mary Robinson's *Memoirs* begins with the recollection of the Gothic minster of Bristol being besieged and largely demolished by an attacking army: 'and the beautiful Gothic structure, which at this moment fills the contemplative mind with melancholy awe, was reduced to little more than one-half of the original fabric' (p. 1).[63] This image of the siege and near destruction of an edifice at once beautiful and deeply inspirational serves as the ruling metaphor of this autobiography. As a renowned actress and later a literary figure, Robinson was surrounded for much of her life by an admiring public and no shortage of would-be suitors. Nevertheless she never escaped a haunting internal loneliness. Such is the self-portrait in the *Memoirs*, in which however strongly outward events indicate a successful career and the author's constant concern with physical appearance suggests a superficial focus, the ultimate impression is of a deeper character destined to suffer alone.

From the opening pages Robinson conveys the sense of being caught up in an ineluctable destiny. She portrays herself much like a heroine in a Gothic novel. From the ruins of the monastery adjoining the minster was erected a mansion, 'a spot ... calculated to inspire the soul with mournful meditation' (p. 2). And, leading the reader from a historical and literal panorama of the grounds, in through the mansion, and finally to the particular room in which she was born, she lays the groundwork for her portentous entry into 'this world of duplicity and sorrow' (p. 3) and into the book:

> In this venerable mansion there was one chamber whose dismal and singular constructure left no doubt of its having been a part of the original monastery. It was supported by the mouldering arches of the cloisters, dark, Gothic, and opening on the minster sanctuary, not only by casement windows that shed a mid-day gloom, but by a narrow winding staircase, at the foot of which an iron-spiked door led to the long gloomy path of cloistered solitude (p. 2).

The ruins and preponderant 'gloom' into which she was born are balanced by the awe and timeless nobility of a Gothic monastery. For an English reader in 1800, such a 'singular' external scene could evoke powerful personal feelings – of spiritual values in decay or transition, of both sympathy and fascination with a fellow human being reared in such an environment. Thus, with respect to her audience and herself, Robinson casts at once a pall and a heroic mist over her narrative.

In this way her *Memoirs* is a gesture aimed directly at the reader, who she hopes will both pity her adversity and admire her success. She is set apart from her brothers at a young age, she writes, by her 'romantic and singular characteristics'. Moreover, 'every event of my life has more or less been marked by the progressive evils of a too acute sensibility' (p. 8). Knowing that to be 'singular' and possessed of 'acute sensibility' was to be cherished during this period, Robinson could count on her reader's sympathetic response to validate and perhaps in some way to make up for those very qualities. Finding herself, because of her beauty and station, immersed at an early age in the London social scene and married at the age of 16, she soon had more reason to feel the 'evils' of constitutional sensibility as well as of youthful innocence. Her husband grew increasingly distant, emotionally as well as geographically, and out of the ruins of her marriage developed her independent spirit. It was during this period of trial, spending most of her time alone, that she began to realize the connection between her profound sensibility and the unlikelihood of marriage as a way of life for her. In a passage which no doubt appealed to her audience's romantic sympathies, she describes how during these early years of her marriage she found solace only with the natural world:

> How tranquil did I feel escaped from kindred tyranny, and how little did I regret the busy scenes of fashionable folly! Unquestionably the Creator formed me with a strong propensity to adore the sublime and beautiful of His works! But it has never been my lot to meet with an associating mind, a congenial spirit, who could (as it were abstracted from the world), find an universe in the sacred intercourse of soul, the sublime union of sensibility (p. 96).[64]

Her *Memoirs*, I would argue, represents her attempt to draw the sympathetic reader into the role of 'associating mind' and 'congenial spirit' which she never found in life. Without a sympathetic comrade in her narrative journey she cannot create the self she desperately wants, just as she cannot alone break through the melancholy mist surrounding her birth. For as Bruss points out, citing R. D. Laing, 'identity . . . is composed not only by acts of self-perception but by "other-perception" as well'.[65] Only by virtue of such 'intercourse of soul', her autobiography implies, can she maintain a balance between her loneliness and melancholy and her heroic independence.

That her lot lay elsewhere than in this world is suggested by her posture throughout the narrative as a victim. Constantly assailed by circumstances and by men, she achieves success only at the cost of genuine camaraderie and tranquillity. In addition to her husband's abandonment and subsequent infidelity in the past, she continues to suffer public suspicion regarding her own honour. As 'the victim of events', she laments that 'of all created beings I have been the most severely subjugated by circumstances . . . ' (p. 83). Hence she endeavours to assure the reader of her innocence, by direct appeals ('solemn asseverations' (p. 83)) and through frequent use of dialogue.

The latter technique serves to heighten the dramatic effect, or more specifically, to engage the reader more immediately in the feeling and image she is trying to communicate. When her husband's debt threatens to put him in jail, an influential acquaintance of his offers to secure her husband's release if Mrs Robinson agrees to be his mistress. After 'every advance he had the temerity to make was by me rejected with indignation' (p. 145), the affair reached a climax the next day in a conversation she recreates for the reader. The man – perfidy and villainy personified – repeats his offer:

I burst into tears.

'You cannot be so inhuman as to propose such terms!' said I.

'The inhumanity is on your side', answered Mr Brereton. 'But I have no time to lose; I must return to Bath ... and I do not wish my name exposed in a business of this nature.'

'Then for Heaven's sake release my husband!' said I. Mr. Brereton smiled as he rang the bell, and ordered the waiter to look for his carriage. I now lost all command of myself, and, with the most severe invective, condemned the infamy of his conduct. 'I *will* return to Bath', said I; 'but it shall be to expose *your* dishonourable, your barbarous machinations ... You have carried outrage almost to its fullest extent; you have awakened all the pride and all the resentment of my soul, and I will proceed as I think proper' (pp. 146–7).[66]

Regardless of how faithful an account this is – and how a twentieth-century reader would respond to her stylized characterization – such a dialogue from a woman's autobiography would doubtless evoke her readers' sympathy for her, particularly since her *Memoirs* is replete with similar sieges upon her independence and honour.

According to Eakin, it is possible 'to understand the writing of autobiography not merely as the passive, transparent record of an already completed self but rather as an integral and often decisive phase of the drama of self-definition'.[67] Robinson's use of dialogue vividly enacts this 'drama' by illustrating the essential linguistic – that is, dynamic and interactive – nature of autobiography. Part of her success in relating in dialogue form such difficult personal moments as the above lies in the fact that this technique underscores the role of relationship in her life. As we have seen, the identity she creates is rooted in the qualities of uniqueness and solitude, both of which are defined linguistically – in terms of one's relationship to the world. Thus, for her autobiography to succeed, it has to render (at least the illusion of) a self, which, as we know from the first section of this chapter, implies an Other – specifically the reader. To this end, the narrator's verbal intercourse with others – usually aggressive men – in the *Memoirs* serves as a sort of negative trope for the sympathetic dialogue she hopes to achieve with the reader. The reader completes the autobiographer's 'self-definition' process by identifying with (in this case) Robinson's 'indignation' and becoming increasingly sensitive to, and engaged in, her feelings and circumstances, as in a personal relationship.

In so far as autobiography is creating at least an image of the self – self-imaging – it is interesting to note Robinson's extraordinary interest in attire. On one level she makes note of dress as a way of marking her maturation from being girlish and obscure to sophisticated and well recognized. More significantly, however, constantly telling us what she wore in public symbolizes her whole mode of self-presentation before the reader. From the standpoint of memory, this element of her narrative at times seems wholly irrelevant, as when she first meets her father-in-law: 'Mr Harris came out to receive me. I wore a dark claret-coloured riding habit, with a white beaver hat and feathers' (p. 58). Robinson is not merely looking back and recalling an image of herself, however. She is looking inward and outward – to her readers – and creating an image. Thus in a very real sense the autobiographer 'dresses herself' for the reader, 'fashioning' a self in language. When she makes her social 'debut' shortly after her wedding, her distinctive attire is the only thing she tells the reader about the event. 'Dressed with peculiar but simple elegance', her appearance

> was so singularly plain and Quaker-like that all eyes were fixed upon me. I wore a gown of light brown lustring with close round cuffs (it was then the fashion to wear long ruffles); my hair was without powder, and my head adorned with a plain round cap and a white chip hat, without any ornaments whatever (pp. 63-4).

Singularity, individuality, is the measure of her success, both as a woman in the public eye and as an autobiographer. Thus it is not surprising that years later as a famous personage she does not fail to point out that 'I was consulted as the oracle of fashions; I was gazed at and examined with the most inquisitive curiosity' (p. 143). In both instances – indeed, at both periods of her life – her clothing, remarkable for its stunning simplicity, sets her apart and even lends her an air of mystery.

Indeed, she uses other women's attire – particularly upper-class women – as a foil to her own as a way of calling attention to a more profound contrast in character. Her husband's sister, Miss Robinson, epitomizes everything that the narrator herself despises. At their very first meeting, Robinson writes,

> Miss Robinson was Gothic in her appearance and stiff in her deportment; she was of low stature and clumsy, with a countenance peculiarly formed for the expression of sarcastic vulgarity – a short snub nose, turned up at the point, a head thrown back with an air of *hauteur*; a gaudy-colored chintz gown, a thrice-bordered cap, with a profusion of ribbons . . . (p. 59).

In contrast to this repugnant ostentation, Robinson herself 'wore a fashionable habit and looked like something human' (p. 61). She notes that during this initial visit at her in-laws, she 'was complimented by the visiting neighbours on my good looks or taste in the choice of my dresses'. While Miss Robinson treated her with 'insolence' out of 'envy' of the narrator's superior beauty and accomplishments, our heroine meanwhile 'endured it patiently' (p. 61). In implicitly contrasting her own nobility of character and spirit with her in-laws' purely socio-economic nobility, Robinson clearly appeals to the Romantic reader's sympathy. She knows that her sense of value lies in her unique individuality, not in inherited fortune or status. During a later visit there, she separates herself from the family by staying at a small cottage on the outskirts of their estate; as with the difference in dress, the literal separation suggests to her a more fundamental distinction:

> I there avoided the low taunts of uncultivated natures, the insolent vulgarity of pride, and the overbearing triumphs of a family, whose loftiest branch was as inferior to my stock as the small weed is beneath the tallest tree that overshades it. I had formed a union with a family who had neither sentiment nor sensibility; I was doomed to bear the society of ignorance and pride; I was treated as though I had been the most abject of beings, even at a time when my conscious spirit soared as far above their powers to wound it as the mountain towered over the white battlements of my then solitary habitation (pp. 96-7).

Robinson makes a similar distinction between herself and another member of the aristocracy, a Signora Albanesi, whom she met while still living with her husband. Despite her husband's wrongdoing, Robinson chose to remain faithful to him. Another sign of her soi-disant unpretentious and unselfish simplicity, this course of action is offered as an illustration of her innate sense of honour, her refusal to let others dictate her morality, and her unassailable, even heroic character. In this light, Signora Albanesi, who dressed in 'satins, richly embroidered, or trimmed with point-lace' and 'was a striking example of beauty and of profligacy' (p. 120), and who 'sacrificed every personal feeling for the gratification of her vanity' (p. 121), was a foil for her own adherence to simple dress and straightforward virtue. As 'the dazzling meteors which fashion had scattered in her way' (p. 121) were waning in her early middle age, Signora Albanesi 'now sought to build a gaudy transient fabric on the destruction of' Robinson. 'At every interview she took occasion to ridicule my romantic domestic attachment . . . and pictured, in all the glow of fanciful scenery, the splendid life into which I might enter' (p. 121).

In contrast to the mean-spirited self-absorption of Signora Albanesi, Robinson gives an account (immediately adjacent to this one) of the Duchess of Devonshire, whose affection and selflessness supported and buoyed Robinson during the several months she spent with her husband in debtor's prison. The narrative presents the Duchess as an example of the sympathetic posture Robinson seeks from the reader: 'frequently the Duchess inquired most minutely into the story of my sorrow . . . she lamented that my destiny was so little proportioned to what she was pleased to term my desert, and with a tear of gentle sympathy requested that I would accept proof of her good wishes' (p. 117). In presenting

Robinson as a woman whose 'destiny' it is to suffer because of her romantic nature – just as she must suffer unjustly for her husband's financial incompetence – the *Memoirs* makes an implicit plea to the reader to respond, like the Duchess, as 'a liberal and affectionate friend' (p. 117).

Indeed, the entire autobiography is couched in terms of a self-defence, one undertaken with a listening friend in mind. She has been ill-treated by those around her as well as by 'destiny'. She writes, 'the world has mistaken the character of my mind; I have ever been the reverse of volatile and dissipated' (p. 53). On the contrary, she says, 'the melancholy propensities' were 'the leading characteristics of my existence' (p. 53). In stating that 'with the candid and sensitive mind I shall, I trust, succeed in my vindication' (p. 53), she implies that reconciliation lies not so much in factual truth or accuracy but in her ability to establish a sympathetic connection with any reader capable of appreciating candour and sensitivity. She suggests that it is the capacity to perceive and validate states of *feeling*, not statements of fact, that makes a good reader. Her narrative assumes her readers will possess this capacity, and it positions the reader with her in opposition to 'the world': 'Ah! how little has the misjudging world known of what has passed in my mind, even in the apparently gayest moments of my existence!' (p. 55). Robinson seems fully aware that understanding her is no easy task, and in this sense her *Memoirs* is less bitter than it is plaintive. In so far as 'telling one's narrative to another helps one find and constitute oneself' as Margulies believes, the narrator longs – aloud – for a sympathetic listener.[68] Her insatiable melancholy and longing for a kindred spirit found occasional solace in Westminster Abbey:

> I have often remained in the gloomy chapels of that divine fabric till I became as it were an inhabitant of another world. The dim light of the Gothic windows, the vibration of my footsteps along the lofty aisles, the train of reflections that the scene inspired, were all suited to the temper of my soul (p. 52).

The entire autobiography testifies to the narrator's Byronic 'temper of soul' – her inexplicable singularity and melancholy. Unable to find comradeship in life, she seeks it through autobiography. This passage makes explicit the suggestion that her 'romantic' dissonance with the world around her is so profound that in order to understand her, the reader must join her in 'another world'.

Whether or not the reader does this, Robinson inherently recognizes that to be known and understood by a sympathetic Other – a relationship of which she all but despaired in life – is profoundly self-affirming. And as David Stewart has shown, 'one's identity is brought into clearer focus through the agency of the other whom he sees to be very like him, yet distinctly not him'.[69] 'I am unique', Robinson seems to be saying to the reader, 'but insofar as you understand and sympathize with me, you participate in my heroic struggle, which is really the struggle of every human being.' Though she never makes a direct appeal to her readers, her dependence on them is implicitly desperate, as she admits having found herself unable to rely on those around her. In women in particular she expresses disappointment: 'I have experienced little kindness from them, though my bosom has often ached with the pang inflicted by their envy, slander, and malevolence' (p. 119). While in debtor's prison, those she thought friends 'neglected all the kind condolence of sympathetic feeling, and shunned both me and my dreary habitation' (p. 119). One of her only experiences of friendship was with the playwright Richard Sheridan. Characteristically, she describes the basis for their mutual affection in terms of his compassion toward and understanding of her. When her infant daughter died Sheridan came to her immediately, expressing 'a degree of sympathetic sorrow which penetrated my soul' (p. 136). Contrasting him to her husband, she once again positions herself as a sufferer by 'destiny': 'I never was beloved by him whom destiny allotted to be the legal ruler of my actions.' The narrative is psychologically subtle and complex, however, so that instead of simply condemning her husband outright, she treats him with a measure of understanding he never gave her: 'I do not condemn Mr Robinson; I but too well know that we cannot command our affections' (p. 136).

When Sheridan uttered his words of sympathy, the narrator says 'I had not power to speak' (p. 136). She is rendered similarly speechless when as an adult she returns to her birthplace and hears the familiar sounds of the cathedral: 'language cannot describe the sort of sensation which I felt' (p. 54). Profound feeling, she seems to believe, renders language inadequate. Her *Memoirs* is an act of communication which, by placing the reader in the position of potential comrade and comforter – such as Sheridan was – relies on a sympathetic Other (reader, listener, friend) to understand it and thereby to complete it. Having been generally disappointed and alone in life – to the point of believing that 'the consciousness of independence is the only true felicity in this world of humiliations' (p. 143) – she has only the reader left to whom to entrust her story, her self. That he is a kindred spirit is the assumption of the whole text; thus she can convey in genuinely moving words many of her deepest fears and longings. Nevertheless, in so far as she identifies herself as a person endowed with an extraordinary depth of feeling, there will always be an element of her story that depends on the language of sympathy. Her *Memoirs* exemplifies Romantic autobiography because instead of inviting a reader's shrewd deconstruction, it makes sense only as an edifice inspired and co-created by the reader's sympathy.

Olaudah Equiano

Olaudah Equiano concludes his autobiography, *Equiano's Travels: His Autobiography: 'The Interesting Narrative of the Life of Olaudah Equiano or Gustavus Vassa the African'* (1789), by stating that 'almost every event of my life made an impression on my mind and influenced my conduct' (p. 158).[70] That this is so is attributable as much to the singularity of the man as to the singularity of the events. Clearly, Equiano makes clear in his prefatory remarks 'To the Reader' (1792) that he hopes his story will help 'put a speedy end to a traffic both cruel and unjust'.[71] However, I would argue that the favourable impact of *The Interesting Narrative* on its original readers hinged less on their anti-slavery sentiments than on their willingness to know and understand the narrator as a uniquely sensitive individual. With remarkable emotional and psychological authenticity, he conveys to the reader in 'almost every event' of the narrative the 'impression' it made on his mind. In this way Equiano acknowledges that while the original experiences remain his own and refer to something he hopes to eradicate, the autobiography depends for its success on the reader's participation in the narrator's suffering and gradual experience of self-creation.

Like the previous two autobiographies discussed in this chapter, *The Interesting Narrative* was written with the assumption that readers would respond sympathetically to the narrator as a real person whose name is on the cover. However, the 'illusion of presence' described by Eakin functions in a different way here. The narrator seeks to separate himself from the character who is a slave as part of his effort to oppugn slavery. According to Annette Niemtzow, 'the slave narrative suggests a paradox: the slave, happily ceasing to be a slave, describes his or her slave self to preserve it just as it is about to cease to be'.[72] An example of this 'contradictory act of recapturing a self that the slave wishes to cast off' is found in Equiano's prefatory address 'To the Parliament of Great Britain'. In this case, the distinction of greater import is that between the pagan self and the Christian – that is, westernized – self brought about by slavery:

> By the horrors of that trade I was first torn away from all the tender connexions that were naturally dear to my heart; but these, through the mysterious ways of Providence, I ought to regard as infinitely more than compensated by the introduction I have thence obtained to the knowledge of the Christian religion.[73]

The fact that the self adopted as a result of slavery 'more than compensated' for the loss of his more 'natural' self indicates Equiano's desire to present an integrated self to the influential men to whom this statement is addressed. Yet, at a time when rational thought and conventional religion were increasingly giving way to individual imagination and feeling, other readers would no doubt encounter as dissonant and unsatisfying his assertion that 'knowledge of the Christian religion' counterbalanced the 'horrors' of being deprived of '*all* the tender connexions that were naturally dear to my heart' (my emphasis).

The conflict between Equiano's irrepressible need to communicate his feelings about slavery and his desire to position himself fully in the western world characterizes *The Interesting Narrative*. According to Chinosole, 'divided and conflicting selves generate the condition for Equiano's narrative posture'.[74] 'Narrative posture' implies linguisticality and relationship to the world and the reader. According to William Andrews in 'The First Fifty Years of the Slave Narrative' (1982), autobiography is about 'the proper relationship between the individual and the world'.[75] If, as Eakin posits, autobiography is an attempt 'to pronounce the name of the self', then Equiano's narrative succeeds to the degree that the listener (reader) who is the object of that speech act appreciates the autobiographer's confusion with respect to self. Angelo Costanzo has illustrated in *Surprizing Narrative: Olaudah Equiano and the Beginning of Black Autobiography* (1987) that the slave narrator must fully engage the reader as sympathetic listener: 'the eighteenth-century black narrator's relationship with listeners and readers was crucial because he had to develop a trust and veracity in himself if he was to be regarded as a legitimate autobiographer'.[76]

One way Equiano sought readers' sympathy is by narrating an event from the naïve perspective he had at the time, a viewpoint of ignorance with which the reader can identify. For instance, after several months of slavery at the hands of other Africans he is taken to the west coast where he sees white men for the first time:

> I was now persuaded that I had gotten into a world of bad spirits and that they were going to kill me. Their complexions too differing so much from ours, their long hair and the language they spoke (which was very different from any I had ever heard) united to confirm me in this belief (p. 25).

He assumes he is 'to be eaten by those white men with horrible looks, red faces, and loose hair' (p. 26). This passage, and many others like it, is by no means simply a memory or recreation of an event; it is quintessentially linguistic and makes sense only as an act of communication. As Chinosole observes, 'by effecting verisimilitude of psychological reactions, Equiano forces us as readers through the same emotional hold he felt'. Moreover, it is written with a specific audience in mind: 'Equiano's narrative technique places white European readers in the position of laughing at Equiano who is stereotyping them with the same myth they have attributed to him.' As a result, 'by the time the reader realizes he has been educated to the real African as opposed to the assumed one, much prejudicial resistance has been worn down by laughter, and he has been hoodwinked into Equiano's point of view'.[77]

In addition to gaining the reader's sympathy by putting him inside the narrator's perspective, Equiano makes it clear that he wants to live as part of his readers' white English world. After having lived in England for three years, he says he felt himself 'almost an Englishman':

> I could now speak English tolerably well and I perfectly under-
> stood everything that was said. I now not only felt myself quite
> easy with these new countrymen, but as men superior to us, and
> therefore I had the stronger desire to resemble them, to imbibe
> their spirit and imitate their manners (p. 43).

As Costanzo has observed, soon after this passage 'he transfers his point of view from "I" and "their" to "we" and "our"'.[78] Indeed, I would argue that the work is driven as much by his desire for acceptance in English society as by his desire to end slavery. Frequently he says that a white man 'took a liking to me' (for example, pp. 75–6) and chronicles in detail his many successes in the white world, including being made captain. While these are part of an effort to win over the reader, it never takes the form of obsequiousness or flattery. Rather, the reader experiences a narrator who has seen the erosion of enormous emotional barriers between himself and white society and who feels kinship with this world, in spite of slavery. At one point the narrator expresses sympathy for his former masters, saying that they are merely pawns like himself of an evil institution: 'had the pursuits of those men been different, they might have been as generous, tender-hearted and just, as they are unfeeling, rapacious and cruel' (p. 73). Thus, by minimizing the differences between himself and white men Equiano attempts to present himself on equal terms with his reader, to invite not only sympathy but dialogue. As Paul Edwards comments in his introduction, 'he ... makes no effort to capture our sympathies sentimentally by presenting himself as a man persistently ill-treated by an irredeemably wicked world'.[79]

The sheer human suffering he endured in slavery is presented in straightforward terms which speak for themselves. This is illustrated in the narrator's frequent desire to die rather than continue living as a slave, moments which set apart *The Interesting Narrative* for the unusually raw psychological experience these moments share with the reader. A low point in his life came when, after having lived in England and

made many friends, and even entertaining hopes of obtaining his freedom, his hitherto kind master unexpectedly sold Equiano. The narrator's descriptions of his feelings during this period are genuinely moving
and remarkable for their psychological realism. Though written in the
past tense, they 'presentify' the experience and the self:[80] 'What tumul-
tuous emotions agitated my soul when the convoy got under sail, and I
a prisoner on board, now without hope! I kept my swimming eyes upon
the land in a state of unutterable grief, not knowing what to do and
despairing how to help myself' (p. 61). When they reached Montserrat,

> a fresh horror ran through all my frame and chilled me to the
> heart. My former slavery now rose in dreadful review to my mind,
> and displayed nothing but misery, stripes, and chains; and, in the
> first paroxysm of my grief, I called upon God's thunder and his
> avenging power to direct the stroke of death to me rather than
> permit me to become a slave, and be sold from lord to lord (p. 62).

During his first passage to England, Equiano's desire for death springs
from profound loneliness:

> I was now exceedingly miserable and thought myself worse off
> than any of the rest of my companions, for they could talk to each
> other, but I had no person to speak to that I could understand. In
> this state I was constantly grieving and pining and wishing for
> death rather than anything else (p. 33).

He aches not for freedom, but communication – someone whose language he shares – and without it he could wish only for death.

This isolation is analogous to his narrative position: he longs to make
himself known to the reader. Without this communication, Equiano
realizes, the autobiographer is effectively dead. A black ex-slave in a
white society received little institutional support; it was on an individual, personal level that he must appeal. Thus, although Equiano
became 'well-known in England as the champion and advocate for
procuring a suppression of the slave-trade', his most efficacious way of
reaching people and escaping isolation was to engage the individual
reader, sitting alone with a book.[81] As Roger Rosenblatt explains,
therefore, establishing a relationship with the reader is an essential
strategy of the slave narrative. Because autobiographer and reader are
both alone, 'whatever else may separate them from each other, their
states of loneliness are mutually recognizable. For the black autobiographer this is a central connection; he is after all not a minority to his
lonely reader'.[82]

Perhaps inherently aware of this natural connection, Equiano does
not try to coerce the reader's sympathy but lets the psychological and
emotional experience speak for itself. As Edwards observes, 'he puts no
emotional pressure on the reader other than that which the situation

itself contains – his language does not strain after our sympathy, but expects it to be given naturally'. Moreover, 'he seems content to let the reader see him as he is, sometimes at a total loss, sometimes ignorant, confused, careless, self-seeking, sometimes rather boastful'.[83] Indeed, the plain style was what appealed to contemporary reviewers. One reviewer praises its 'truth and simplicity', and the *Monthly Review* for June 1789 writes that 'the narrative wears an honest face; and we have conceived a good opinion of the man, from the artless manner in which he has detailed the variety of adventures and vicissitudes which have fallen to his lot'.[84] Thus, for example, during the early moments of his captivity, when he sees the vast ocean, the white race and savage brutality to blacks all for the first time, when the only familiar thing left is the land itself, he is deprived even of this. Thrown on to a ship – a huge vessel the likes of which he had never seen before – stripped of everything familiar to him, his ignorance is the reader's ignorance:

> I now saw myself deprived of all chance of returning to my native country or even the least glimpse of hope of gaining the shore, which I now considered as friendly; and I even wished for my former slavery in preference to my present situation, which was filled with horrors of every kind, still heightened by my ignorance of what I was to undergo (p. 26).

The 'making-present' (which, as Eakin has shown, is another word for communication) of the slave experience – illustrated by the narrator's use of 'present' in the above passage – helps to establish 'an intimate relationship with the reader'. According to Costanzo, because black autobiographers 'relied heavily on the emotional appeal produced by the graphic scenes of slavery they described', the reader and slave narrator often developed 'a close dialogue'. 'The autobiographer', he contends, 'speaks directly to readers as a close friend who wishes to understand his life and explain it to himself and to readers for some beneficial effect upon his own life and that of theirs [sic].'[85] In addition to seeking the reader's sympathy, then, the autobiographer conveys an altruistic sympathy toward the reader.[86] In this way, the desire for and the agency of sympathy makes *The Interesting Narrative* less historical than rhetorical, an attempt to 'pronounce' rather than recreate the self.[87]

Costanzo shows that oratorical and rhetorical techniques were commonly used in slave narratives as part of their conception as spiritual autobiography. When 'Equiano looks back on his life and describes his personal struggles for freedom and identity and religious salvation', it is not so much a record of his past as an act of communication with the reader in the present with a view to having an impact on the future.[88] Costanzo elucidates the intensely personal, interactive nature of such writing:

black authors who used the practices of oratory in their works kept
the reader at their elbows while they were writing. They were
aware of what type of effect they might have on the reader with
their use of words, and they wanted to be certain that their ideas
and appeals would produce the intended effects.[89]

His rhetorical flourishes often erupt into anger directed at those most
resistant to the anti-slavery message. Interestingly, even more than the
physical hardship, Equiano decries the deprivation of camaraderie and
sympathy which slaves endure: 'O, ye nominal Christians! . . . are the
dearest friends and relations, now rendered more dear by their separation from their kindred, still to be parted from each other and thus
prevented from cheering the gloom of slavery with the small comfort of
being together and mingling their sufferings and sorrows?' (p. 32).

Part of the reason for Equiano's references to forgiving his former
masters and his explanation of misfortune as being part of a divine plan
stems from the belief that one's own conversion can have a beneficial
impact on others. More important, however, is his desire to be recognized and understood as a member of the white, Christian world. Only
by achieving this image can he engage not merely the reader's pity, but
his fullest sympathy. As Costanzo puts it, 'he knew that people might be
sympathetic to the story of his victimized life, but whether white readers would be convinced of the narrator's mental and spiritual talents
was questionable'. To this end, the narrator takes pains to illustrate that
he is more intelligent, civilized and trustworthy than other blacks and
even some whites. For example he refers to what a 'curious' (p. 40)
mind he always had and how much he loved to read. A great part of the
narrative consists of detailed accounts of his acumen and leadership as
businessman and sailor, such as the time he was 'the principal instru-
ment in effecting [the] deliverance' (p. 109) of the entire crew during a
shipwreck. Occasionally he uses dialogue to increase the dramatic effect. After the shipwreck, while others advised against setting out again,
he was singular in his fearlessness: 'These things did not deter me. I
said, "Let us again face the winds and the seas, and swear not, but trust
to God"' (p. 115). If he seems heroic at times it is because he must try to
compensate for the racial and social odds against him: 'because he
might be excluded from the human race by many of his readers, Equiano
has to maintain his individuality in his work so that he may appear as a
human being'.[90] One incident epitomizes the degree to which his assimilation into the white world, and the (white) readers' sympathetic
identification, would determine the success or failure of his autobiography. While he was in Georgia, a woman wanted a burial service for her
child who had just died: 'not able to get any white person to perform it,
[she] applied to me for that purpose'. He finally consented and, before

'a great company both of white and black people', he 'performed the funeral ceremony to the satisfaction of all present' (p. 117).

According to both Costanzo and Andrews, *The Interesting Narrative* is unique among early black autobiographies because of the way Equiano manages to position himself firmly in the white world without watering down his goal of rousing efficacious sympathy for his own suffering and the suffering of all slaves. His endeavour represents the tremendous obstacles to sympathy that slave narrators had to overcome, for his 'situation as a black man living in a white world never allows him to identify and merge completely with the western community at large'.[91] Nevertheless, Equiano's is more successful than other early slave narratives in bridging the gap. After all, he was well aware of the disadvantages and advantages of western civilization: its technology and religion, as much as its slavery, made him who he is. Unlike other eighteenth- and early nineteenth-century black autobiographers, 'by defining himself as a bicultural man, he found the means to imagine his relationship to the world in terms that did not require his becoming either totally coopted or totally alienated from the Western socio-cultural order'.[92]

The way in which he cries out against slavery illustrates how he was part of both worlds. He complains of the folly, as well as the immorality, of the slave trade: 'how mistaken is the avarice even of the planters! Are slaves more useful by being thus humbled to the condition of brutes than they would be if suffered to enjoy the privileges of men?' (p. 73). As a member of white society he can argue against slavery from a practical, economic standpoint, even though as a former slave he cannot tolerate it on any grounds. Without mitigating his emotional pitch, he logically points out the inconsistencies in the thinking that perpetuates slavery: 'you stupefy them with stripes and think it necessary to keep them in a state of ignorance, and yet you assert that they are incapable of learning' (p. 73). It is interesting to note that early in the narrative, before he had gone to England, the narrator grouped himself with the slaves – 'Is it not enough that we are torn from our country and friends . . . ' (p. 32) – whereas after becoming Anglicized he identifies with both worlds and, as in the above passage, the slaves become 'they'. Even at this point, however, he does not group himself as a 'we' with whites. As Andrews observes, 'he was outsider and insider and somewhere in between'.[93]

Indeed, Andrews argues that Equiano 'used his bicultural perspective to write an analysis of the *process* of acculturation'.[94] Aware, therefore, that his success in fighting the slave trade depended on his success as an autobiographer, he likewise knew that the reader's sympathy was instrumental to both endeavours. He could not create the autobiographical self alone, but was reliant on the reader's willingness to embrace him as a human being and to be moved to respond in a concrete way for the melioration of all humanity. His narrative status as both Englishman and ex-slave allowed him to fashion a self at once bizarre and comforting to the reader. The prominent place of sympathy in society, a phenomenon dependent equally on similarity and difference, allowed his readers to participate in that self-creation.

At the outset of this chapter, I posited that the primary interest in all three autobiographies examined here is that they represent a challenge to sympathy. Shifting the locus of meaning from a purely referential notion of self to the realm of the psyhcological and moral imagination means that the autobiographer's life is allowed to assume new life in the imagination of the reader. In this way, Romantic autobiography becomes less a matter of narrative than an interactive phenomenon. *The Memoirs of the Life of Daniel Mendoza*, Mary Robinson's *Memoirs* and *The Interesting Narrative of the Life of Olaudah Equiano* are all works of the imagination designed for a readership – intended to create an image and an impression of the narrating self. The reader for whom these works achieve the greatest impact are those whose understanding and compassion are equally elicited, for it is when the intellectual and emotional faculties are seamlessly interwoven within the reader that the narrator and the reader become engaged in two sides of the same creative act. Reading these Romantic autobiographies demonstrates the crucial relationship between communication and creation, between creating and reading a life.

Notes

1. J.-J. Rousseau (1988), *Confessions*, J. M. Cohen (tr.), Harmondsworth: Penguin, 17.
2. J. Foster (1844), 'On a Man's Writing Memoirs of Himself', in *Essays on Decision of Character, & c.*, Hartford: S. Andrus, 4.
3. D. A. Stauffer (1941), *The Art of Biography in Eighteenth Century England*, Princeton: Princeton University Press, 134.
4. R. F. Baumeister (1986), *Identity: Cultural Change and the Struggle for Self*, New York: Oxford University Press, 64, 63.
5. Stauffer, *The Art*, 166.
6. Ibid., 166.
7. While widespread and illustrated across philosophical and literary discourse, this shift in emphasis was by no means either sudden or complete. Two works written in the first half of the nineteenth century betray the desire to cling to the notion of biography as a means of 'fixing' virtue: *An*

Essay on the Study and Composition of Biography (1813) by J. F. Stanfield, excerpts appear on pp. 60–71 in J. L. Clifford (ed.) (1962), *Being as an Art: Selected Criticism: 1560–1960*, New York: Oxford University Press; and Foster, 'On a man's'. Both point to 'the progress of human character' as being the only worthy subject matter of all biographical or autobiographical writing. Both writers clearly demonstrate a psychological interest – Foster asserts that one undertakes to write one's memoirs not 'to enumerate mere facts and events of life' but as a means of grasping the 'states of the mind' (p. 3). But for all their emphasis on the factors that go into the shaping of an individual mind, they reveal a fundamental wish to use the individual as a means of understanding human character in general. For Stanfield, 'the two great ends of biography are – to obtain a deeper insight into the principles of the human mind, and to offer examples to practical observation and improvement' (p. 66). The goals of writing and reading biography centre on self-improvement and generalization rather than understanding a unique personality for its own sake.

8. Stauffer, *The Art*, 180, 172, 268.
9. D. Marshall (1988), *The Surprising Effects of Sympathy: Marivaux, Diderot, Rousseau and Mary Shelley,* Chicago: University of Chicago Press, 168, 169.
10. P. M. Spacks (1976), *Imagining a Self: Autobiography and Novel in Eighteenth-Century England,* Cambridge, MA: Harvard University Press, 22.
11. Spacks, *Imagining*, 18, 20.
12. Ibid., 302, 310.
13. P. De Man (1979), 'Autobiography as De-Facement', *Modern Language Notes,* **94**, (5), December, 920.
14. G. Gusdorf (1980), 'Conditions and Limits of Autobiography', in J. Olney (tr. and ed.), *Autobiography: Essays Theoretical and Critical,* Princeton: Princeton University Press, 35.
15. J. V. Gunn (1982), *Autobiography: Toward a Poetics of Experience,* Philadelphia: University of Pennsylvania Press, 7.
16. Gunn, *Autobiography*, 23.
17. Ibid., 22.
18. Ibid., 8, 9. Elizabeth Bruss describes this process in terms remarkably similar to Gunn's 'displayed self': 'to be a "self" at all seems to demand that one display the ability to embrace, take in, one's own attributes and activities – which is just the sort of display language makes possible' (quoted in P. J. Eakin (1985), *Fictions in Autobiography: Studies in the Art of Self-Invention*, Princeton: Princeton University Press, 219).
19. Gunn, *Autobiography*, 20.
20. D. Stewart's (1956) *Preface to Empathy,* New York: Philosophical Library, 36, develops the notion of 'deliberate identification and consciousness of difference' as the 'two phases' of empathy. See also C. R. Rogers's (1951) notion of the 'as if' quality in *Client-Centered Therapy,* Boston: Houghton Mifflin.
21. Gunn, *Autobiography*, 21. See ch. 2 of *Autobiography* for more detailed discussion of Gadamer's 'fusion of horizons'.
22. Ibid., 9. For a more extensive discussion of the implications of *autos, bios* and *graphie*, and specifically of the 'shift of attention from *bios* to *autos* – from the life to the self –' (p. 19), see J. Olney's two essays in J. Olney

(ed.) (1980), *Autobiography: Essays Theoretical and Critical,* Princeton: Princeton University Press.
23. Eakin, *Fictions,* 209.
24. Ibid., 181.
25. Ibid., 190, 191.
26. Ibid., 276. Philippe Lejeune (1989) has convincingly argued that 'it is the nature of autobiography to create this illusion' of direct communication between autobiographer and reader in *On Autobiography,* K. Leary (tr. and ed.), with foreword by Paul John Eakin, Minneapolis: University of Minnesota Press, 233.
27. This is not, of course, a new concept; it is its application to autobiography which is fresh. Heidegger, for example, argued that truth resided *in* language, not *by* language: 'words and language are not wrappings in which things are packed for the commerce of those who write and speak. It is in words and language that things first come into being and are', in *Introduction to Metaphysics* (1953), as quoted by J. Stewart (1983), 'Interpretive Listening: An Alternative to Empathy', *Communication Education,* 32, October, 385. Stewart himself argues for the linguisticality of the self: 'Learning to speak does not mean learning to use a pre-existent tool for designating a world already somehow familiar to us; it means acquiring a familiarity and acquaintance with the world itself and how it confronts us' (p. 384).
28. Eakin, *Fictions,* 213–14.
29. Ibid., 220.
30. Ibid., 197. See D. Bleich (1978), *Subjective Criticism,* Baltimore: Johns Hopkins University Press.
31. D. Stewart, *Preface,* 154, 4.
32. R. Elbaz (1988), *The Changing Nature of the Self: A Critical Study of the Autobiographical Discourse,* London: Croom Hill, 6.
33. E. Beneviste (1971), *Problems in General Linguistics,* M. E. Meek (tr.), Coral Gables: University of Miami Press, 225.
34. J. Stewart, 'Interpretive Listening', 386.
35. Ibid., 389.
36. Ibid., 383.
37. Ibid., 382.
38. Ibid., 383; Elbaz, *The Changing,* 153.
39. R. C. Arnett and G. Nakagawa (1983), 'The Assumptive Roots of Empathic Listening: A Critique', *Communication Education,* 32, October, 372, 375.
40. R. L. Katz (1963), *Empathy: Its Nature and Uses,* New York: Free Press, 97.
41. B. J. Mandel, 'Full of Life Now', in J. Olney (ed.), *Autobiography: Essays Theoretical and Critical,* Princeton: Princeton University Press, 69.
42. P. Jay (1984), *Being in the Text: Self-Representation from Wordsworth to Roland Barthes,* Ithaca: Cornell University Press, 25.
43. Lejeune, *On Autobiography,* ix, 30.
44. Ibid., 233.
45. E. Bruss (1976), *Autobiographical Acts: The Changing Situation of a Literary Genre,* Baltimore: Johns Hopkins University Press, 26–7.
46. J. Olney, 'Autobiography and the Cultural Moment: A Thematic, Histori-

cal, and Bibliographical Introduction', in J. Olney (ed.), *Autobiography*, 24.

47. A. Margulies (1989), *The Empathic Imagination*, New York: W. W. Norton, 142–3.

48. Lejeune, *On Autobiography*, 14 (Regarding 'the identity ("identicalness") of the name (author-narrator-protagonist)', 'the autobiographical pact is the affirmation in the text of this identity, referring back in the final analysis to the name of the author on the cover').

49. Mandel, 'Full of Life Now', 55.

50. Ibid., 72. The idea of 'co-creation' frequently appears in autobiography theory. For Paul Jay autobiography is 'a narrative created in the present' (Jay, *Being in the Text*, 25), implying the reader's active part in the process. Bruce Mazlish makes it central to his psychoanalytical approach to the genre. 'We, as readers', he writes, 'can and must create [meanings] for ourselves out of the experiences that [the autobiographer] presents to us' (pp. 36–7). His notion of autobiography as 'binocular' entails the creation of two selves, the reader's and the author's, in the act of reading autobiography. Mandel stops short of using the text in this way as a tool for the reader's own self-analysis: B. Mazlish (1970), 'Autobiography and psychoanalysis: Between Truth and Self-Deception', *Encounter* 35, July–December, 28–37.

51. Mandel, 'Full of Life Now', 69.

52. In light of Mandel's inherently sympathetic approach, it is instructive to compare Mandel's account of his reading experience to psychologist Carl Rogers's description of the way the empathic therapist assists the client in communicating his story. The key, says Rogers, is 'to assume, in so far as he is able, the internal frame of reference of the client, to perceive the world as the client sees it, to perceive the client himself as he is seen by himself' (Rogers, *Client-Centered Therapy*, 29).

53. C. R. Rogers, as quoted in Stewart, 'Interpretive Listening', 380.

54. R. Pascal (1960), *Design and Truth in Autobiography*, London: Routledge and Kegan Paul, 59.

55. Margulies, *The Empathic*, 132, xii.

56. Bruss, *Autobiographical Acts*, 163.

57. Eakin, *Fictions*, 225, 227.

58. M. Buber (1965), *The Knowledge of Man: A Philosophy of the Interhuman*, M. Friedman and R. G. Smith (tr.), London: George Allen and Unwin.

59. J. Olney (1972), *Metaphors of Self: The Meaning of Autobiography*, Princeton: Princeton University Press, 30, 270.

60. D. Mendoza (1951), *The Memoirs of the Life of Daniel Mendoza*, with introduction by P. Magriel (ed.), London: B. T. Batsford. All subsequent citations are from this edition.

61. Not surprisingly, Mendoza's memory of losses is not as vivid as it is of successes. While he reports the loss to a fighter named Jackson as simply having 'terminated in his favour', it was in fact a sound and humiliating defeat in which Jackson 'grabbed the mop of hair' which Mendoza sported and 'held Mendoza where he wanted him, and pounded him at will' (p. 11).

62. Olney, *Metaphors*, 34.

63. M. Robinson (1894), *Memoirs of Mary Robinson*, from edition edited by

her daughter, with introduction and notes by J. F. Molloy, London: Gibbings. All subsequent citations are from this edition.

64. As an illustration of the extent to which Robinson's was a distinctly Romantic character, compare the following passage from Byron's *Manfred*, written 16 years after the publication of Robinson's *Memoirs*:

> From my youth upwards
> My spirit walked not with the souls of men,
> Nor looked upon the earth with human eyes;
> The thirst of their ambition was not mine,
> The aim of their existence was not mine;
> My joys, my griefs, my passions, my powers,
> Made me a stranger; though I wore the form
> I had no sympathy with breathing flesh. (II.ii.50–7)

See also Shelley's notion of the 'antitype' in his essay, 'On Love'.
65. Bruss, *Autobiographical Acts*, 13.
66. For a similar use of dialogue in portraying herself as a virtuous heroine besieged by villains, see *Memoirs*, 73–7.
67. Eakin, *Fictions*, 226.
68. Margulies, *The Empathic*, 142.
69. D. Stewart, *Preface*, 19.
70. O. Equiano (1967), *Equiano's Travels: His Autobiography: 'The Interesting Narrative of the Life of Olaudah Equiano or Gustavus Vassa the African'*, P. Edwards (abr. and ed.), New York: Frederick A. Praeger. All subsequent citations are from this edition unless otherwise indicated.
71. MS of Eighth Edition (Norwich: Printed for the Author, 1794), v.
72. A. Niemtzow (1982), 'The Problematic of Self in Autobiography: The Example of the Slave Narrative', in J. Sekora and D. T. Turner (eds), *The Art of Slave Narrative: Original Essays in Criticism and Theory*, Macomb, IL: Western Illinois University, 96.
73. MS of Eighth Edition (1794), viii.
74. Chinosole (1982), 'Tryin' to Get Over: Narrative Posture in Equiano's Autobiography', in Sekora and Turner, *The Art*, 53.
75. W. L. Andrews (1982), 'The First Fifty Years of the Slave Narrative', in Sekora and Turner, *The Art*, 8.
76. A. Costanzo (1987), *Surprizing Narrative: Olaudah Equiano and the Beginning of Black Autobiography*, New York: Greenwood Press, 15.
77. Chinosole, 'Tryin' to Get Over', 47, 47, 47–8.
78. Costanzo, *Surprizing Narrative*, 51.
79. P. Edwards, 'Introduction', xvii.
80. Elbaz believes that 'autobiography is a discourse not about the "I" but about a series of "he's"', it 'cannot allow for the presentification of the self'. In response to this refutation of 'the mystified consistency and continuity of the "I"' (Elbaz, *The Changing*, 11–12), Eakin argues that the unverifiability of the self does not necessarily prevent the autobiographer from rendering self-presence. However illusory, 'the voice of presence in the text' is at the heart of the reader's experience of successful autobiography (Eakin, *Fictions*, 277).
81. *Gentleman's Magazine* (1792), as quoted in Costanzo, *Surprizing Narrative*, 43.

82. R. Rosenblatt, 'Black Autobiography: Life as the Death Weapon', in Olney, *Autobiography*, 180.

83. Edwards, 'Introduction', xvii, xvi–xvii.

84. As quoted by Costanzo, *Surprizing Narrative*, 44, 43.

85. Ibid., 19, 32, 19.

86. On the relationship between altruism and sympathy, see M. L. Hoffman (1981), 'Is Altruism Part of Human Nature?', *Journal of Personality and Social Psychology*, 40, (1), 121–37, and L. Wispé (ed.) (1978), *Altruism, Sympathy and Helping: Psychological and Sociological Principles*, London: Academic Press.

87. Paul Jay, in summarizing De Man (1979), asserts that 'the action proper to autobiography . . . is not historical but rhetorical' (Jay, *Being in the Text*, 18).

88. Costanzo, *Surprizing Narrative*, 50.

89. Ibid., 33.

90. Ibid., 15, 66.

91. Ibid., 66.

92. Andrews, 'The First Fifty', 22.

93. Ibid., 22.

94. Ibid., 20.

CHAPTER FIVE

'I' to 'I': encountering the Other and the challenge to sympathy in the Romantic lyric

Oh, how I feel, just as I pluck the flower
  And stick it to my breast – words can't reveal;
But there are souls that in this lovely hour
  Know all I mean, and feel whate'er I feel.[1]

  ... (I speak bare truth,
As if to thee alone in private talk).[2]

Coleridge spoke for an entire generation of poets and readers when articulating his belief that poetry 'is purely human – all its materials are *from* the mind, and all the products are *for* the mind'.[3] By linking the mind from which poetry springs and the mind for which it is intended, he suggests the inherent reciprocity between poet and audience. It is a goal of this chapter to show that the English Romantics regarded the most 'appropriate' reader, and the one for whom poetry was written, as one capable of sympathy. As a result, the lyric poetry written between 1790 and 1850 is characterized by an intimacy and emotional intensity which, I will argue, stems from the assumption of an actively sympathetic reader. The detailed psychological states rendered and the extreme emotional states depicted are what stimulate readers' sympathetic imagination, often precisely because they pose a challenge to sympathy.

It is emotional content, rather than form or style, which characterizes the Romantic lyric. Writing in the *Eclectic Review* in 1816, Josiah Conder declared that 'poetry interests never as the simple record of events, but as it exhibits human feelings and develops human passions'.[4] Mill views lyric poetry as 'feeling confessing itself ... bodying itself forth in ... representations of the feeling in the exact shape in which it exists in the poet's mind'.[5] The giving of physical form to bare emotion ('bodying itself forth ... shape') suggests the reader's role within the Romantics' conception of poetry. Walter Scott confirms this notion in an essay in which he claims that all art represents the simultaneous effort to express, or embody, emotion and 'to communicate, as well as colours and words can do', those feelings to other minds.[6] In so far as 'communication' means not only imparting and conveying (ideas, images, thoughts, feelings) to another but also the interchange between two people, it aptly captures the way in which the Romantic lyric invites an intimate, flesh and blood connection with readers. Alexander Smith believed that poetry's expression of emotion could not be understood apart from its effect on the reader or listener. In his essay, 'The Philosophy of Poetry' (1835), Smith argues that poetry is the expression of emotion and it must 'transmit that feeling from one mind to another . . . creating a sympathetic participation of it in the mind of the hearer'.[7]

A key quality of the Romantic lyric, then, is that it excites, or 'bodies forth', a corresponding emotion in the reader. One reviewer, writing in 1814, describes as 'best' those artists who 'make us feel as well as see their work, and excite sympathy as well as admiration'.[8] James Montgomery frequently expressed a similar view, as in his review of Wordsworth's *Poems, in Two Volumes* (1807), in which he praises Wordsworth for 'awakening unknown and ineffable sensations in the hearts of his fellow-creatures'. Such poems as 'Tintern Abbey', he says, 'have taught us new sympathies'.[9] Emphasizing its subjective nature, Hegel understood the lyric as a sort of emotional meeting ground between poet and reader. In giving objective expression to his inner life, the poet aims 'to arouse and keep alive in the hearer the same sense and spirit, the same attitude of mind, and the like direction of thought'. Works 'are the more lyrical', he continues, 'the more they emphasize . . . the inner state of soul in which the poet tells his story and give us the whole circumstance in such a way that the poet's mood itself has a living echo out of them in us'.[10]

This 'living echo' is anything but a passive response. In order for the lyric to achieve its full impact, the reader's imagination must be moved to new and profound levels of activity. Hegel asserts that as readers 'we are not to contemplate this or that object from the outside but to be inwardly conscious of the heart which has put itself into it and so to be moved by that consciousness to have the same mode of feeling or meditation'.[11] According to Wordsworth, a poem can be correctly read and understood only through a partnership between poet and reader, in which understanding hinges on the reader (who 'cannot be carried like a dead weight') 'exert[ing] himself' and 'read[ing] with the feelings of the Author'.[12] '[T]he exertion of a co-operating power in the mind of the Reader' represents the only 'adequate sympathy'.[13] In so far as this co-operative, interactive process extends the limits of subjective awareness into the unknown of the Other, the centre of sympathetic activity is the imagination.

Raised in the rural village of Helpstone, John Clare felt a deep-seated need for communion, or co-operation, with the natural world. His lyrics manifest a similar need for the reader's co-operating faculties – namely, imagination and feeling. 'Pastoral Poesy' is about the reciprocal relationship between poet and nature, and suggests that reader and poet must also achieve an interchange of feeling. The phrase, 'social loneliness', is a paradox which encapsulates what the speaker in 'Pastoral Poesy' finds in nature.[14] He describes his surroundings:

> Unruffled quietness hath made
>   A peace in every place,
> And woods are resting in their shade
>   Of social loneliness.

'True poesy', according to the speaker, lies not in words but images which 'stir' hearts. Language is efficacious only if understood, and nature, which speaks in:

> A language that is ever green,
>   That feelings unto all impart,

epitomizes the potential for expressing and communicating feeling. Just as natural beauty in a sense would not exist without appreciative beholders – for beauty is a judgement – so the language of feeling is meaningful only to the degree that it brings a corresponding 'image to the mind' of listeners and readers. The concept of 'self-creating joy' embodies the paradox on which the entire poem rests. Nature itself creates the joy it imparts, just as the poet is the author and source of his feeling; but the listener and reader participate in the creation of the pleasure that 'stirs' them in so far as they contribute a sympathetic sensibility to the encounter. This exchange between nature and poet, poet and reader, depends on silence and solitude – the solitude of nature and of reading. Paradoxically, only in solitude can one know genuine sympathy – with nature and with the Other:

> I feel where'er I go
> A silence that discourses more
>   That any tongue can do.

The solitude of nature inspires the poet, yet what the poet creates springs from within. Only in lyric utterance can these 'silences' be proclaimed and the speaker's 'elevated' feelings expressed and shared. Only in lyric solitude can reader and poet coexist in intimacy.

The speaker illustrates this interactive dynamic by a poet's response to a storm, which:

> Is music, ay, and more indeed
>   To those of musing mind
> Who through the yellow woods proceed
>   And listen to the wind.

With 'musing mind' the poet 'meets' the storm 'as some strange melody'. Using the poet's active mind as a model, the speaker wants such oneness with the world around him as to 'impress' his 'own heart' on every experience, so that 'poesy's self' becomes 'a dwelling joy/Of humble quietness' within him. 'Poesy's self' is not identical with the poet, but corresponds to a mode of existence in which subject and object move into and out of separateness and unity. The speaker envisions a merging of his creative faculties and emotions with the sources of inspiration – nature – thereby in effect rendering the inanimate world alive, or giving it a 'self'. So, too, the poet's language of feeling imparts feeling to the sympathetic reader, who is capable of at once being moved by the poem and half-creating it. The reader, too, must 'listen to the wind' in order to transform the poet's language of nature into the 'strange music' of feelings. By virtue of such active listening, the reader likewise trans-forms the lyric utterance into the language of human relationship.

For Romantic poets, the lyric achieves its full impact and meaning only when its emotional and psychological content is produced afresh within the reader. This activity not only yields insight and understanding; it likewise gives pleasure. This is why for Archibald Alison, in his *Essay on the nature and principles of taste* (1790), the connection between emotion and taste is paramount. In demonstrating the interconnection between pleasure and the exercise of the imagination, Alison is careful to distinguish between 'Simple Emotions', which are produced by any quality felt to be beautiful or sublime, and 'Emotions of Taste', which represent a more profound kind of emotion: 'Whenever ... [a] train of thought, or [an] exercise of the imagination is produced, we are con-scious of an emotion of a higher and more pleasing kind.'[15] Although his comments do not pertain exclusively to lyric poetry, they are espe-cially illuminating with respect to the lyric. For, according to Alison, successful poetry links the reader's mind and heart: it acts as a catalyst for feeling in so far as it excites the imagination. The power of poetry lies in how the reader's imagination is affected, 'beyond what the scene or description immediately before him can of themselves excite'. The poem or 'object itself appears only to serve as a hint to awaken the imagination, and to lead it through every analogous idea ... It is ... when we are carried on by our conceptions, not guiding them, that the deepest emotions ... are felt; that our hearts swell with feelings'.[16]

Francis Jeffrey confirms this view of reading as an emotional and intellectual interaction in his essay on Thomas Campbell:

> The highest delight which poetry produces, does not arise from the mere passive perception of the images or sentiments which it presents to the mind; but from the excitement which is given to its own internal activity, and the character which is impressed on the train of its spontaneous conceptions.[17]

Reading is not guided or forced, but led by the ideas and feelings stimulated by the poem:

> the writers who possess the greatest powers of fascination ... [are those] who most successfully impart their own impulse to the current of our thoughts and feelings ... The object is, to awaken in our minds a train of kindred emotions, and to excite our imaginations to work out for themselves a tissue of pleasing or impressive conceptions.[18]

The successful lyric establishes a bond with the reader by stimulating the imagination such that the reader is moved to reproduce for himself the poet's emotional state. 'The chief delight of poetry consists, not so much in what it directly supplies to the imagination, as in what it enables it to supply to itself ... in setting it agoing, by touching its internal springs and principles of activity.'[19] Like Alison, Jeffrey considers this psychological *movement* (a metaphor constantly reinforced by such terms as 'train', 'agoing', 'internal springs' and 'activity') to be poetry's 'highest and most delightful effect'.[20]

For Romantic readers, the poet and the 'I' of a poem were identical. Successfully reading a lyric poem therefore demanded nothing short of the reader's relating to the poet as one human being to another. This was part of what Richard Altick has shown to be a larger movement in the Romantic period, during which 'the literary work ceased to be an artistic object and was transformed into the person of its creator'.[21] Thus one critic of *The Excursion* (by no means the most personal or lyric utterance of the period) could praise Wordsworth for allowing 'such familiar and complete access to his heart'.[22] According to M. H. Abrams, 'the widespread use of literature as an index ... to personality was a product of the characteristic aesthetic orientation of the early nineteenth century'.[23] This shift, Donald Goellnicht observes, 'led to a poetry more private, introspective, and subjective, despite the fact that it was disseminated to a larger reading public'. Unlike the situation during most of the eighteenth century, when a poet spoke to the severely limited sector of society who were educated and to whose 'shared foundation of knowledge and attitudes' the poet could confidently appeal, in the early nineteenth century 'the democratizing of education and higher literacy rates' shifted the focus in the reading of lyric poetry away from the universal, the commonly held values, to the individual, the particular and the idiosyncratic.[24] The inner life of feeling, rather than social attitudes or opinions, formed the basis for first person effusion. Consequently, while Gray's 'Elegy' and Goldsmith's 'Deserted Village' can be seen as expressions of a particular speaker, they are by no means akin to the complex self-exploratory expression of the 'Immortality Ode' or 'Frost at Midnight'.

The intense personalizing and psychologizing of the creative process transformed reading into a relationship-building activity, and therefore one grounded in the absolutely unique character of the poet/speaker and reader. As one reader put it in 1816, 'the only converse to be held with a poet's mind, is that of sympathy. The feelings of the reader must be strung to a pitch in unison with those of the poet himself, or they will not vibrate in reply'.[25] Romantic readers felt they were engaging in a dialogic relationship with a person, not a 'text'. Hazlitt recognized that reading poetry engaged the entire self in an active process. 'The light of poetry', he wrote, 'brings every moment of our being ... in startling review before us.'[26] '[S]tartling' emphasizes the Romantic lyric's unusual, often disarmingly revealing character. What Francis Jeffrey praised in Crabbe's poetry – its illustration of 'the eternal and universal standard of truth and nature, which every one is knowing enough to recognise'[27] – was to the Romantic sensibility inimical to lyric poetry because it is impossible to form a personal relationship with the 'universal'.

In fact, sympathy is most engaged by the unique and idiosyncratic precisely because it presents a greater challenge, particularly when it takes the form of 'startling' emotional and psychological detail. Few poets manifest this quality more explicitly than Clare. Because his lyrics are so personal, they invite sympathy; because they are so raw in emotional and psychological pain, they challenge sympathy. Clare had an unusual fear of falling into obscurity, of losing his sense of self. His lyrics served, in a way, as an antidote to such loss: 'A very good commonplace counsel', he wrote,

> is ... always to keep self in the first place lest all the world who always keeps us behind it should forget us all together – forget not thyself and the world will not forget thee – forget thyself and the world will willingly forget thee till thou art nothing but a living-dead man dwelling among shadows and falsehood.[28]

After being committed to an asylum at the age of 44, according to Geoffrey Grigson, Clare 'was cut away from the stimulus or comfort of the few friends of his Helpstone days who had been in communion with him'. His 'emotional and spiritual starvation' forced him to rely exclusively on the comfort and companionship of nature and his own imagination.[29]

The poems of this period are characterized by expressions of wretchedness and desolation so blunt as to be at once painful and compelling, such as in the lines:

> My mind is dark and fathomless, and wears
> The hues of hopeless agony and hell,

and

> Life is to me a dream that never wakes;
>   Night finds me on this lengthening road alone.

Such lines present a challenge to the reader's sympathy – and hence to
the escape from solitude which Clare so desperately sought – because
the emotions and psychological states rendered are so severe and stark.
Part of the reason why contemporary readers could so readily sympathize with these poems was that they were aware of Clare's having been
committed to an asylum. As a result, his frequent use of self-referential
language and personal pronouns would have had a powerful impact on
readers' sympathy toward the 'I' they identified with Clare himself.
Lines such as:

> My life hath been one chain of contradictions,
> Madhouses, prisons, whore-shops –

have the effect of autobiography on the sympathetic reader, for whom
Clare wrote out of the depths of his isolation.

Clare's best lyrics demonstrate that he implicitly recognized the interconnection between personal identity and human relationship. Both 'I
Am' and 'John Clare', lyrics steeped in singularity and solitude, ultimately affirm the self precisely by virtue of the speaker's absolute alienation. Rooted in stark self-revelation, they demand to be read with
intimacy and meditation. In 'John Clare' the speaker equates emotion
with awareness: 'I feel I am, I only know I am.' Yet in the next line he
characterizes his life as 'dull and void'. 'Dull' denotes 'unfeeling' and
'depressed . . . without life or spirit', which contradicts both the central
assertion, 'I am', and the poignant sensibility displayed by the speaker
in reflecting on his life.[30] '[E]arth's prison', he claims, 'destroyed' his
'soaring thoughts' and led him to the point of absolute emptiness and
alienation. This was not always the case:

> I was a being created in the race
> Of men, disdaining bounds of place and time . . .
> A soul unshackled like eternity.

At first the poem seems riddled with contradiction: for instance, how
can a mortal creature disdain the bounds of time and place? The contrast between three disparaging references to 'earth' and two positive
references to 'soul' suggests that the way to understand the poem is to
understand the speaker as a man who sees himself as more spirit than
body, but who has lost his spirit. The final line, 'But now I only know I
am, that's all', plainly renders his desperate state of mind: he is nearly
(but not quite) suicidal. Lacking spirit, he lacks inspiration and feels an
inner void. Yet this unalloyed emptiness contains the seeds of its own

anodyne. For its very starkness – 'that's all' – at once challenges and invites the reader's sympathetic entry into the 'void' in the form of shared emptiness and grief, and hope that the spirit in him/her may once again soar 'like a thought sublime'.

In 'I Am', too, the speaker's hope lies solely in the unearthly nature of his being, but he bewails less the corrupting influence of earth's 'vain and soul-debasing thrall' than the state of dereliction and failure into which he has been cast. He conceives of his identity in terms of others: 'I am: yet what I am none cares or knows.' Hence a great demand is placed on the sympathetic reader who is willing to disprove the poem's assertion that 'none cares'. This first line recalls the passage quoted earlier in which Clare counsels 'self-identity' in order that one not be forgotten by others. In that context, and in contrast to 'John Clare' in which the statement 'I am' is disparagingly yoked with 'that's all', in this poem 'I am' represents a defiant assertion:

> And yet I am, and live with shadows tost
> Into the nothingness of scorn and noise,
>   Into the living sea of waking dreams,
> Where there is neither sense of life nor joys,
>   But the vast shipwreck of my life's esteems.

The poem contravenes the speaker's purely subjective identity as 'self-consumer of my woes'. In the speaker's disordered experience of those 'dearest' to him having become 'strange' and of longing 'for scenes where man has never trod' – in short, having to seek solace in the unfamiliar, the Other – the poem places enormous demands on the reader's sympathy. In both poems, the speaker's emptiness cannot be filled, but only shared for a time by the reader. Solitude and relationship are linked, as the speaker's expression of emptiness creates space for the reader to participate in that grief by intensely imagining it and repro-ducing it in him/herself.

Like Clare's lyrics, Shelley's 'Stanzas: Written in Dejection, near Na-ples' is most noteworthy for its element of apparent contradiction. Steeped in solitude and isolation, it nevertheless hinges on human rela-tionship; despite being at the very extremes of emotional and psycho-logical experience, it nevertheless engages readers' sympathy on the most basic level. In contrast to the soothing harmony all around him –

>   Like many a voice of one delight,
>   The winds, the birds, the ocean floods,
> The City's voice itself, is soft like Solitude's –[31]

the speaker 'sit[s] upon the sands alone', longing in vain for sympa-thetic human connection:

> How sweet! did any heart now share in my emotion.

He describes his life and his spirit as utterly desolate and joyless:

> Alas! I have nor hope nor health,
>   Nor peace within nor calm around.

Like the careworn speaker in 'I Am', he sees death as a sweet release from his pitiful state:

> I could lie down like a tired child,
>   And weep away the life of care
>   Which I have borne and yet must bear,
> Till death like sleep might steal on me.

His attitude is less bitter and tormented than it is detached and clear-minded: inured to suffering to the point of being all but numb ('despair itself is mild'), he has resigned himself to death because at least in death he might once again *feel*. His images of the experience of death are ghastly and vivid:

> ... I might feel in the warm air
> My cheek grow cold, and hear the sea
> Breathe o'er my dying brain its last monotony.

It is almost as if he comes alive in the process of imagining his death, a phenomenon which suggests what happens to the reader's sympathy. The Romantics believed that reading a lyric successfully demands that one sympathetically imagine the speaker's experience; in this poem, therefore, one can either gloss over the speaker's unusually intense state of mind – thereby failing to 'read' the poem at all – or one can imagine his extreme isolation and his slow death in all its detail. Precisely because the experience is so unfamiliar, the imagination is vigorously engaged in an effort to forge a sympathetic connection with the speaker – that is, to understand the speaker's feelings within the context of his life experience and of one's own.

Sympathizing with such extreme isolation and despair, then, is actually pleasurable – more pleasurable, I would argue, than sympathizing with another's joy or success. This is not because sympathy exclusively 'means' identifying with painful emotions: it does not. Rather, it is because the act of bridging two unfamiliar worlds, or consciousnesses, produces its own pleasure, partly out of the belief that a lyric expresses actual experiences and is written in order to be felt and understood by another. According to Alison, even those who indulge in contemplating 'gloomy or melancholy thought [and images] find a pleasure which more than compensates for all the pain which the character of their thoughts may bring'.[32] The 'emotion of taste' evoked by successful poetry, as a deeper and 'higher' species of pleasure, provides 'an almost inexhaustible source either of solemn or cheerful meditation'.[33] What is important, as Jeffrey likewise believed, is that the reader's mind and heart be active in working through the 'tissue of pleasing or impressive conceptions'.[34] Pain can be as 'impressive' as pleasure; indeed, both Alison and Jeffrey would argue, it can produce its own kind of pleasure when the sympathetic imagination is thoroughly engaged. Thus, though lyrics such as Clare's and Shelley's pose a challenge to sympathy, for Romantic readers lyric poetry is satisfying only to the degree that the imagination is actively engaged in the effort to feel, understand and even reproduce the poet's experience. In a sense, sympathy is only truly itself when there is a challenge to the imagination; it cannot take place without the existence of a distinction, or gap, between self and Other.

The way in which Romantic writers and readers on the whole envisioned the reader's participation in a poem's subjectivity demanded active self-involvement on the part of the reader's own subjective experience and emotion. By grounding itself in sympathy, Romantic hermeneutics advocates a reciprocal process of creating meaning. Romantic metaphors for the reader's role in lyric resonate with many twentieth-century definitions of sympathy which turn on the notion of vibration and reverberation, a musical metaphor especially apt for the lyric. Recent studies of sympathy illustrate that the interrelationship between persons similarly demands, as Martin Buber puts it, 'an intensive stirring of one's being into the life of the other'.[35] Sympathy is not self-abnegation. Hence Barbara Herrnstein Smith's notion of reading as a cognitive encounter with oneself: 'the interpretation of poetry often becomes the occasion for our recognition and acknowledgment of otherwise inaccessible feelings'.[36] Robert Katz claims that in empathizing 'we reverberate to the emotions of the other person'.[37] According to Katz, 'when we have sympathetic feelings in our encounters with others, we become even more sharply aware of ourselves'.[38] Describing the psychoanalytic dynamic, Theodor Reik says that the therapist must 'vibrate unconsciously in the rhythm of the other person's impulse'.[39] As the Romantics understood, the process of knowing and understanding another is inseparable from knowing oneself.

Because the mode of inquiry was personal rather than textual, the speaking 'I' of the lyric was not menacing to Romantic readers, but corresponded to an actual person reaching out to each individual reader. In so far as the lyric 'I' implies the presence of a listening Other ('you, the reader'), far from threatening to absorb the reader it represents an emptiness – on both personal and aesthetic levels – to be entered into by the reader through sympathy. The lyric is conducive to a shared ego, rather than imposing a transcendental one. However, far from dissolving all difference between speaker and reader, the Romantic lyric celebrates it, for the sympathetic dynamic on which it depends hinges on the distinction between self and Other. Psychoanalysts Beres and Arlow posit that in order for the therapist successfully to understand the analysand his/her identification must be 'transient'. 'The empathizer preserves his separateness from the object' in order that he may 'go on to interpretation and insight', the concluding stages of the empathic process. 'The capacity to separate self from nonself' is equally critical for patient and therapist as for 'all human interaction'. The empathic process, conclude Beres and Arlow, 'finds its highest social expression in the shared aesthetic experience of the artist and his audience'.[40]

Part of the shared experience is a mutual need for separation, or distance, in order to achieve understanding. For the poet it is the externalizing of emotion into language, and for the reader it is sympathizing with those emotions while maintaining a distinct identity. In an article comparing psychoanalysis and the creative process, Beres argues that both poet and analysand must employ a 'synthetic activity' which takes place at a remove from the 'chaos' of actual experience. For poet and analysand alike, there must be a 'distance . . . between the experience and its contemplation or analysis. Without this distance there is only the momentary relief or discharge of energies, the irruption of instinctual impulses – there is not the insight, imaginative awareness which constitutes the true content of the aesthetic experience or the analytic revelation'.[41] One way of looking at this distance in terms of Romantic lyric is that while the lyric is experienced as a natural utterance, it is actually 'fictive discourse', or 'a representation of an act of self-expression'.[42] As such, this process corresponds to what Wordsworth describes as the distillation period in which raw emotion must be 'contemplated' prior to 'successful composition'. The poem itself, Wordsworth avers, renders an emotion 'kindred' to the original and one which 'does itself actually exist in the mind'.[43] According to Anne Williams, the lyric 'I' provides an 'air of reality', ensuring that, whether the poem is an unmediated utterance, as the Romantics often understood it, or the representation of actual feeling, the reader's sympathetic process is in no way hindered. 'It is as if the "I" were an empty space in the world of the text which the reader irresistibly enters.' Once 'empathy is established, the speaker's language temporarily becomes our language, his experience ours'.[44]

Along with the need to 'externalize' emotion, according to Beres, the other component of the poet's and analysand's 'act of creation' is the need to communicate with a sympathetic listener. In a psychoanalytic version of what Schleiermacher meant when he said that 'every act of understanding is the reverse of an act of speaking',[45] Beres argues that the mere presence of the analysand implies the presence of the analyst. So, too, the lyric speaker implies a listening Other, or reader, whose sympathetic activity makes meaningful the spoken (or written) expression of feeling. As Beres puts it, 'it is an established psychoanalytic dictum that whatever the analysand says or does in the analytic session has reference to the analyst and even with these unformed productions the analysand is in communication with the analyst, whether on a verbal or nonverbal level'.[46] To comprehend 'unformed productions' and 'nonverbal' signs, an interactive approach relies on a decidedly unscientific kind of subtlety and intimacy which echoes Romantic hermeneutics. Barbara Hardy paints a strikingly similar parallel between the lyric and actual relationships: 'in the life we live outside poems feeling is not always articulate, but can also work through touch, gesture and look. Lyric can get close to such silences'.[47] If, as psychologist Gregory Siomopoulos puts it, the 'transmission of emotion' is 'the most human kind of communication', then the Romantic lyric 'may be viewed as a developmentally advanced edition of the primordial sharing situation'.[48] Analogous to the profound dialogue and relationship which occurs in psychotherapy, the Romantic lyric can be understood as 'a mutual communication experience'.[49]

Consequently, while Romanticism is often understood as an effort to dissolve the boundaries between the mind and the external world – to launch a frontal attack on the dualism of self and Other – the 'Other Romanticism', according to Paul Privateer, 'underscores the instability of the "autonomous self"' by pointing to its dependence on the sympathetic Other. This voice within Romantic literature says that 'the power of the Romantic imagination is evident not only in what it creates and orders but also in all its dialogic forms, in all the contradictions, apparent meaninglessness, disruptions, silences, absences ...'.[50] Along the same lines, Tillotama Rajan sees the attempt to 'decenter' its own discourse as a powerful element of the Romantic movement. This is particularly problematic in the lyric, traditionally taken to be a purely subjective, univocal effusion. In the drama, writes Rajan, 'the presence of the other' is 'an explicit condition' and 'makes us aware that all utterance is incipiently dramatic: a communication to an other ... which forces the language of the self to pass through an external detour and thus to be decentered'. In the same way, the monological notion of the lyric is an illusion, since the reader is not merely an echo within the poem but a person who exists outside the poem. Thus Coleridge's attempt in his conversation poems to 'turn monological effusion into dialogue' or Shelley's use of the lyric in drama exemplifies 'a larger movement in Romanticism toward making the lyric interdiscursive'.[51]

It is in part the instability of the autonomous self which leads to dialogic interplay between poet and reader, to a sharing of the burden of creating meaning and the lyric self. I would argue that this dialogic element of Romanticism actually manifests itself most efficaciously in the lyric, and that what Rajan keenly identifies as Romantic poetry's 'attempt to delyricize discourse' can be understood as a desire to empower the reader by giving him a share in the subjective creative process. Situating the subjective voice 'in a more objective space' (as we saw with psychotherapy in earlier chapters), makes the creative process dynamic by making the sympathizing reader a co-creator.[52] According to Tzvetan Todorov, Romantic poetry favours symbol over allegory because while allegory 'transmits meaning', symbol's meaning is discovered 'indirectly', 'only in a secondary phase' through the reflective medium of 'the mind of the receiver'. The 'valorization' of 'process' or 'becoming' over 'being', Todorov implies, demands an active and sympathetic reader.[53] In this way, Goellnicht demonstrates that Keats anticipated many of the ideas of reader-response criticism, advocating the 'removal of the author from a position of authority' and believing that 'the reader acts as cocreator of the work, with the reader's imagination supplying the part of the text only implied but not written'. Neither 'a fixed, closed entity' nor a dominant, all-absorbing ego, the poem, 'acted upon by the reader, becomes a flowing texture . . . a process of individual self-discovery for the reader as for the poet'.[54]

To the Romantic sensibility, the dark regions of singularity – epitomized by solitude and alienation – are insatiably attractive. Wordsworth was deeply fascinated by the singular – extreme individuality – and the lyric subject's encounter with the unfamiliar, the Other. Such seminal encounters, he felt, provided a basis for the 'process of individual self-discovery' described above. The widespread desire to know another human being for his or her own sake was new in the Romantic period. As Foucault argues in *The Order of Things* (1966), 'it is the presence of man as a concept that distinguishes the beginning of a new *episteme* in the nineteenth century'.[55] Hence in Wordsworth's poetry epistemology and ontology often merge as knowledge of another becomes intertwined with self-revelation. Often the lyric speaker is so inexplicably moved by a relatively brief experience with another human being – whom he does not otherwise know well – that that Other becomes a lasting part of the speaker's consciousness: 'Resolution and Independence', the blind beggar episode in *The Prelude*, and 'The Ruined Cottage' are only a few of many such instances in Wordsworth's *œuvre*. Focusing specifically on three short lyrics in which the speaker is mysteriously touched and changed by an ostensibly unremarkable figure ('She Dwelt Among the Untrodden Ways', 'Stepping Westward', and 'The Solitary Reaper'), I hope to show that the event hinges on an act of sympathy. The speaker's transformation of the utterly insignificant into the strange and noteworthy simultaneously transforms the speaker himself by virtue of extraordinary emotional and psychological activity. Mover and moved, the speaker engages in reciprocal relationship, if only momentarily, with these strangers. Briefly shifting the focus of our analysis from the reader's sympathy with the speaker to the speaker's own sympathetic encounter with another serves to highlight the potentially problematic nature of the sympathetic relationship between reader and lyric subject.

'She Dwelt Among the Untrodden Ways' illustrates an experience of the Other as simultaneously alien and compelling – engaging, at least in part, *because* elusive. According to the speaker's testimony, the 'Maid' was at once ordinary and unique: she was undistinguished, yet luminous. Her paths were so remote as to be considered 'untrodden' altogether.[56] And her life could not objectively be called remarkable for she was praised by none and loved by 'very few'. The poem, however, is about the capacity for subjective feeling to overturn the standards of objective judgement and transform impression into understanding. The speaker's description of her is anything but the conventional lover's panegyric to his beloved. The second stanza:

> A violet by a mossy stone
> Half hidden from the eye!
> – Fair as a star, when only one
> Is shining in the sky,

paints a portrait of enigmatic beauty and character. This object of his affection – and wonder – was not dazzling to him, but 'half hidden'. She did not stand out among a starry sky, but rather was like a single star. Both metaphors indicate one who provoked meditation rather than awe or desire, one whose value can be appreciated not through comparison but by quiet observation.

The only use of present tense in the poem comes in the penultimate line: that she '*is* in her grave' (emphasis mine) suggests that for the speaker her death carries perpetual possibility for his relationship to her. His painful experience of Lucy as dead and gone confirms her Otherness when alive, and so in a sense keeps her present to him. According to Buber, sympathy is 'a bold swinging – demanding the most intensive stirring of one's being – into the life of the other'.[57] Just so, the sympathy which prompted the speaker's awareness and reflection while she 'lived unknown' to others likewise moves and 'stirs' him at her death. 'The difference' which serves as the measure of his grief is commensurate with his understanding of her 'difference' – her singularity – as quintessentially separate and Other, though sympathy granted him brief excursions beyond the barriers of subjectivity. Thus the quality which makes her at once obscure and elusive provides the very basis for the speaker's desire to know her and his appreciation for her unique identity.

Far from being a straightforward means to insight and understanding, sympathy can be an experience of darkness with brief moments of illuminating affirmation. Like the sojourning speaker in 'Stepping Westward', the reader of lyric must be capable of imaginative excursions beyond his own subjective experience – 'in a strange land'. The darkness inherent in such encounters is transformed by simple human interconnection into a visionary landscape capable of 'leading him on':

> the greeting . . . seemed to give me spiritual right
> To travel through that region bright.

The 'sound' of her voice, mentioned three times, carries its 'echo' in his mind as he continues his journey:

> Its power was felt; and while my eye
> Was fixed upon the glowing Sky,
> The echo of the voice enwrought
> A human sweetness with the thought
> Of travelling through the world that lay
> Before me in my endless way.

The spoken word has power to move – that is, to evoke emotion as well as to inspire one in a pilgrimage. This characteristic Romantic yearning, the notion of being on a lifelong spiritual journey through a 'wildish' or 'heavenly destiny', inspired equally the processes of writing and reading poetry. Sympathy links speaker and listener, making foreboding conditions 'bright' and 'glowing' and rendering a stranger's remark a mark of 'human sweetness'.

Sound plays a central role in 'The Solitary Reaper', in which the speaker shows listening to be a profound link between distinct individuals – a bridge from the purely subjective to the realm of understanding and fellow-feeling. The first stanza emphasizes solitude: the 'solitary Highland Lass' is 'single', 'by herself' and 'alone'. So engaged by the young woman that he is brimming with emotion, the speaker exhorts the reader to 'Behold' and 'listen!' and at any rate to maintain a reverence for her solitude: 'Stop here, or gently pass!' The only way to understand her, the speaker seems to be saying, is to meet her as she herself is: in quiet meditation. Although singing, she is lost in feelingful thought. Listening 'motionless and still', the speaker is nevertheless psychologically active. He merges his meditative silence with her meditative song, speculating and longing to understand it:

> Perhaps the plaintive numbers flow
> For old, unhappy, far-off things,
> And battles long ago:

> Or is it some more humble lay,
> Familiar matter of today?
> Some natural sorrow, loss, or pain,
> That has been, and may be again?

Whatever its particular meaning, he feels that it must spring from grief. Yet he experiences it as a 'welcome' and 'thrilling' break in the silence. Despite the painful feeling he gets, he derives pleasure from the encounter because he recognizes that what takes place in passing has sparked a more enduring sense of understanding and interconnectedness with the young woman. Moreover, this peculiar kind of pleasure, as Jeffrey and Alison describe it, stems from the heightened activity of, and even challenge to, the imagination.

Sympathy with unpleasant or painful emotion as 'The Solitary Reaper' illustrates, can be pleasurable because the speaker's understanding is not a result of analysis but a product of sympathetic listening. Schleiermacher's hermeneutics centres around his equation of interpretation and understanding. 'The success of an act of interpretation depends', he wrote, as much on 'one's ability for knowing people' as on 'linguistic competence'.[58] As communication psychologist John Stewart conceives it, 'language – or more accurately "languaging" – is a mode or medium of human be-ing; it is not a tool or system we use but a way we be who we are'.[59] As a consequence, the listener must be attuned less to a hidden meaning behind another's words than to the meaning which emerges and is developed at that moment by virtue of the listening dynamic. The reaper's solitary labour and the speaker's own wandering are interconnected, therefore, not so much by the singing as by his response to it – inquiring, reverent, receptive. The speaker's sympathy is what transforms the reaper's 'languaging' into meaningful communication and temporarily unites them.

Although the encounter involves no verbal exchange (as, for example, in 'Stepping Westward'), the experience is no less dialogic or inspiring. Nor is it silent, for her 'melancholy strain' fills the speaker's heart such that it seems 'the Vale profound is overflowing with the sound'. Her song is what captures his attention; the desire to understand it is what haunts him. Although he knows her song will end, she sang 'As if her song could have no ending'; and although he must eventually move on:

> The music in my heart I bore,
> Long after it was heard no more.

Her lyrical strain communicates with him by virtue of his sympathetic presence, a model for what must be the reader's simultaneously receptive and active attitude. Whether or not he actually understands the song is less important than that he reciprocates the woman's meditative attitude.

What is uniquely Romantic about these Wordsworth lyrics is that the simple and unremarkable encounter excites the speaker's (sympathetic) imagination to a profound degree, revealing the extraordinary complexity of his inner life of feeling and reflection. Encountering the Other presents one with the possibility for understanding. Only by listening – and 'reading' (literally and figuratively) – with one's whole being can the stranger be transformed from object into subject, and oneself from observer (or reader) into co-participant. As Reik has discovered in conducting psychotherapy, genuine sympathy entails bringing one's entire emotional and psychological 'reservoir' into play and, frequently, feeling pain may be the only way to achieve an understanding of another person. According to Reik, 'to spare ourselves pain sometimes involves sparing ourselves psychological insight'[60] and the fruits of human relationship. All three Wordsworth poems end by reaffirming the enduring power of the Other to affect and effect the speaker. But however profound a 'difference' the other person made in his life, in each poem the speaker is left to confront his sole, individual self. Similarly, the reader enters and feels the lyric experience, and then re-emerges to reflect and interpret and contextualize. In this way, the Romantic lyric enacts the very process it invites.

Coleridge's 'Dejection: An Ode' epitomizes the Romantic lyric's profound affirmation of the primacy of feeling. Yet the poem hinges on, and is inspired by, the very opposite: the failure of the imagination and of feeling. What disturbs the speaker is having sight without insight, hearing without inspiration, experiencing the sensual without the emotional. Indeed, sight and sound figure prominently in the poem, suggesting that there are two types of sense: the kind which the speaker literally sees and hears, and a deeper illumination, or 'glory' – the 'sweet voice', the 'luminous mist' – springing from within the depths of human passion. It is the loss of this latter species of awareness which the speaker mourns. As we will see, however, the 'dejection' engulfing the speaker is precisely what infuses the poem with the very quality he longs to regain.

The opening stanza locates the poet in a state of anticipation: the swollen, 'dull' clouds and 'tranquil' atmosphere parallel his own 'dull pain', that mental state in which he awaits the 'rain and squally blast'.[61] Highlighted by the juxtaposition of the actual calm and the imagined storm, ambivalence underlies the opening lines, as the poet questions the very value of his lyric utterance, his

> Aeolian lute,
> Which better far were mute. (ll. 7–8)

He passionately wishes for the storm to transport him from his lethargy:

> oh! that . . .
> Those sounds which oft have raised me, whilst they awed,
> And sent my soul abroad,
> Might now perhaps their wonted impulse give,
> Might startle this dull pain, and make it move and live! (ll. 15–20)

In movement is life, he seems to suggest: accustomed to inspiration through communion with nature, the poet now feels bereft because unmoved. It is not the weather so much as his own lifeless spirit which oppresses him. And it is not the nature of the feeling so much as its intensity which he equates with being alive: 'startle' recalls Hazlitt's use of 'startling' to emphasize the lyric's often disarmingly stark depiction of feeling. Just so, to 'startle' a 'dull pain' implies making the pain more sharply felt.

The second stanza describes in forceful detail the tormented emotional state which, as we saw in the first stanza, causes him to doubt the very enterprise of writing this poem:

> A grief without a pang, void, dark, and drear,
> A stifled, drowsy, unimpassioned grief,
> Which finds no natural outlet, no relief,
> In word, or sigh, or tear –

'A grief without a pang', like a 'dull pain', might almost be an oxymoron, except that his depiction is so vivid. '[V]oid', 'drowsy [and] unimpassioned' generate an image of emptiness and numbness, while 'stifled . . . find[ing] no natural outlet, no relief/In word, or sigh, or tear' suggests bottled emotion in need of, but denied, verbal or physical expression. It is at once a feeling and not a feeling; or rather, it is a sensation which seems to defy articulation and understanding: 'I gaze – and with how blank an eye!' Like the speaker in Shelley's 'Stanzas', his senses work, but not that deeper sense which gives meaning and life to the sensual images and experiences. Thus he sees with detail the 'thin clouds' and the stars, and even:

> Those stars, that glide behind them or between,
> Now sparkling, now bedimmed, but always seen. (ll. 33–4)

His imagination, however, like the 'balmy and serene' evening air, is utterly stagnant and lifeless. Accustomed to reading and passionately transforming the world around him, the speaker can only acknowledge the natural beauty, not feel it.

The third stanza, which begins with a raw and aptly laconic assessment of the problem as he sees it – 'My genial spirits fail' (l. 39) – expresses in stark terms the poet's sense of hopelessness regarding the possibility of his 'lift[ing] the smothering weight from off my breast'. 'It were a vain endeavour', moreover, for him to expect to regain his emotional vitality from natural objects, because:

> I may not hope from outward forms to win
> The passion and the life, whose fountains are within. (ll. 45–6)

Though, as he indicated in the first stanza, he would *like* for the natural world to rouse his imagination and keen depth of feeling, he knows that it is only the poet's feelingful rendering of the world and of his experiences which ennoble and animate those 'outward forms'. As a consequence:

> we receive but what we give,
> And in our life alone does nature live. (ll. 47–8)

He contrasts the things of 'higher worth', which 'from the soul itself must issue forth', with what the:

> inanimate cold world allowed
> To the poor loveless ever-anxious crowd. (ll. 51–2)

Like 'the sensual and the proud' (l. 70) in stanza five who are bound to the phenomenal world and incapable of imaginative activity, these 'loveless' masses are limited to a purely mundane and petty ('ever-anxious') existence. Interestingly, what they patently lack is precisely what the speaker himself grieves the loss of in himself: the capacity to conceive:

> A light, a glory, a fair luminous cloud
> Enveloping the Earth – (ll. 54–5)

The poet seems to make every effort to distance himself and the nature of his dejection from the very readers whose sympathetic understanding might affirm that feeling through their own imaginative activity. As we have seen, it was a commonly held belief that poetry's 'highest . . . effect can only be produced by the poet's striking a note to which the heart and affections naturally vibrate in unison; by rousing one of a large family of kindred impressions'. According to Jeffrey, 'the emotions connected with common and familiar objects, with objects which fill every man's memory', are those most conducive to exciting the reader's sympathetic imagination.[62] In light of this, one might argue that the feelings and psychological states depicted in Coleridge's poem are too extreme and esoteric to evoke sympathy. After all, the speaker emphasizes the fact that the 'beautiful and beauty-making power' (l. 63) he longs to regain belongs only to 'the pure' of heart, from whose 'sweet voice' all beauty 'flows':

> All melodies the echoes of that voice,
> All colours a suffusion from that light. (ll. 74–5)

The challenge to the Romantic reader was to participate in the poem, to find a way to read with the kind of emotional vitality and inspired imagination that the poet himself claims to have lost. The reader, in other words, must co-create by virtue of sympathizing with the poet's loss of creative power. This is a daunting task when the poet has set himself apart as a gifted being.

However, like the lyrics by Clare and Shelley, the poem enacts a sort of humanization of the poet: his power is subject to human loss, a phenomenon with which all can identify:

> There was a time when, though my path was rough,
>   This joy within me dallied with distress,
> And all misfortunes were but as the stuff
>   Whence Fancy made me dreams of happiness:
> For hope grew round me like the twining vine,
> And fruits, and foliage, not my own, seemed mine. (ll. 76–81)

The highly idiosyncratic nature of a poet's loss is tempered by the simple pathos of a man's sadness over joy once effortless now turned sour. The pain is rendered in terms so raw and detailed that the reader's imagination is actively engaged in connecting the speaker's unique and extreme circumstances with the universal experience of longing, confusion and grief. Where he/she cannot bring his/her own experiences to bear on the poet's situation, the reader's emotional and psychological horizons are broadened by the imaginative effort to enter into the unfamiliar and unusual. If, as Alison and others believed, the more the imagination is stimulated, the stronger is the emotion received from that activity, then the reader who is challenged by 'Dejection' to *think* in deeper and more complex ways about his/her own experiences of pain and emptiness will likewise *feel* more acutely the pain and pleasure of sympathy.

In recognizing at the beginning of stanza seven that the predicted storm has been 'rav[ing] unnoticed' (l. 97), the speaker implicitly connects the hoped for storm with his detailed account of the 'affliction' which 'bow[s him] down to earth' (l. 82). The 'scream/Of agony by torture lengthened out' (ll. 97–8) which he attributes to the wind applies equally to the preceding stanzas. The analogy between the wind and poetic creation, a metaphor at the center of the Romantic ethos and suggested by the opening stanza's 'Aeolian lute', is the basis not only for this stanza but for the poem as a whole. Addressing the wind ('Mad Lutanist!'), he is also summoning his own imaginative powers – the font of passion which he feared was dry. Just as the wind transforms the tranquil spring evening into 'Devils' yule' (l. 106), the poet's imagination, obviously roused into activity (signalled by the sudden flurry of exclamation marks), begins to weave lurid images of pain, horror, even madness – images not merely fantastical, but allied to intense emotion and suggestive of a larger psychological portrait. He hears within the 'deepest silence' of the wind the sound:

> of a rushing crowd,
> With groans, and tremulous shudderings . . . (ll. 114–16)

and a tale:

> of a little child
> Upon a lonesome wild,
> Not far from home, but she hath lost her way:
> And now moans low in bitter grief and fear,
> And now screams loud, and hopes to make her mother hear. (ll. 121–5)

Far from stock devices, these images challenge the limits of readers' emotional identification: they are by no means the simple 'echo of our familiar feelings' which Jeffrey believed effective poetry must be.[63] As Alison made clear, however, the 'higher and more pleasing kind' of emotion is produced when the imagination is spurred into activity and the reader must, as Wordsworth put it, 'exert himself'.[64] It is in this way, I submit, that 'images and affections that belong to our *universal* nature'[65] are imbued with fresh meaning by the lyric: the very challenge to the reader's sympathy sets in motion the imaginative activity (or 'vibrating' in unison, a term shared by Romantic and twentieth-century sympathy theorists) which unites the familiar and universal with the individual and idiosyncratic.

Stanza eight, which ends the poem with a rousing wish for perpetual joy and peace for his beloved (to whom the poem is addressed) punctuates the poem's success in the terms outlined by Beres and Arlow. The speaker 'externalizes' or achieves distance on the experience which first gave rise to his lyric effusion, while at the same time communicating his pain and grief to a sympathetic listener. Indeed, the two activities are interdependent, and in this final stanza he continues to manifest the emotional energy so evident in the preceding stanza, as his imaginative activity, far from self-absorbed or 'dull', carries him further outside himself into his beloved's present and even future circumstances. Still anxious about 'the smothering weight' – 'small thoughts have I of sleep' (l. 126) – the speaker none the less manages to lift himself into the very 'joy' that he longs to rekindle by entering into her world and creating a picture of happiness as he conceives of it:

> To her may all things live, from pole to pole,
> Their life the eddying of her living soul! (ll. 135–6)

Like a whirlpool, the perpetual going out and bringing back – giving and receiving – which he envisions between 'her living soul' and 'all things' implies a sympathetic interchange in which one's inner life feeds and is nourished by the external world. In the same way, sympathy enables the poet to extricate himself from the paralysis of his 'unimpassioned grief' and set his imagination in motion again.

These lyrics make clear that where the poet's rich and complex life of feeling is supplanted by a sense which is 'dull and void' ('John Clare') or at best a 'dull pain' ('Dejection') is a place 'Where there is neither sense of life nor joys' ('I Am'). In a preponderance of Romantic lyrics, the poet's grief over the loss of feeling and inspiration becomes itself the source of poetic inspiration – for the poet and, consequently, for the reader. Twentieth-century psychology has confirmed the Romantics' belief that the imagination is most stimulated by what is unreal or absent, and sympathy is most profoundly engaged by extremes of pain and loss. It is by virtue of the challenge to the reader's imagination and sympathy, therefore, that the Romantic lyric generates the possibility for human interchange and relationship – with readers then and now.

Notes

1. J. Clare (1935), *The Poems of John Clare*, J. W. Tibble (ed.), 2 vols, London: J. M. Dent, vol. 1, 265.
2. W. Wordsworth (1805), *The Prelude, or Growth of a Poet's Mind*, E. De Selincourt (ed.), corrected by S. Gill (1970), London: Oxford University Press, 187.
3. S. T. Coleridge (1936), 'Poesy or Art', *Coleridge's Miscellaneous Criticism*, T. M. Raysor (ed.), London: Constable, 205.
4. D. H. Reiman (ed.) (1972), *The Romantics Reviewed: Contemporary Reviews of British Romantic Writers*, 9 vols, New York: Garland, Part A, vol. 1, 377.
5. J. S. Mill (1976), 'What is poetry?', in F. M. Sharpless (ed.), *Essays On Poetry by John Stuart Mill*, Columbia, SC: University of South Carolina Press, 12.
6. W. Scott (1834–36), 'An Essay on the Drama', in *The Miscellaneous Prose Works of Sir Walter Scott*, 21 vols, Edinburgh and London: Robert Cadell, vol. 6, 310.
7. A. Smith (1835), 'The Philosophy of Poetry', *Blackwood's Edinburgh Magazine*, 38, 829.
8. Reiman, *The Romantics*, Part A, vol. 1, 140.
9. Ibid., 334.
10. G. W. F. Hegel (1975), *Aesthetics: Lectures on Fine Art*, 2 vols, T. M. Knox (tr.), Oxford: Oxford University Press, vol. 2, 1129, 1134.
11. Hegel, *Aesthetics*, vol. 2, 1134.
12. Scott, *Prose Works*, vol. 3, 82; E. De Selincourt (ed.) (1935), *The Early Letters of William and Dorothy Wordsworth (1787–1805)*, Oxford: Oxford University Press, 306.
13. Letter to Catherine Clarkson, in A. G. Hill (ed.) (1984), *Letters of William*

Wordsworth, Oxford: Oxford University Press, 172; *Prose Works*, vol. 3, 81.

14. All Clare references from *The Poems of John Clare*, (1935) 2 vols, with an introduction by J. W. Tibble (ed.), London: J. M. Dent.
15. A. Alison (1815), *Essay on the Nature and Principles of Taste*, Edinburgh: George Ramsay, vol. 1, 160.
16. Alison, *Essay*, 58–9.
17. F. Jeffrey (n.d.), *Essays on English Poets and Poetry from the Edinburgh Review*, London: George Routledge, 185.
18. Jeffrey, *English Poets*, 186.
19. Ibid., 309.
20. Ibid., 309.
21. R. D. Altick (1965), *Lives and Letters: A History of Literary Biography in England and America*, New York: Alfred A. Knopf, 99.
22. Reiman, Part A, vol. 1, 357.
23. M. H. Abrams (1958), *The Mirror and the Lamp: Romantic Theory and the Critical Tradition*, New York: W. W. Norton, 227.
24. D. C. Goellnicht (1989), 'Keats on Reading: "Delicious Diligent Indolence"', *Journal of English and Germanic Philology*, 88, (2), April, 191.
25. J. Conder, in Reiman, Part A, vol. 1, 366.
26. W. Hazlitt (1934), *The Complete Works of William Hazlitt*, P. P. Howe (ed.), 21 vols, London: J. M. Dent, vol. 5, 3, 5.
27. Jeffrey, *Essays*, 309.
28. John Clare, from a folio manuscript book which he kept during his five-month stay at home in Northborough after escaping from Epping Forest asylum and before being recommitted for the rest of his life to Northampton asylum, as quoted in G. Grigson's (1949), 'Introduction' to *Poems of John Clare's Madness*, London: Routledge and Kegan Paul, 20.
29. Grigson, *Poems*, 40.
30. *Webster's New Universal Unabridged Dictionary*, (1983), New York: Simon and Schuster, 563.
31. All Shelley references from D. Perkins (ed.) (1967), *English Romantic Writers*, New York: Harcourt, Brace and World, 979–80.
32. Alison, *Essay*, 164.
33. Ibid., 166.
34. Ibid., 66; Jeffrey, *English Poets*, 186.
35. M. Buber (1965), *The Knowledge of Man*, M. Friedman and R. G. Smith (tr.), London: George Allen and Unwin, 81.
36. B. H. Smith (1978), *On the Margins of Discourse: The Relation of Literature to Language*, Chicago: University of Chicago Press, 36.
37. R. L. Katz (1963), *Empathy: Its Nature and Uses*, New York: Free Press, 5.
38. Katz, *Empathy*, 9.
39. T. Reik (1949), *Listening with the Third Ear: The Inner Experience of a Psychoanalyst*, New York: Farrar, Straus, 468.
40. D. Beres and J. A. Arlow (1974), 'Fantasy and Identification in Empathy', *Psychoanalytic Quarterly*, 43, (1), January, 33–4, 47.
41. D. Beres (1957), 'Communication in Psychoanalysis and in the Creative Process: A Parallel', *American Psychoanalytic Association Journal*, 5, 412–13.
42. B. H. Smith, *On the Margins*, 24; A. Williams (1984), *Prophetic Strain:*

The Greater Lyric in the Eighteenth Century, Chicago: University of Chicago Press, 13.

43. John O. Hayden (ed.) (1982), *William Wordsworth: The Poems, Volume One,* Harmondsworth: Penguin Books, 886.

44. Williams, *Prophetic Strain,* 15.

45. F. D. E. Schleiermacher (1977), *Hermeneutics: The Handwritten Manuscripts,* Heinz Kimmerle (ed.), J. Duke and J. Forstman (tr.), American Academy of Religion, Texts and Translations Series, Missoula, Montana: Scholars Press, 97.

46. Beres, 'Communication', 411.

47. B. Hardy (1977), *The Advantage of Lyric: Essays on Feeling in Poetry,* Bloomington: Indiana University Press, 16.

48. G. Siomopoulos (1977), 'Poetry as Affective Communication', *Psychoanalytic Quarterly,* 46, (3), July, 499, 512. 'The ontogenetic paradigm from which human communication and symbolization emerge', this 'primordial sharing situation', seems closely related to Shelley's understanding of poetry as being 'connate with the origins of man' ('A Defence of Poetry', in Perkins, *English Romantic Writers,* 1072).

49. Beres, 'Communication', 413.

50. P. M. Privateer (1991), *Romantic Voices: Identity and Ideology in British Poetry, 1789–1850,* Athens, GA: University of Georgia Press, 227, 226.

51. T. Rajan (1985), 'Romanticism and the Death of Lyric Consciousness', in C. Hosek and P. Parker (eds), *Lyric Poetry: Beyond New Criticism,* Ithaca: Cornell University Press, 205, 195, 206.

52. Rajan, 'Romanticism', 206.

53. T. Todorov (1982), *Theories of the Symbol,* C. Porter (tr.), Ithaca: Cornell University Press, 169, 201, 206.

54. Goellnicht, 'Keats on Reading', 210, 200, 197, 199.

55. As paraphrased by P. J. Eakin (1985), *Fictions in Autobiography: Studies in the Art of Self-Invention,* Princeton: Princeton University Press, 204.

56. All Wordsworth references from John O. Hayden (ed.) (1982), *The Poems, Volume One,* Harmondsworth: Penguin.

57. Buber, *The Knowledge,* 81.

58. Schleiermacher, *Hermeneutics,* 101.

59. J. Stewart (1983), 'Interpretive Listening: An Alternative to Empathy', *Communication Education,* 32, October, 385.

60. Reik, *Listening,* 506.

61. All Coleridge references from Perkins, *English Romantic Writers,* 432–4.

62. Jeffrey, *English Poets,* 309.

63. Ibid., 186.

64. Alison, *Essay,* 160; Wordsworth, *Prose Works,* 306.

65. Jeffrey, *English Poets,* 309.

Index

Gramley Library
Salem Academy and College
Winston-Salem, N.C. 27108